SOME PEOPLE . . .

* achieve the top ranks of the corporate power structure.
* go in and ask for raises and promotions—and get them.
* give speeches that win applause, approval and respect.
* make a dynamic first impression.
* know how to put other people at ease.
* have all the right connections.
* get things done.

Some people, you might say, just seem to have been born winners.

But if you really believe that, Lloyd Purves is about to let you in on a secret. What divides the winners from the losers is nothing more complicated than *self-confidence*.

Most people never realize their potential for success. They drift along, trapped by self-doubt, racked by misgiving and apprehension.

But with the techniques and examples in this book, you'll discover how to find your strengths, know weaknesses, and make the most of what you've got with . . .

THE POWER OF SELF-CONFIDENCE

The Power of
SELF-CONFIDENCE

By Lloyd Purves

ZEBRA BOOKS
KENSINGTON PUBLISHING CORP.

ZEBRA BOOKS

are published by

Kensington Publishing Corp.
475 Park Avenue South
New York, NY 10016

First printing: August 1985

Printed in the United States of America

This book is dedicated to the self-confident men and women who make this world a better place for all of us.

Table of Contents

Cecil Atwood's written plan made things happen fast — Feed your self-confidence — Focus self-confidence on what you want — How Harvey Cross focused self-confidence on what he wanted and got it — Stick to essentials — How to use self-confidence to pinpoint what is important — Travis Mays' index card system — Use your self-confidence every day — Work on a level of reality — How Jerry Harris faced reality — Now for the nitty-gritty — How to keep your self-confidence constructive as you use it — Make a self-power inventory — Confidence keys.

Chapter 3. Self-Confidence as Self-Concept

How do you see yourself? — Be your own best friend — Ten ways to prove that you have what it takes — You can like yourself no matter what your circumstances are today — Why C. K. Martin liked himself — You can change your circumstances and environment — You don't have to apologize to anyone — You don't need flattery — You can get rid of crutches — How Sidney Atteberry controlled his attitude at age sixty — Why hobble yourself? — How to rid yourself of destructive self-concepts — What Warren Millet did to rid himself of a destructive self-concept — One weak spot need not be fatal — How to develop a positive self-concept — How Laverta Hartman shed a crippling jealousy — You are all you own — A self-concept test — Confidence keys.

Chapter 4. Sixteen Ways to Whip
a Nagging Inferiority Complex

1. Respect yourself — Terri Holden turns frustration

**Chapter 5.   Key Self-Confidence Techniques
             to Influence People**

Chapter 6.   How to Build a Self-Confident Attitude

Attitude re-defined — Ten ways to control your attitude — How Delvin Manor changed a depressing attitude to one of enthusiasm — How Doyle Parsons resisted outside pressures and controlled his attitude — Your attitude belongs to you — How to make your attitude work for you — How Mary Woolsey learned not to be afraid of being vulnerable — Marshal the facts — How to maintain a self-confident attitude against competition — A reference checklist for you — Confidence keys.

**Chapter 7.   How to Use Self-Confidence
to Multiply Your People Power**

What the term "people power" means — How you can develop people power — Give yourself a chance — Throw away your mask — Refuse to accept every no as final — Refuse to let a negative response throw you — Refuse to set yourself up for failure — Repetition builds people power — Put them to work at the first signal — Keep some secrets of your own — How Molly Rinker multiplied her people power — Who needs people? — People are the key — How Tom Ligon increased sales with people as the key — People want self-confident leaders — What self-confident people power means to you — What self-confident people power meant to Ollie Lyles — What your people power means to others — Your people power expands in the leader's role — You will enjoy people power — Your associates and friends will applaud your people power — Why Mildred Gilliam's friends applauded her — You have a self-obligation — How

Fred Stephens fulfilled an obligation to himself and won a raise — An exercise to check where you stand — Confidence keys.

Chapter 8. Self-Confidence Methods to Make a Strong First Impression

The first minute counts the most — How to handle the all-important first minute — Take the initiative — Example 1: When meeting only one or two people for the first time — Example 2: Be a friend — Example 3: Make your position known — Example 4: Be prepared — Example 5: Ask for action — How Kay Underwood makes the first minute count — How to come on with self-confidence — People expect you to be assertive — How to avoid a flabby beginning — How to make a strong first impression under scrutiny — Key 1: Recognize that it is to your advantage to be evaluated — Key 2: New people are looking for strong friends — Key 3: You are an insider already — Key 4: You have a head start — Key 5: You can lay the groundwork for further action — Your self-confidence wins instant confidence from others — How to make the most of a strong first impression — Holding onto the advantages a strong first impression gives you — Use the follow-up technique — How R. W. Rimmer used self-confidence to capitalize on a strong first impression — How to win friends with a strong first impression — Flo Massey's technique to win friends — The exposure technique — The first impression lasts a long time — Confidence keys.

11

Chapter 9. Self-Confidence Procedures to Make you a Leader

Control your thought processes — Thirteen steps to control your thinking — Never be undone by a mistake — Wesley Stemmons' procedures after a mistake — Every leader bleeds a little — Decide what you want as a leader — Avoid the shotgun approach — Go after big goals first — How to deal with ridicule and discouragement — How Harold Ames handled ridicule — How to get up when you get knocked down — How Leonard Ross got up after being knocked down — Be your own leader — The leader who likes himself wins the most — Confidence keys.

Chapter 10. Techniques to Build a Winning Personality Through Self-Confidence

Act like a winner — Acting like a winner pays big for Fay Pellham — Talk like a winner — Build a personality that you like — Hold down outside influence — Virgil Harper shakes an outside influence — Go with the winners — Don't feel guilty about winning — Be your own best example — Reveal your own true self — Face tough situations fast — Don't overrate everybody you meet — What happened when Harvey McAlister stopped overrating everybody else — Make a working list of your winning traits — Concentrate on the strong points in your working list — Confidence keys.

Chapter 11. Enthusiasm as a Component of Self-Confidence

Enthusiasm generates self-confidence — Enthusiasm

excites people — Norm Lambert's hot "throwed" rolls — The more excitement, the more self-confidence — What happened when Carolyn Fay got excited — Enthusiasm, like self-confidence, is contagious — The more people you enthuse, the more you gain — How to get enthusiastic — How Karen Rupp won when she got enthusiastic — Don't wait for enthusiasm to strike — How to stay enthusiastic — Max Raider's secret for staying enthusiastic — Controlled enthusiasm adds to your self-confidence — When you act enthusiastic, you become self-confident — Enthusiasm gives zip and fire to your self-confidence — A checklist to keep your enthusiasm boiling — Confidence keys.

Chapter 12. How to Use Self-Confidence to Win Respect

Respect yourself first — Do your best, forget the rest — Confidently act as if respect is your due — How Marie Riggs regained her self-respect — Respect is your right — You cannot demand respect — Clifford Adams learns that you can't demand respect — Respect is more than flattery — Betty Abbot rejects flattery — How to team self-confidence with respect — You don't have to learn tricks — Rick Hauser finds that respect goes deeper than tricks — How to develop personality traits that win respect — Attitudes that build self-confidence and win respect — Confidence keys.

Chapter 13. Self-Confidence Secrets to Handle Problem People

Expect to meet a few disgruntled and bitter characters — Keep your sense of proportion — Keep your dignity — The day Glenn Ramey won with dignity — The loudmouth is insecure — How Joe Hardie subdued a troublemaker — Your self-confidence can soothe the savage beast — Let the man blow off steam — How to amaze the belligerent with your self-confidence — How J. C. Barber surprised the belligerent with his self-confidence — How to win the respect of problem people — Confidence keys.

Chapter 14.　How to Use Self-Confidence to Get a Head Start

How to get a head start by being your own competitor — More ideas on how to create your own opportunities — How to hit the first lick in a tight competitive situation — How Wayne Kimball hit the first lick to nail down a big sale — How to use self-confidence to stay ahead — Using self-confidence makes it look easy — Apology makes your self-confidence sound weak — Martin Erwin makes an important speech look easy — A head start guarantees a quick response — How a confident head start stacks the odds in your favor — Jimmy Mingo stacks the odds in his favor — How to sharpen your self-confidence for a head start — Confidence keys.

Chapter 15.　How to Sharpen Your Contacts With Self-Confidence

Why you need strong contacts — A word about weak contacts — Plan your contacts with bold self-confidence — Be more than a name dropper! — Keep away from people who try to belittle you — How insurance salesman Kip Rucker used bold self-confidence and sharpened his contacts — How to strengthen old contacts with self-confidence — Lee Nickels' method to keep old contacts sharp — Powerful contacts expand your self-confidence — Self-confidence makes your contacts mutually profitable — How Gina Pasko makes her contacts profitable for everybody — Why worthwhile contacts welcome your self-confidence — Ten confident ideas to widen your contacts — Confidence keys.

Chapter 16. Nine Ways to Use Self-Confidence to Get What You Want

1. Know what you want — Patti Wallis moves off dead center — 2. Make a written self-commitment — 3. Establish time frames — How Paul Nash makes time work for him — 4. Power techniques to leap from goal to goal — 5. Don't impose limits on your self-confidence — How J. C. Stuart shoots high — 6. Self-confidence methods that influence people — How Florence Taft emphasizes the positive — 7. Accept your ability to gain what you want — Expect good results — 8. Start with what you have — 9. Consider the advantages — Confidence keys.

Chapter 17. How to Develop Confident Speech Power

What your speech says about your self-confidence — Confident speech gives you credibility — How to use speech mechanics to add confidence — Use words economically — How Jess Brazeal learned to speak confidently — Tone is important — Body language adds power to speech — Stick to easy-to-grasp words — Use words that get to the point — Use action words that generate confidence — Confidence keys.

INTRODUCTION
WHAT THIS BOOK WILL DO FOR YOU

Self-confidence is one of the most important elements in man's makeup. It often contributes more to mankind's well-being and happiness than any other factor in the personality. It is one of the basic traits that determine how much success will be attained, how much esteem will be enjoyed, and how an individual will feel about one's own self. It influences the outlook on life and shapes attitudes. It is the driving force that takes men and women where they want to go and enables them to become what they want to be. Self-confidence lifts the vision and sets goals that far exceed most people's expectations, then supplies the power to surpass these high goals. Yet there are many who fail to recognize and accept this great wellspring of power which is theirs. They drift along filled with misgivings and self-doubt. This need never be your lot. You do not have to live in the cage of self-doubt. Your days do not have to be racked by fear or filled with apprehension. The secrets, techniques and examples in this book will show you how to get and develop self-confidence. And it will show you how to make the most of it.

You are not condemned to live in a world of personal misgivings and self-doubt. Self-confidence is your birthright. This book with its examples and case histories, can help you claim that right. Here are a few samples of what you can expect.

* In chapter one, how Marty Loren regained her self-confidence after a demeaning personal problem.
* In chapter two, how Harvey Cross focused self-confidence on what he wanted and got it.
* In chapter five, how Elmer McElhaney closed his big deal when he took his self-confidence power for granted.
* Chapter seven tells how Fred Stephens fulfilled an obligation to himself and won a fat raise.
* In chapter eight, how R. W. Rimmer used self-confidence and capitalized on a strong first impression.
* In chapter nine, how Leonard Ross moved from the low man on the totem pole in his company to the top when he used self-confidence to establish leadership.
* Chapter eleven details how Karen Rupp won her first promotion with an adroit combination of enthusiasm and self-confidence.
* Chapter fifteen tells how salesman Kip Rucker sharpened his contacts and boosted his income while enhancing his social life with self-confidence.
* Chapter sixteen shows how Patti Wallis moved off dead center and got what she wanted.

* Chapter seventeen describes how Jess Brazeal learned to speak confidently.
* Chapter eighteen highlights how Leona Choate uses imagination and keeps her self-confidence working for her.

This is a meat and potatoes book. For instance, in the first chapter you are given techniques and ideas that can enable you to get as much self-confidence as you want. Then in chapter two, methods and suggestions on how to use your self-confidence are set forth. This book gets you right into the values and purposes of the self-confidence that you can have today.

A feeling of self establishes your place in the throbbing and stirring events that whirl around all of us each and every day. With this in mind, chapter three identifies self-confidence as positive self-concept. This is right on target. If you are going to live and work the way you choose, if you are going to get what you want, then you must perceive self-confidence as a highly personal matter. The lack of self-confidence (a weak self-concept) is a crippling disability. It is a self-imposed handicap. This chapter and the other potent chapters in this book can ensure that you will never be a self-victim.

The rewards of self-confidence, along with more ideas and techniques, as well as additional examples, quizzes, self-tests and other aids to capitalize on the miracle power of self-confidence, are in every chapter of this exciting book. Chapter four, for example, explores sixteen ways to whip a nagging inferiority complex; chapter five gives you techniques to influence people with your self-confidence.

Self-confidence is a special kind of force. For example, chapter seven deals with techniques that you can use to multiply your people power with your own brand of self-confidence as the motivating force. In like manner, chapter eight not only explains how to make a strong first impression with self-confidence, but tells you how to capitalize on this amazing maneuver.

This book puts the spotlight on you. Each chapter is organized around the principle of self-confidence. The guidelines are designed to make you a winner. Chapter nine supports this thesis with the emphasis on self-confidence procedures to make you a leader. Chapter ten furthers this point by developing techniques to build a winning personality loaded with self-confidence.

Enthusiasm has been extolled as a personality trait that will overcome just about every problem imaginable. It will not quite do all this. But, as pointed out in chapter eleven, enthusiasm is a component of self-confidence. This chapter shows you how to inject enthusiasm into your self-confidence to make it even more dynamic and compelling.

Chapters twelve and thirteen have a common thread. Chapter twelve is entitled "How to Use Self-Confidence to Win Respect" and chapter thirteen details secrets to handle problem people. You can hardly have one without the other.

Succeeding chapters present orderly and important steps in the development of a strong, self-confident personality. Each chapter reinforces the other as it makes its own logical and valuable contribution to your campaign to magnify the power of your self-confidence.

The closing chapters keep up the fast and exhilarating pace. Each makes a telling contribution to the singular power and the many uses of self-confidence. The final chapters add fire to the book with topics designed to keep your self-confidence strong and alive.

Any one chapter in this book is worth more to you than the price of the book. Each is a storehouse of techniques and ideas to give you extra self-confidence and all the satisfaction that self-esteem brings. Read it with confidence and put it to work for you today.

Chapter 1
How You Can Get Self-Confidence

Self-confidence is an abstract quality much akin to faith and trust. Like many other abstract qualities, self-confidence is as strong as iron and as stubborn as a mule. It is self-possession, a reliance on yourself with a satisfying feeling that you are fully capable of handling any circumstance which may confront you. There are other connotations, but our concern is with *your* self-confidence. This is a personal asset that can and does move mountains. You can have just about all you want of it and you can have it just about when you want it.

It would be self-destructive to assume that self-confidence is nothing more than blindly plunging into any situation without regard for consequences. This priceless attribute is more than brashness. It is sense and reality rolled into a ball of determination. With all of this in mind, it is easy to see that you must have a clear understanding of what self-confidence is before you can get and develop it. A simple dictionary definition puts it in a nutshell: *Confidence in one's self and in one's powers and abilities.*

Isn't that what you want—confidence in yourself and in your powers and abilities?

You have a personal portion of powers and abilities plus the desire and ambition to build the confidence to make the most of these vital traits. Otherwise you would not be reading this book. So let's get right into some basic steps after this observation.

IT CAN BE DONE

No, it is not easy for some to crawl out of his or her shell. It's much easier to seek associates who make no demands on your intellect than it is to align yourself with bright people who assume that you are self-assured. It's much easier to back off from opportunity than to confidently risk an occasional failure. The shadows are always softer than the sunlight, but no roses grow there.

I've watched two men over the years who both started working for the same giant company in a Texas city. Each of these men, whom we shall call Joe and Harry, were highly trained and well qualified when they started with this company. Joe turned down three out-of-town promotions because, as he explained, he was afraid that he might not be able to handle a new job in a new town. Harry eagerly accepted the first promotion offered and went on from there.

Where are these men today? The company apparently decided that since Joe didn't have the confidence in himself to move ahead, that perhaps their confidence in him might have been misplaced. Joe is still on the same job and performing it as well as ever. But his lack of confidence in himself and his "powers and abilities" has closed the door forever as far as his employers are concerned. And who can blame them? Harry, on the other hand, is a vice-president at thirty-five and still confidently moving up.

Developing powerful self-confidence may not always be the easiest thing in the world to do, but it can be done. The rewards are enormous. Here are some steps that you can take now to ensure that you get your share.

NINE STEPS YOU CAN TAKE NOW

Step 1: Reinforce Your Self-Image

You will never be more self-confident than you think you are. This book will not, by itself, give you self-confidence. Your self-confidence depends on you and your self-image. You can, indeed, take the suggestions and experiences in this book and construct a strong self-image and acquire the abundance of self-confidence that goes with it. The ideas and case histories are here for you to put to work. Let's begin with this:

YOU ARE IMPORTANT

You are important. Not because you just happened to be born on this planet, but because you have the ability to produce, to serve, to lead and to direct your life. In the process of developing and maintaining your self-image, don't fall into the trap of feeling that you are important only if everybody you meet sees you as someone important. What is important to many people may not be important to you at all. Their image of you doesn't count that much. Of course, it is comforting to have the approval of others, but self-approval is what gives you a worthy self-image. Don't be a self-victim by judging yourself by outside standards and comparisons. What you think, what you want, and what you do is the deciding factor in reinforcing your self-image. Here are some keys that can give you the self-image that rightfully belongs to you.

* ACCEPT THE FACT THAT
YOU ARE INTELLIGENT

You may not have all the intelligence in the world, but you don't need that. You have plenty of intelligence or you would not be concerned with self-confidence and your self-image. Every person has somebody running around out there who is smarter than he is in some areas. Your concern is not how intelligent other people are. Your concern is to accept the fact that you are intelligent and then go from there. You will be surprised at how much the truth of this little idea can do for your self-image.

* BEING AFRAID IS NOT
A SIGN OF HELPLESSNESS

Fear is a normal, protective reaction to the strange and unfamiliar. It is nature's way of keeping you out of trouble. It is not a sign of helplessness, nor is it a signal to quit. It is an indication that you should proceed with the intelligence you command toward the goal or object you want.

HOW MARTY LOREN OVERCAME HER DISABLING FEAR

You can use fear effectively, rather than let it weaken or destroy your self-image. A young mother, Marty Loren, whom I have talked with frequently, reached a point in her life where, after a demeaning marital problem, she could not get out of the house to buy groceries, run her kids to school or ball games, or engage in simple social activities alone. Her facial expression often reflected the agony and turmoil that this unrealistic fear was causing her. The fear was real enough to her. Home, with the doors closed and windows barred, was the only place where she felt safe from further hurt. However, this lady used the natural intelligence she had. She sought out an excellent clinic where a knowledgeable staff soon made her see that it was her sorry self-image that had really backed her into a corner. Her hurts had been severe, but the ongoing damage was being caused by the fearful low esteem she was suffering as a result of real or imagined humiliation during her marital troubles. As soon as my young friend recognized her problem, being afraid no longer made her feel utterly helpless. It took awhile, but once she saw that she was still a qualified and able individual, her self-image was restored and became stronger than before. Today she manages a successful business and fills an exciting role as a career woman and

mother. Being afraid can be painful, as this successful lady will attest, but as she demonstrated it is not
a sign of helplessness. When you understand fear
and keep it in perspective, you can use it constructively. This way your self-image will become even
more positive.

* LIKING YOURSELF IS PARAMOUNT

If you dislike yourself, everybody is going to know
it. Your self-image is about as inconspicuous as a
broken leg. There is no way that a sorry self-image
can be hidden. On the other hand, when you have a
clean, healthy liking for yourself and what you are
doing, everybody is going to know it. You will feel
good about yourself, and your friends and associates
will share that feeling. What you see in yourself and
how you see yourself is of paramount importance, because that is how you will be perceived by others.

There is a simple way to verify this. Observe the
people around you. You will easily see that the
people who like themselves are the happy and successful ones. Or to paraphrase it, you will see that
the people who are happy and successful are the ones
who like themselves.

The answer to the problem of self-dislike is to
change whatever is causing that problem. If this bugaboo is haunting you in the slightest, you probably
already have a keen idea of its cause, so you have a
pretty good idea of where to go to work on it. The
thing to keep in mind is that *you are important*.
With this obvious fact reinforcing your self-image,
you can use the techniques and ideas in this book to
develop a self-image that is second to none.

Here is a final thought that you should engrave in stone: How you see yourself—your self-image—is how you are going to be seen by everybody you meet. When you like yourself, others are going to like what they see.

STEP 2: DO SOMETHING YOU FEAR

We have already made the point in step one that being afraid is not a sign of helplessness. But since fear is such a factor in an inferiority complex (the opposite of self-confidence), it deserves further study. Step two will deal with how to get rid of the fear. The most effective technique to get rid of this debilitating syndrome and move on to a working self-confidence is to do something you fear. If this thought disturbs you, here is something you can do right now to prove to yourself that you can gain self-confidence and put fear in its place.

MAKE TWO LISTS

Make two lists. List the thing or things that you fear to do on the left-hand side of a large, clean sheet of paper. On the right-hand side list the worst thing that could happen to you if you did the thing you fear. Here is a brief example:

The Fear That Blocks My Self-Confidence	*The Worst Thing That Could Happen to Me if I Did It*
1. Meeting strangers	1. The worst that could happen would be that some oaf might rebuff me or otherwise be rude.

*So what? You don't need such characters anyway. The answer is just to relax and treat a stranger like a friend. Most of them will respond in like manner. You can't lose and you can win new friends and much more.

2. Making a speech

2. The audience might not like my speech.

*The best of speakers sometimes fall on their faces. To date, there is no record of one having been murdered. It takes practice to make a really great speech. Keep at it, because *nothing builds self-confidence faster than public speaking.*

3. Asking for a raise

3. The boss might say no.

*Yes, the boss might say no, but he won't think less of you for asking for a raise. After this, he will be watching you, so do more than he expects. Then go back later with solid reasons why you are worth more. The boss will listen.

4. Controversial subjects

4. Somebody might disagree with me and become upset.

*If somebody doesn't disagree with you occasionally, you aren't saying much. Disagreement over an idea (controversial subject) is not rejection of you as a person. Lively discussion can be fun. Try it. It also builds self-confidence.

5. Driving in heavy traffic	5. I might have a wreck.

*Well, you might. Nearly everybody who drives a lifetime has a traffic mishap. Most are minor and few of the total are fatal. Get yourself a good driving instructor if you lack skill and get into it. When you return home safe and sound you will have the confidence to go where you want next time.

These simple examples will serve as models. When you list a confidence-robbing fear, note, just as we have, the worst thing that could happen to you. Then write in your own words why the fear is unjustified and what you can do about it. Getting it down in black and white makes it easy to see that you can do something about such fear. Self-confidence is too important and too much fun to surrender to a hobgoblin.

STEP 3: REWARD YOURSELF

It is not uncommon for those with little or no self-confidence to feel culpable if they do not defer to just about everybody in everything. They feel worthy only when they make a personal sacrifice. Instead of concentrating on getting and building a healthy self-confidence, they focus on avoiding a feeling of guilt and selfishness. Consequently, their attitude and behavior reflect a pattern of negative thinking. This makes them easy targets for more demanding individuals (and institutions) who are intent on their own self-interests.

There is a gratifying remedy for this state of mind. First, try to list one good reason why you should not be entitled to a fair share of the rewards of this life. You won't find one. Now, with that settled, use your native self-confidence (you were born with it, remember?) and stop deferring and backing up. To enhance the good feeling you will get from so much as the smallest act of self-confidence, reward yourself with a tangible gift.

CARLA HILTON'S SELF-REWARD

Carla Hilton started putting this technique to use five years ago when she surprised herself by firmly saying no to a pushy co-worker who often asked to "borrow" five dollars for lunch. Of course, this impudent young lady had a faulty memory and often forgot to repay Carla.

Carla felt so good about her newfound confidence that she rewarded herself by buying an unusual demitasse cup she had seen in a gift shop. She had wanted to start a collection of such cups, but up to the time she said her first "no" she hadn't felt that she deserved such luxury. Carla's self-confidence has grown since she decided she was entitled to her share of this priceless trait. And so has her cup collection. She now proudly exhibits one hundred dainty and beautiful cups and saucers in an antique glass cabinet. She considers this display of self-rewards a constant reminder that she can have self-confidence and the goodies that go with it.

The moral of Carla's story is obvious.

STEP 4: BREAK THE CIRCLE

A lack of self-confidence can be habit-forming. When you observe people who are afflicted with an inferiority complex, you can see that they do the same destructive things over and over again. They get in a rut. Their mentality stays in a hole. There is no apparent effort to change their way of thinking and doing until some inner force sparks them to take charge and turn their attitude around. Then their self-image changes and they are on the road to getting the self-confidence every man, woman and child needs and is entitled to. The circle of self-humiliation has been broken.

What is it that brings about such a change? What is it that jars a meek and miserable soul out of a rut of despair and changes him or her into an outgoing, productive person? It can be any of a number of things: a good book, a religious experience, a wise friend, study, counseling, maturity, and on and on. But one factor is always first and foremost. There must be a firm personal commitment to grasp self-confidence and to make the most of it. Simply put, if you do not have all the self-confidence you want, nobody can force it on you. *You* are the key. Yours will be the benefits.

To get you on the road, start by doing something that you would like to do. Play tennis. Take a girl or guy to dinner and leave a big tip. Talk to an important figure. Take a trip to a new town. Call on a mean customer. Climb a mountain.

After you break the circle once, let your self-confidence take you where you want to go. You will like the trip.

STEP 5: ANALYZE YOUR CONFIDENCE PROBLEM

One of the most difficult things for anyone to do is to be wholly objective in analyzing his own problem. We all tend to favor ourselves by rationalizing our faults and weaknesses. However, when we fall into this trap we do nothing to correct the problem. We compound it and make it more difficult unless we are completely honest with ourselves.

How do you find and analyze a confidence problem that may be robbing you of all or part of your self-confidence? Look these questions over, add some of your own. When you've spotted the problem, you are ready to do something about it.

* Are you uncomfortable because you lack advanced formal education?
* Are you afraid of sounding foolish?
* Do you avoid new situations?
* Are you afraid of disapproval?
* Are you self-conscious about your appearance?

* Do you worry that you may not be a brilliant conversationalist?
* Does a deprived childhood haunt you?

Let's analyze these sample questions and see if they are truly impossible barriers to a sound self-confidence.

There are thousands of successful, confident people who have little formal academic training. In this day and age any determined person can overcome this handicap. There are excellent libraries, evening classes at any level, superior newspapers, educational television, and willing people to help you. So if you feel that you are handicapped by your lack of education, you can correct that. Not everything is learned only by the very young in ideal classroom surroundings. Further, the educated person will not look down his nose at everyone who doesn't have a Ph.D. The more educated your friends, the more they will appreciate your bold self-confidence.

The fear of sounding foolish is no more valid than the worry over a lack of advanced formal education. Everybody sounds foolish at one time or another. Besides, you may not sound foolish at all. This may be nothing more than a foolish fear handicapping your self-confidence. Forget it.

New situations and challenges add zest to life. As soon as you have met one or two head on, your growing confidence will make the others easy.

It is unreasonable to always expect approval. It is also unreasonable to let this fear slow down your self-confidence. As we have touched on, anybody who does anything is going to deal with some disapproval.

35

Go with your convictions and watch your self-confidence grow.

Your appearance is good enough if you are clean, well groomed and mannerly. If you have that, you have enough to build a load of self-confidence that will make people look at you most favorably.

A brilliant conversationalist is also a good listener. You don't have to be glib and entertaining all the time. Quiet self-assurance is also a most desirable trait. Work on that and your conversation will take care of itself.

A deprived childhood is a weak excuse. I know. I've been there. I'll agree a deprived childhood is a rough trip, but it should not be a life sentence. In fact, it might just have made you tough enough to handle a hot brand of self-confidence.

When you analyze your confidence problem, have identified it and taken it apart, write down your plan to handle that problem. The act of doing that much will give you the confidence to keep going until your self-confidence is where you want it to be.

STEP 6: BE OBJECTIVE
IN YOUR OPINIONS

An opinion is not positive knowledge. It is a view, belief or judgment that you hold. It may be hard for you to explain just how or why you hold a particular opinion. On the other hand, you may feel so strongly about an opinion that you can defend it vehemently. Whatever else an opinion is, it is yours. Your self-confidence demands that you value your opinion, for it is akin to an idea. It is yours. You are entitled to it.

Still, there is another demand that self-confidence makes. It demands that you deal with reality, that you recognize and accept reality when your opinion does not hold to what your reason tells you is true. We would all like for the world to be what we see in it, that is, our opinion of it. But if our opinions choose to ignore reality, then we are in trouble and our self-confidence is likely to take a beating from time to time.

Does this mean that you should never entertain an opinion? No, indeed. The mind would have to be blank and the spirit vapid if you never held an opinion. As we have said, your self-confidence demands that you value your opinion. The thing to do is form your opinions on reality. Do not adopt or cling to self-defeating opinions. This is where the danger lies and where your self-confidence might be shaken up.

Let's take a quick look at a few self-defeating opinions that are heard all too often. These opinions are really meaningless, but for fearful, careless people they take on an importance they do not deserve. Here are examples.

* I'm just not smart enough.
* I'm an ugly duckling.
* All minorities are greedy and parasitic.
* It's easy for him to make money.
* I never really had a chance.
* Rich people are no good.
* All poor people are lazy.
* You can't get a solid education today.

* Big corporations are crooked.
* There never was an honest politician.
* There is no use trying to get ahead.
* There is little or no opportunity today.
* Nobody loves me.

Embracing such self-defeating opinions cannot help but erode self-respect and self-confidence. Cherish your opinions, but be objective in evaluating them. When your opinions are based on reality, you can use them to build a real self-confidence.

STEP 7: MAKE YOUR OWN DECISIONS

Making personal or business decisions can be an excruciating experience. A decision is a commitment to action. The hesitant and doubtful personality cringes and stutters at the prospect. This is a sure sign of no confidence. It is a punishing, torturous feeling.

Developing the ability to make decisions and to act on them is a necessary aspect of getting and building a storehouse of self-confidence.

WHAT HAPPENED WHEN NORBERT FABER BEGAN MAKING DECISIONS

Norbert Faber, who now owns a thriving retail establishment, worked as a shoe salesman in a small store for seven years. This despite the fact that he held a degree in business administration and had the financial backing to do about whatever he wanted to do in the business world. He was worrying aloud about this at lunch one day with an attorney friend. His friend bluntly told him that he would never accomplish much of anything until he learned to make a quick, clean decision and then go from there. Norbert was uncomfortable for the rest of the meal. However, the next day he called his friend to thank him for waking him up. He had resolved to take full responsibility for himself, Norbert said, and already was feeling more confident and excited than he had in over seven years. Six months later Norbert was in business and had decided to keep on expanding.

When you make your own decisions, stick with them and act on them. You, too, will feel an exhilarating surge of self-confidence and self-power. Nobody can do it for you, but neither can anyone else reap the rewards for you.

STEP 8: TAKE THE RESPONSIBILITY FOR YOU

That you must take responsibility for yourself is so patently obvious that a lengthy discussion is not in order. How else can you hope to get and develop self-confidence?

If self-responsibility is a frightening prospect for you, here are ways you can begin to become a self-reliant, self-responsible person today.

Start with something small and easy. After all, no matter how self-confident one may be, everything he undertakes is not monumental. Life is filled with small duties, little decisions, and many, many small achievements. You don't have to climb the highest mountain. Recognizing and accepting that is, in itself, an act of self-confidence. Here are some small areas where you can begin taking responsibility for yourself and for your self-confidence:

Break your routine. Shop at a different store. Go to a new movie. Join a social club. Go to lunch with a new friend. Buy something you've been wanting a long time. Take a vacation in another country. Fix dinner for somebody you admire. Pay somebody a nice compliment. Go to evening school.

As you break your routine and do the unusual, your sense of responsibility will grow and your self-confidence will keep right up with it. You will not only gain self-confidence but you will have fun in the process.

WHY GILDA ROMAN NO LONGER SITS HOME ALONE

Gilda Roman had so little confidence that she had almost become a recluse. She lived alone and went to work every morning and came home every night. A weekly trip to a nearby grocery was the extent of her activities. Finally, after a particularly lonely weekend, she took action. She knew that she owed it to herself to be more responsible for her own welfare. She ate out every night the next week, bought new clothes, and joined a singles' club. As she took on more and more responsibility, her self-confidence grew. Her whole attitude toward herself and the people around her became positive and healthy. Gilda Roman no longer sits home alone. She is invited out often. And she has a new and bigger job—

which often happens when self-responsibility is demonstrated. This not only develops your self-confidence, it also gives your associates a like measure of confidence in you.

STEP 9: DON'T INSIST
ON A PERFECT SELF

Don't insist on a perfect self before you take hold of self-confidence. If you were perfect you couldn't stand it and neither could anybody else. That is a bit too much to be comfortable with, or to expect.

The writer who waits for perfection never gets past the blank first page. The athlete who waits on perfection never gets into the first game. The teacher who waits until the lesson is perfect never gets to the classroom. The businessman who demands perfection in himself watches the competition steal his customers. The man who waits for the perfect self-confidence never gets it. The man who gains great self-confidence is the man who goes with what he has and builds on that.

There is a difference between the healthy pursuit of self-confidence and a nitpicking striving for perfection. The first leads to a productive, satisfying life; the other can be lonely and frustrating.

HOW W. C. LeKAMP'S
NEUROTIC QUEST FOR PERFECTION
PUT HIM IN THE HOSPITAL

W. C. LeKamp, sales manager for a thriving wholesale distribution company, insisted on perfection from himself and from his men. He considered perfection and the resultant stress and ulcers the personal price that he had to pay for success. His productive salesmen were smarter than that. They left and found jobs where results were expected, but where they were not constantly hassled to be mannequins of perfection. As you might guess, W. C. Le-Kamp wound up in the hospital. He is out now but, on his doctor's advice, is no longer driving himself or his salesmen to be or do the impossible. W. C. feels better and he is building a competent sales force now that he understands the difference between high standards and a neurotic quest for perfection in everybody and everything. He no longer suffers frustration and self-doubt as before.

A little moderation helps anybody's self-confidence. You don't have to be average. You can do better than that. And you can have a supreme self-confidence without being a compulsive perfectionist.

CONFIDENCE KEYS

* You have "powers and abilities."
* You are important.
* You have intelligence.
* You can use fear effectively.
* Liking yourself is paramount.
* Your self-image is what others see in you.
* You can get rid of fear.
* Reward yourself.
* Analyze your confidence problem.
* Don't be afraid to have an opinion.

* Making decisions is a vital aspect of self-confidence.
* You are responsible for you.
* Don't insist on self-perfection.
* Build on what you have.

Chapter 2
How To Use Self-Confidence

Here is the pay-off. The more you use self-confidence, the stronger it gets, the easier it is to use, and the more it just naturally becomes a part of your everyday personality. The sooner you start using your self-confidence, the sooner you can begin enjoying all of the satisfying benefits that self-confidence brings. The pay-off is your entitlement. Here are ideas that you can put to work right now.

LABEL YOURSELF #1

To use your self-confidence to greatest advantage you must take a good look at yourself and who you are. Self-confidence dictates that you be intensely interested in you. This is the way it should be. Remember that nobody is going to be interested in you if you are not interested in you. This is not to say that you should have no interest in anyone but yourself. The self-confident man is always interested in other people, their ideas, their welfare, their activities and their thinking. Nevertheless, self-confidence begins with you, its primary focus must be on you. But the wondrous thing about self-confidence is that it is all-encompassing. When you label yourself #1 you take your rightful place in a busy, exciting world full of busy, exciting people. You make friends, your spirit is vibrant, your outlook positive. You know where you stand and what you can do. You know who you are. OK. So who are you? Here are four pertinent points.

* You are unique, one of a kind. There is nobody else in the world like you. There is nobody else who can live your life. You are you and your life belongs to you exclusively.

* You are the one who must decide what you want, when you want it, and how you will get it. You are #1, the head of You, Inc.

* You are the one who decides what you want to be. You may ask questions, seek counseling, or wish for guidance, but it is you who must weigh the balances and make the determination. In this matter, as with all else affecting your life, you are #1.

* You are the one to decide when to get started on the road to full self-confidence and the goals you have set for yourself. Others may encourage, plead or push, but only #1—you—will be the one to take the first step. This is your privilege as well as your responsibility.

Now that you are wearing the proud label of #1, let's get into the specifics of using self-confidence. Following is a thought that deserves primary consideration. Self-confidence is built upon its truth.

SELF-CONFIDENCE IS FOR WINNING

It may be hard to believe, but it's true: There are people who don't want to win. They have so little self-confidence, such a poor opinion of themselves, that the thought of being a winner fills them with guilt. They feel so unworthy that the simple little three-letter word w-i-n makes them uncomfortable. They would rather have a substitute word such as fortunate or lucky. It is sad, but there are those who find rewards in failure. Their satisfaction is found in such weak-kneed expressions as these: "I'm just not lucky"; "Nobody expects me to win"; "I've never been a winner"; "Why should I win when there are people so much smarter?" And on and on.

Of course, it is unlikely that you would ever entertain the wish not to win. Your interest in a winning self-confidence is manifested by your study of and interest in this book. But if ever you face a project and feel the faintest hesitation about winning, here is a simple, workable solution to that bag of qualms. *Get started on it at once.* Throw yourself wholeheartedly into whatever project or undertaking you are contemplating. The exhilarating feeling you will get when you accomplish something in spite of an irrational temptation to "succeed in failing" will drive home the reason that self-confidence is for winning. Here is another thought that should wipe out any negative feelings about winning. What good is self-confidence if you use it swatting flies? Self-confidence—a gift of life—is not for squandering. It is for winning.

HOW STEVE REITER
BECAME A CONFIDENT WINNER

Steve Reiter wanted to be a minister. He put off implementing his desire for two years with such excuses as, "I can't speak well enough," "I can't think on my feet" and "The good Lord didn't make me very smart." Finally, after hearing a rousing sermon by a missionary on leave, Steve realized that he had been courting failure. He then went to his father and explained, "Dad, I hope that you will understand. I don't want to be an architect like you. I want to enter the seminary and be a preacher." To Steve's surprise his father happily agreed and then financed his son's way through school. Today Steve is an evangelist winning converts and fame wherever he goes. His self-confidence knows no bounds, and he has instilled this precious attribute in many self-doubters along the way. Winning with self-confidence has a snow-balling effect.

Here is another winning thought for the self-confident to watch: Strong self-confident individuals like to do what they want to do. If they want to play golf or bridge, they may spend a great deal of time at it. If they like to fish, they can spend an awful lot of time at that. The list is endless. But the point is that if you really want to use your self-confidence in the most productive way, then you cannot be so busy doing what you want to do that you neglect what you can do.

Self-confidence is the most individualistic miracle extant. Its uses defy imagination, yet the personal qualifications necessary to be a self-confident winner are everyday stuff. Here is a list of personal qualities to illustrate for you that you have all it takes to be a confident winner today.

* Ambition
* Determination

* Desire
* Some intelligence (not all there is)
* Willingness to learn
* Self-interest
* Self-respect
* Planning
* Some pride
* Action

None of these are unusual traits. They are about what you would expect to find in your friends or the people you work with every day. Let's give particular attention to the last item on the list: action. No matter how much self-confidence is involved, nobody wins until they take action.

HOW TO USE SELF-CONFIDENCE
TO MAKE THINGS HAPPEN

The first thing to fix firmly in your mind as you set about to use your self-confidence is that you live in the present. If your self-confidence was faulty yesterday, that is over and done. With this much decided let's take a look at specific steps that you can take to make things happen today.

1. Back to the matter of decision-making. Before you can do much of anything, you have to decide what is important to you. When it comes to using self-confidence, it is not what Aunt Mamie wants, what your parents want (dear as they may be), what the boss wants, or what anybody else may want. It is what you want and that must be your decision. Now this is not to suggest that you do not owe other people polite and kind consideration. You do, and it

should be accorded them, but you do not owe them your life. Further, if your self-confidence means anything to you it means that you are the one to decide what you want. Nothing much will ever happen until you decide that it will. Don't forfeit this responsibility for a mess of pottage.

2. Action is a key word when it comes to using your self-confidence to make things happen the way that you want them to happen. You can make grand and profound decisions all day long, but until you take action they will mean nothing. Once the decision is made, your self-confidence will demand action. If action is not forthcoming, self-confidence will shrivel and die. Self-confidence cannot be built on good intentions and sharp decisions unless they are supported by intelligent and forceful action.

Of course, this does not mean that once you reach a decision that you should immediately jump up and flail out in all directions. Reason and logic are always a part of self-confidence. Once you have decided to make something happen then you must decide how you will make it happen, when you will make it happen and where you will make it happen. The pen and the pencil are mighty good tools to keep your self-confidence on track and moving ahead. Let's see how Cecil Atwood decided to buy his first new car and the action plan he followed.

HOW CECIL ATWOOD'S WRITTEN PLAN MADE THINGS HAPPEN FAST

Cecil Atwood was a new graduate engineer away from home on his first job with the Big Machine Tool Company. It had taken all the money he had to go to school so he still had no car. His decision had been to pay cash for his new automobile. Now after one year on the job he still lacked two thousand dollars to buy the car that he had his eye on. He had selected his car. Now he decided when and how he would take action. His written plan looked like this.

1. Have cash for car within six months.
2. Purchase from Town and Country Motors.
3. How to do it.
   a. Give up ski trip vacation ....$ 500.00
   b. Sell bike......................... 1000.00
   c. Moonlight Saturdays and Sundays on
      Willow Lake for Edgerton Construction
      —five weekends at $100 .... 500.00

Cecil had his car within three months instead of six. He confided that writing out when, where and how had given his self-confidence such a boost that it had been easier and quicker than he expected. Mr. Atwood is enjoying his new car and his healthy self-confidence. He is entitled. He made it happen.

FEED YOUR SELF-CONFIDENCE

Yes, you have to feed and care for your self-confidence if you expect it to always be ready when you need it. Here are some general ideas on the care and feeding of your self-confidence.

* Keep organized. Be on time. Eat right. Respect your body. Don't put yourself in a strait jacket, but do establish some positive order. Adopt a system that gets your work done, leaves time for a bit of leisure

and, of great importance, time for study and ideas.

* Commit yourself to something. It may be a plan to become president of your company or to sing in the church choir. Whatever it is, if it is something that is important to you, your self-confidence will grow as you commit yourself wholeheartedly to it.

* Tackle new activities and experiences. You can keep organization in your life and still avoid monotony and boring repetition. Your self-confidence thrives on new friendships, new places, fresh projects and a change of pace. New activities and new experiences need not be monumental to give your self-confidence an emotional and intellectual boost. When you try something new, you can accomplish something new. This is the kind of use that self-confidence thrives on.

FOCUS SELF-CONFIDENCE ON WHAT YOU WANT

When we talk of how and why you should focus your self-confidence on what you want, we are not indulging in an essay on selfishness. What we are talking about is your responsibility to yourself. You have a needle-sharp responsibility to be as strong as you can as well as sweet as you can. Self-confidence can accommodate both areas of your life. You can't do much of anything for anybody until you use self-confidence to pay your debt to you.

You hear and read a lot about helping others get what they want and how, in turn, they will give you what you want. There is a certain amount of selfish truth in this popular philosophy. If you will note, however, by and large the people who profess and preach this approach are, in fact, focusing on that all-important end result—what they want. There is nothing wrong with that. Any self-confident person should extend a helping hand whenever he can, but never at the expense of his own goals and needs. There is something inherently political and wrong with a demand that requires that you sacrifice what you want (thus leaving your self-confidence open to question) in order to help others. The self-confident man will help all he can within reason, but not with great expectations of reward and not at the total expense of what he wants.

The way to focus your self-confidence on what you want is to first decide what it is that you want above all else and then devote yourself and your intellect to it. Sound simplistic? The idea is, but implementing it requires thought, planning and effort. Here again the pen helps. Write down your plan step by step and then follow it confidently. Here is a sample. Suppose that you are in accounts receivable, but you want to be the comptroller of your firm. Lay it out along these lines.

What I want: To be comptroller.

Present qualifica-
tions:
1. Degree in accounting.
2. Three years' experience.

Steps to reach goal:
1. Further study.
2. Pass CPA examination.
3. Ask for tougher jobs.

4. Press for advancement at
every opportunity.
5. Keep my superiors aware of
my goal and what I am do-
ing to reach it.

Your visual plan can be as simple or as complicated as you like. The key is to keep your eye on
what you want. Here's how one ambitious young
man did that.

HOW HARVEY CROSS
FOCUSED SELF-CONFIDENCE
ON WHAT HE WANTED AND GOT IT

Harvey Cross was a high-school graduate with a
wife and year-old daughter. He drove a truck for a
lumber company in the town of ten thousand popula-
tion where he grew up. His burning ambition was to
be a building contractor. He had little training in this
field, but the local high school had recently started
vocational classes as a part of its evening program for
adults. Harvey went to see the teacher who adminis-
tered the vocational training classes. When he left he
had a written list of the subjects he was to pursue for
the next two years, subjects such as carpentry, blue-
print reading, drafting, wiring and plumbing. Next
he and his young wife worked out a budget that
would allow them to set aside some money for the
day Harvey was ready to embark on his new career.
With each step Harvey's self-confidence grew. At the
end of his two-year program Harvey took a job with
an established contractor to gain on-the-job experi-

ence. Three years later he struck out on his own. Today Harvey Cross Houses is going strong with Harvey confidently buying new equipment and adding new crews regularly. Harvey Cross focused his self-confidence on what he wanted and bolstered it with a workable plan. This is a most commendable way to use your self-confidence.

STICK TO ESSENTIALS

It is hard to put self-confidence to good use if it is permitted to float about like a butterfly on a summer day. You can avoid this. Here are key items to keep in mind as you stick to essentials while you use and build your self-confidence.

* Don't try to get everything you want all on the self-same day. No matter how much self-confidence you garner, you are still going to have to consider physical and time limitations. Deal with the essentials first. After that you can ladle as much frosting on the cake as you like.

* Establish obtainable objectives. If you lack the qualifications to reach an objective, you will put an intolerable strain on your self-confidence if you insist on using it before you are prepared. One of the essentials in using self-confidence is to examine your personal qualifications for a proposed objective. This is no cause for alarm. Since you are smart enough to realize the importance of self-confidence, you have plenty of intelligence to equip yourself to go after anything you want. A word of caution: When you examine your qualifications, don't put yourself down. You have plenty going for you right now. When you

reach one objective you can always step up to a bigger one. This is a healthy, painless way to use self-confidence. It is the way to establish obtainable objectives.

* Don't be distracted. Once you have made up your mind as to what is essential, don't take side trips to please a friend or satisfy a whimsy. You use your self-confidence most forcefully when you stay on track. That is one of the essentials.

HOW TO USE SELF-CONFIDENCE
TO PINPOINT WHAT IS IMPORTANT

The first observation to make when we speak of how to use self-confidence to pinpoint what is important is this: We are talking about what is important to you. Of course, you owe your fellow man and all the world something, but—we can't say this too often—until you do something for yourself, you can't do much for anyone or anything else. The record of important accomplishments by the man who doesn't use his self-confidence for his benefit, as well as for the benefit of those around him, is like hips on a snake. Hard to find.

Pinpointing what is important to you is a DIY (Do It Yourself) project. If somebody else does it for you, you won't be happy with it and your self-confidence will go begging. On the other hand when you put your self-confidence to work and pinpoint what is important to you on that basis, then your self-confidence will expand and grow. Self-confidence is like your brain; only you can make it work, and the more you work it the sharper it becomes.

You may mentally pinpoint what is important to you or you may create your own visual aid to speed the process. Here is how one young man did it.

TRAVIS MAYS' INDEX CARD SYSTEM

Travis Mays listed ten things of great importance to himself on ten three-by-five index cards. He then selected the five least important and discarded them. Next he studied the five remaining cards and eliminated three of them. This left two cards. He threw out the "get married" card and kept the "go back to school" card. His self-confidence was put to the test when he told his girl, but she concurred. Travis earned his degree and married his girl two years later. Travis used his self-confidence to win two ways: He pinpointed what was most important and got his girl, too.

Pinpointing what is most important should not be an excruciating thing to do. Your mind and your self-confidence will tell you what is important (what you really want). Then it is time to map your strategy and move quickly.

USE YOUR CONFIDENCE EVERY DAY

Self-confidence is not something only for emergencies, high moments and glorious flights. It is for everyday use. You live in an everyday world. Much of what is required of us is routine stuff: getting out of bed, going to work, paying the bills, educating the children, sitting quietly in church, keeping in touch with family and friends, and dealing with each day. This in itself is no small thing in a complicated, swirling world such as ours. You need an abundance of self-confidence to handle all this comfortably. Here is the most comforting thought of all: When you use your self-confidence every day, it is always there when big opportunities come, when emergencies arise, when glorious challenges are faced. Don't let it rust like a can in the ditch.

WORK ON A LEVEL OF REALITY

Ambition and desire are admirable virtues. However, they are not immune to reality. Self-confidence must be based on a level of reality. This in no way hints that self-confidence has rigid limitations. It does mean that no matter how much self-confidence you have, there is no sense in using it in unwinnable wars. The most renowned mortal who ever lived had his limitations. But consider this: No matter your handicaps or limitations (real or imaginary), your self-confidence can still make a magnificent achiever of you. I personally know the man in this true story that follows.

HOW JERRY HARRIS FACED REALITY

Jerry Harris had a consuming interest in horses. His dream was to become a trainer, a cowboy, a rodeo performer, and an owner of horses. At the age of fifteen, Jerry broke his neck in a diving accident. He has been paralyzed from the shoulders down for over thirty years. Yet Jerry's self-confidence did not die. He knew that he could never ride or handle horses again. This was beyond reality. Jerry faced his plight with a sense of reality. He would not abandon his beloved horses. He attended horse shows, rodeos and fairs in his wheelchair. Painfully, slowly, he learned to type. He began to write about horses. His articles have been published internationally. His self-confidence has added years to Jerry's life. His doctors are amazed. When you put your self-confidence to work on a level of reality, surprising things do happen.

NOW FOR THE NITTY-GRITTY

How can you be sure that you are using your self-confidence realistically? If your answers to the following questions are a resounding yes, you are on solid ground.

* Do you take pride in what you are doing?
* Do you enjoy what you are doing?
* Are you doing what you want to do?
* Does your training and background qualify you for what you are doing?
* Will your financial resources see you through?
* Do you have a definite goal?
* Will your life be better if you do this thing?
* Will you be better off financially, emotionally or physically once you have attained your goal?
* Are you determined to stick with your objective?
* Are you prepared to pay the price of success?
* Will you keep working once your immediate goal

is reached?
* Do you appreciate that self-confidence is a journey and never the end?

If your answer is yes to these twelve questions, you are using your self-confidence on a level of reality. As long as your feet are on solid ground, self-confidence will take you where you want to go.

HOW TO KEEP YOUR SELF-CONFIDENCE CONSTRUCTIVE AS YOU USE IT

No matter how desirable a strong personal trait may be, it becomes a handicap when perversely used. Self-confidence used abrasively or boorishly makes the best intentions appear antagonistic and insulting. Such use incites needless resistance and produces negative results all around. You can avoid this risk by using a modicum of diplomacy and courtesy along with the strongest dose of self-confidence. You don't lose a thing when you use self-confidence in this manner. Such an application makes your self-confidence stronger and more effective.

Obviously, you will want to keep your self-confidence constructive. The following guide lines will keep you on course.

KEEP A POSITIVE OUTLOOK. You keep a positive outlook when you accept the fact that you have all the confidence a winner needs, when you know that your views and goals are honest and legitimate, and that people will be happy to see you succeed. This isn't much but, like many simple truths, it is enough.

DON'T BE AFRAID. Fear entertains the negative. It is destructive and demoralizing. Go back and reread step two in chapter one. Fear costs too much. You can't afford it. It was said of one poor soul that he was more afraid of life than death. This will never be your lot, because your interest is in a strong, constructive self-confidence.

LEAVE ROOM FOR A POSSIBLE MISTAKE. You may make one. that does not mean that you are through and done forever. One angry fellow said of another that he was as dogmatic as an evangelist with a third-grade education. If he's right in this observation, the dogmatic man is going to be in bad shape when he realizes that he has finally made a mistake. You will keep your self-confidence constructive and powerful when you leave room for a possible mistake as you use it.

TAKE THE HIGH ROAD. Self-confidence is not petty stuff. There are no tricks, no subterfuge or deceptions in your self-confidence. It is a constructive force to be used for constructive purposes. It is the high road to success and personal power.

TAKE THE LONG ROAD. By this we mean that end results should be the primary concern of constructive self-confidence. Of course, instant fame and quick success do come, but the end result is what counts. Every self-confident man and woman appreciates this. It is what will make your constructive self-confidence most worthwhile.

USE THE TALENTS YOU HAVE. Don't worry about what you don't have or what the other fellow does have. It's what you have that will keep your self-confidence productive and constructive. As

Henry Van Dyke said. "Use what talents you possess. The woods would be very silent if no birds sang there except those that sang best."

MAKE A SELF-POWER INVENTORY

There is nothing that conveys a sense of self-worth more than self-confidence does. The feeling of power and well-being grows every time you use your self-confidence. A quick inventory of your self-power assets will show that you have plenty of personal power to put your self-confidence to bold use. Get a scratch pad or make mental notes. Forget formal education, degrees, academic honors and social position. Look at all you have in addition to these prized credits. Here is a partial list that you can add to as you make your own self-power inventory. The order of the list is random.

Respect	Enthusiasm	Comfort
Home	Common Sense	Incentive
Family	Vision	Persistence
Friends	Energy	Motivation
Freedom	Mind	Faith
Choice	Experience	Ambition
Opportunity	Competitiveness	Talent
Positive Attitude	Mobility	Desire
		Goals

CONFIDENCE KEYS

* Label yourself #1.
* You are one of a kind.

* Self-confidence is for winning.
* Don't neglect what you can do.
* Make things happen.
* Action is a key word.
* Feed and care for your self-confidence.
* Commit yourself to something.
* Pinpoint what is important to you.
* Work on a level of reality.
* Keep your self-confidence constructive.

Chapter 3
Self-Confidence as Self-Concept

Read this chapter twice. Your self-confidence can never be any better than your self-concept. You must drill this into your mind with the intensity of a blowtorch. The importance of a wholesome, positive self-concept cannot be overstated. With this firmly in mind, let's examine this.

HOW DO YOU SEE YOURSELF?

First, if you do not like what you see in yourself, remember that you are not made of stone. You are a warm, living, viable creature subject to the change of your heart and your will. No matter how weak your self-confidence is, *you* can make it strong. No matter how strong your self-confidence is, *you* can make it stronger still. This is a demonstrable truth with living examples of healthy self-concepts all about you.

Regrettably, there are those who are burdened with a deplorable self-concept and are unable to identify their problem. They suffer from a destructive feeling of inadequacy, but have never looked within themselves to diagnose their problem. Then there are those struggling to face their problem who are never sure of the answer. Here are simple questions to help you see yourself. If your answer to any of these questions is yes, you can identify your problem and go to work on it today. The purpose of a diagnosis is to make the patient well. Self-diagnosis has the same application. When you use these questions, use them to make your self-concept strong or stronger. The prescription is the same for a sagging self-confidence or a booming one.

1. Are you uncomfortable when you meet new people?
2. Do you feel that you are not as "good" as anyone else?
3. Do you compulsively compare yourself with everyone you meet?
4. Do you almost never take part in group conversations?
5. Do you make excuses when invited out socially?
6. Are you painfully self-conscious in a crowd?
7. Do you worry over what other people may be thinking of you?
8. Do you often feel left out?
9. Are you unhappy with the way you feel around people?
10. Do you worry about how you look?
11. Does a slight compliment lift you to the ceiling?
12. Can you accept a gift without protesting?

If you see yourself in any of these questions, don't despair. You are still in charge of you. There is much that you can do. Begin with this.

BE YOUR OWN BEST FRIEND

This book is about you. Of course, there is a thread of psychology in the subject. This is natural and necessary, but there is no high-flown medical jargon, no psychobabble. This book is about the person who should be your best friend—you.

The Second Commandment, which Christ said was like unto the First is, "Thou shalt love thy neighbor as thyself." Now let us paraphrase that. "Thou shalt love thyself as thy neighbor." This is high authority that we are to have due regard for ourselves. Otherwise, the commandment, "Thou shalt love thy neighbor as thyself," would be devoid of meaning. This should dispel any pangs of doubt about the validity and wisdom of the admonition to be your own best friend.

Being your own best friend does not mean being self-centered, wholly selfish, or withdrawn. It is the realization and conviction that your self-concept must be positive and outgoing before you can offer anything of substance to anybody else. Nobody wants your neurosis.

You can be your own best friend. Here are ten ways to prove that you have what it takes not only to be your best friend, but also that you can have a healthy and happy self-concept.

TEN WAYS TO PROVE THAT
YOU HAVE WHAT IT TAKES

These topics are not for anyone else's benefit. They are for your benefit alone. You don't have to prove anything to anybody else. Use these as a checklist to make sure that your best friend is you. If you detect or suspect a deficiency in any area, put the remedy to work. There is no medicine as effective as self-therapy.

There are as many ways to prove that an individual has what it takes to maintain a healthy self-concept as there are people on the streets. Here are ten simple ways for you to prove that you have what it takes and more.

1. You can like yourself no matter what your circumstances are today.

Proof: You don't have to be wealthy, socially prominent, exceptionally intelligent, or anything besides a normal everyday, conscientious human being, to be an admirable person. We could make a list running several pages of just such ordinary men and women who have left their imprint on history. But that is not necessary. Your best examples can be found right where you live and work. Count the people around you who are well adjusted and content with themselves. What do they have that you don't have or can't get?

It is true that aggressive, ambitious people are seldom totally self-satisfied. They are always reaching. This, though, is another reason that you can like yourself.

WHY C. K. MARTIN LIKED HIMSELF

One of the most respected and best adjusted men I ever knew was C. K. Martin who was a life insurance salesman for one of the top companies in our country. His income was adequate, but far from spectacular. His lifetime avocation was teaching a Sunday school class. His creed was service to mankind. He liked that and he liked himself. Though Mr. Martin has been gone a long time, there are still men in my town who boast that C. K. Martin was their teacher and friend. I am one of them. Mr. Martin would tell you that yes, indeed, you can like yourself. No matter what your circumstances are today, that is a prerequisite of a positive self-concept.

2. You can change your circumstances and environment.

Proof: If you feel trapped, you can do something about it. It may take some time and it will take planning and study. Nobody can sentence you to an unhappy situation. Here's how you can change your circumstances and your environment.

A. Be specific. Decide exactly what you want and where you want to be.

B. Dedicate yourself to getting what you want and living where you want. Be single-minded about it.

C. Plan. Plan by the day, week, month and year. Set time limits on your goals and keep track of your progress.

D. Don't feel sorry for yourself. Self-pity turns people off. If you doubt this, ask yourself how you feel about a man who habitually complains and feels sorry for himself. Honestly, don't you want him to change his self-concept or just go away?

3. You don't have to apologize to anyone.

Proof: Nobody else can decide what is important to you. Being and doing what is important to your self-concept is your job. Do you know anyone else better qualified to handle this job than you?

4. You don't need flattery.

Proof: Conversely, your strong self-concept will resent insincere compliments or meaningless praise. You have what it takes to get along without anything as fragile and useless as flattery.

5. You can get rid of crutches.

Proof: You don't have to prop up a keen self-concept with crippling habits or demeaning artificial crutches. If you have to have a drink to convince yourself you're one of the guys, that's a crutch. If you take pills to boost your confidence, that's a crutch. You are the only one who has what it takes to get rid of crutches. It takes will power, but without will power nobody builds much of a self-concept anyway.

6. You can say no.

Proof: The ability to say no is as important to a power-filled self-concept as the ability to say yes. During a lifetime you will be exposed to all kinds of propositions and temptations. If you say yes to all of them, your self-concept will suffer. One sure way to prove that you have what it takes is to say no when your intellect tells you to say no!

7. You can take action.

Proof: The beauty of this land that we live in is not that we have to do anything, but that we are free to do anything. Action to do what you want and to get what you want is a great contributor to a robust self-concept. It is proof that you have what it takes to control your life and your self-concept.

8. You can control your attitude.

Proof: The power to control other people is a fascinating subject, but the enormous power that you have over yourself is the key to a most productive self-concept. You have what it takes to change your attitude. An attitude is a mental or an emotional position with regard to a fact or condition. If your attitude is one of depression or hopelessness, then your self-concept has no chance. But you can change your attitude by harnessing the immense power that you have over yourself. Here is how one man did it.

HOW SIDNEY ATTEBERRY
CONTROLLED HIS ATTITUDE
AT AGE SIXTY

Sidney Atteberry had retired from his job and from life at age sixty. He had been a highly productive independent businessman for years, but he had quit. He had, as he said, earned his rest. His attitude was one that told his family and friends that they could expect nothing more from him because he was old and retired. After three months of hibernating, Atteberry saw the sun shining one morning and realized that he had lost his friends, his family and his self-respect. He went back to work as a volunteer consultant, joined a civic club, became active in his church again and rejoined his family and friends. Almost immediately he felt better and became happier. Now he goes about making speeches on the importance of the right attitude. Sidney has what it takes, but he had lost it all for a while.

9. You can forgive yourself.

Proof: Yes, be hard on yourself. Discipline is a hallmark of self-confidence and self-concept, but this does not mean that you should self-destruct if you make a mistake or fall on your face. You can forgive yourself and get up and go on. You forgive others, so you can be your own best friend and forgive you. Do not excuse yourself. *Forgive* yourself and go on to prove that you have what it takes.

10. You can make a self-investment.

Proof: The biggest and most profitable investment you can ever hope to make will be a self-investment. You can be aggressively ambitious; you can read, study, plan and act for your benefit. Others will profit too from your self-investment. When you invest in self-concept, you have a lot to share. You will have what it takes and then some when you invest your time and talents in you. And this leads to an interesting question.

WHY HOBBLE YOURSELF?

When all the evidence points to the fact that you have the necessary equipment to do just about anything that you want to do, why hobble yourself with a weak self-concept? There are those confused souls who have such a low opinion of themselves that they fear a strong self-concept. An excuse is easier to come by than a high-powered, productive personality. It is also a hobble that keeps self-concept shackled to the ground. It is not for you. Today is not the last day of your life. It is the day to kill excuses. This is not a preachment; it is a fact.

HOW TO RID YOURSELF OF DESTRUCTIVE SELF-CONCEPTS

A destructive self-concept is partial suicide. A part of you is destroyed. But if you have a destructive concept of yourself, you can get rid of it. After all, you gave it to yourself; you can get rid of it. If you have any destructive self-concepts, you know what they are. They worry you. They bug you. You can identify them. The hard part will be to admit them. Once you have admitted you have a destructive self-concept, then you are ready to do something about it. Here are some ideas.

* Recognize that any poor self-concept is an emotional problem. Nobody is beating you over the head, but the hurt is real enough all right. Changing an emotional problem is changing your mind, which is changing the way you view the problem. For example, if you are suspicious of everybody because you think that they may be so much stronger than you that they are going to do you in, that is an emotional illness. The way to correct this is to change your mind about other people. They haven't done you harm yet. View them as they are: hard-working, ordinary folk who are too busy with their own affairs to have time to go around plotting and planning against you or anyone else.

It has been said that fifty percent of the people who are driven to seek medical help are suffering

71

from self-induced illnesses. They have an emotional problem; their self-concept is destroying them. You don't belong in this category. As a productive, studious individual, you can't afford any part of a destructive self-concept.

* Build yourself a little pedestal and put yourself on it. I don't mean that you should sit on an imaginary throne and idolize yourself. Instead, accept the fact that you are a whole, competent person and give yourself some standards. Build your pedestal on some personal principles and stick by them. Climb on that throne and don't let anything knock you off. Here's an example.

WHAT WARREN MILLET DID
TO RID HIMSELF OF
A DESTRUCTIVE SELF-CONCEPT

Warren Millet hated himself because he was prone to exaggerate and lie for no reason. He knew it was wrong and he knew that it made him feel badly about himself. He vowed to put himself on a pedestal of truth and stay there. Every time he felt the urge to boost his ego with stupid exaggeration or blatant untruths, he remembered he had built a pedestal for himself. It must have worked magnificently. Warren no longer has this destructive habit or a destructive self-concept. He enjoys his self-respect and the solid opinion he has of himself. More, his friends and associates like Warren better also.

* Have a private brain-storming session with yourself.

You know what a brain-storming session is. It's a

group problem-solving technique where everybody spontaneously throws in ideas. You will be the whole works at your private brain-storming session. Explore every idea pertaining to any destructive self-doubts that may be haunting you. Write them down. Your ideas should cover such areas as: What's causing my self-doubts? What am I afraid of? Why do I feel this way? Put down every idea that crosses your mind no matter how trivial it may seem. After this, do the same with ideas for getting rid of the harmful self-concept. Study both lists, isolate the bugaboo that is causing your problem. Then choose the solution from the problem-solving list your brain-storming has produced.

The brain-storming technique has solved some big problems. Your private brain-storming session can help you if you have a self-concept problem. This technique points the finger at the heart of the problem and brings forth a solution to rid you of any destructive opinions about yourself. Don't be afraid to stir the black pot.

ONE WEAK SPOT NEED NOT BE FATAL

Everybody has a flaw of some sort, but it is rarely fatal. What can be fatal is worrying over it until your reason takes leave. The way to deal with your weak spot is to eliminate it, or if it is of such a nature that this is a physical impossibility, then work around it. You work around it by centering your activities where you can accomplish the most. Whatever you do, don't think that you are a failure because of a flaw (one weak spot). If you label yourself on this basis, you are doing yourself a great injustice.

Mark Twain had trouble with spelling. That was his weak spot, but it didn't keep him from becoming a famous and much-loved writer. He disposed of this weak spot by saying that he wouldn't give a damn for a man who couldn't spell a word more than one way. Obviously, Mark Twain knew how to deal with a weak spot.

HOW TO DEVELOP A POSITIVE SELF-CONCEPT

Paul Bryant says that to be good, a man must do something every day to help himself. That, in a nutshell, is the way to develop a positive self-concept. Your life cannot be a circus of confusion if you are going to do anything worthwhile. Doing something worthwhile for yourself is the place to begin. This is how you help yourself. This is how you develop a positive self-image.

Doing something worthwhile doesn't necessarily mean loading yourself with massive, difficult assignments when you get up each morning. Instead, it is taking a daily step toward your goal or goals, maintaining a schedule of study and planning, reinforcing your daily schedule, and capitalizing on workaday opportunities. It is staying in charge of your life.

If you feel good about yourself, that is a sign that your self-concept is on a positive track. If you think your self-image is in good shape but you still have some tremors of misgivings, here are some danger signals and the remedies you can apply to further develop a robust self-concept.

Danger signal. You avoid giving a direct, straight answer when you are asked a question.

Remedy. The way to get rid of this tell-tale signal is to realize that a question is not an attack against you. Nobody is trying to expose your ignorance or lay your fears open. Usually a question seeks nothing more than an honest answer. If the question is not frivolous or malicious, then it deserves an honest answer. If you don't have the answer, don't feel put down. Say that you don't know. Otherwise, answer the question forthrightly. Squirming and talking about everything under the sun instead of answering the question in point says more about you than any incorrect answer could. Questions are not bullets aimed at your heart. Practice answering them in a relaxed, routine manner. You don't have to be profound or bombastic to be impressive or helpful. Treating questions as a normal part of human communication will not only get rid of this danger signal; it will help develop a positive self-image.

Danger signal. You don't like to offer an opinion.

Remedy. This signal and the remedy is akin to the preceding one. When you hesitate or try to avoid giving an opinion, you are saying that you don't think your opinion counts and thereby saying, "I don't count." Go back and reread the discussion on answering questions. Handle this problem the same way. Your opinions do count and you count. When you accept this basic idea, your self-concept will be positive and outgoing.

Danger signal. You are suspicious of everybody's motives.

Remedy. Only a fool believes everybody and everything. It is even more foolish and destructive to be paranoid and believe in nobody. Anyone who is suspicious of everybody else's motives is defensive and often antagonistic. There is no such thing as being happy, self-respecting and positive while full of suspicion and cowering in a defensive posture. Like all emotional illnesses, the problem of constant suspicion of others is best treated by the victim. You can handle this issue by asking why anybody could be after your skin, and what the whole world could possibly gain by doing you in. A realistic answer to these questions can set you on the road to the positive self-concept that is yours to claim.

Danger signal. You are jealous of self-confident outgoing people.

Remedy. There is no such creature as a jealous man or woman with a strong self-concept. Jealousy and envy are signs of insecurity and personal apprehension. The quickest way to be rid of these confidence-destroyers is to ask yourself what you gain by indulging them. Try this. Write down three true benefits jealousy and envy can contribute to your self-concept or, for that matter, three benefits that they can bring to any areas of your life. There won't be one. When you look at jealousy in this light, you can rid yourself of it. Then you are a big step closer to your own positive self-concept.

HOW LAVERTA HARTMAN SHED
A CRIPPLING JEALOUSY

Laverta Hartman was jealous of her older sister, Mary, who lived only two blocks from her. Mary had many friends, went to parties and other social functions regularly, and frequently entertained in her home. Laverta loved her sister and resented the jealousy that hampered their relationship. She discussed her problem with her doctor. He suggested that she forget her jealousy and give a party herself with her sister as the guest of honor. The thought infuriated Laverta momentarily, but she agreed. The party, of course, was a warm success. It gave Laverta cause for a better self-concept and it made her aware that her sister was not only helpful, but that she loved her dearly. Laverta put her improved self-concept to work enriching her life. She now teaches classes on how to make and entertain friends. She no longer suffers from a crippling jealousy and her self-concept is bright and shiny, as a self-concept is supposed to be.

When you recognize these or any other danger signals that something is hurting your self-concept, identify the culprits and apply the remedy. A positive self-concept is too important to you for you to surrender it without a fight.

YOU ARE ALL YOU OWN

You may be a millionaire, you may control many assets, and you may direct the activities of many people, but you are all you own. You may lose everything else, but nobody can take away your self-confidence and destroy your self-concept without your express permission. You are all you own. That is enough. As long as you keep your confidence, your self-respect and a vigorous self-concept, you can recover anything else you may temporarily lose. This is something to hang on to.

A SELF-CONCEPT TEST

Nobody wants their lives to be a waltz danced in a graveyard. A self-concept test will illustrate to you that your life, wherever you are and whoever you are, can be productive and rewarding. Here's a simple concept test for you. Use it, enlarge upon it, and build upon it. You will find plenty to like in yourself even if some of the questions hit home. Remember you are in charge.

1. Do you cave in and do favors for others though you don't want to?
2. Does it annoy you when a friend gets a promotion or wins an honor?
3. Do you feel resentful when your wife or husband is praised?
4. Do you feel guilty when you take time to do something you enjoy?
5. Do you feel that you are always on the outside looking in?
6. Do you turn down invitations when you really want to accept them?
7. Do you hate yourself for acting like a coward?
8. Are you inhibited about winning and succeeding?
9. Are you worried that you won't be liked?
10. Do you always identify with the underdog?
11. Do you conceal your true feelings?
12. Are you hiding from yourself?
13. Are you overly impressed by titles?
14. Do you seek sympathy?

15. Do you find it difficult to keep a commitment to yourself?

None of these questions should make you fold up. They are designed to make you stronger. If you see yourself in any of these questions, don't despair. When you have isolated the problem, you can do something about it. Go back and reread the section, "Ten Ways to Prove That You Have What It Takes." You will find plenty of proof that you can overcome any deficiency one of these questions might have uncovered. Be a hero about it. As Ralph Waldo Emerson said, "Self-trust is the essence of heroism."

CONFIDENCE KEYS

* Your self-confidence can be no better than your self-concept.
* You are not made of stone.
* You can make your self-confidence strong.
* You are in charge of you.
* Be your own best friend.
* You don't have to prove anything to anybody but you.
* You can prove that you have what it takes.
* Don't hobble yourself.
* A defective self-concept is partial suicide.
* Your life cannot be a circus of confusion.
* Do something worthwhile for yourself.
* You are all you own.

Chapter 4
Sixteen Ways To Whip A Nagging Inferiority Complex

Let's first identify "inferiority complex" by looking at the two words. When we clearly understand the meaning of the words *inferiority* and *complex* we begin to see the enormity of the problem. An inferiority complex is indeed a painful, crippling affliction. Our definition will illustrate this.

To be inferior is to be of low value, to possess little merit, and to be insignificant and of minimal importance. It is to be of a low or lower rank.

A complex is something that is made up of complicated or interrelated parts; it also may be a group of forces that exert a dominating influence upon the personality and/or an exaggerated reaction to other people, or to a particular subject or situation.

Now we come to inferiority complex. Here is how a best-selling dictionary defines it. "An acute sense of personal inferiority resulting in either timidity or through overcompensation in exaggerated aggressiveness."

As anyone who has ever suffered from this debilitating condition can tell you, it is a persistent nagging illness. But it can be whipped. That is our concern. It responds best to self-therapy. The following techniques and ideas can get the victim on the road to recovery through his own determined effort.

1. RESPECT YOURSELF

You can't do much for someone that you do not respect, especially if that someone is you. If a sneaky bit of inferiority complex is keeping you from feeling enthusiastic about yourself, here is something to keep in mind: You don't have to be the biggest dog in the fight to have self-respect. You don't have to base your self-respect on great accomplishments, making large amounts of money, or always being the best in everything. All men have limitations, physical, mental and spiritual. Self-respect derives from doing the best that you can with what you have where you are. When you do that much you have every right to self-respect and respect from your fellow man. When you do that much you can feel good about yourself. How you feel about yourself determines whether you respect yourself.

There are numerous causes, real and imaginary, that account for an individual's loss or abandonment of self-respect. Let's examine a few.

* Frustration. The sense of despair that comes from frustration can easily degenerate into a loss of self-respect if you do not keep an objective view of your life. When one is stuck in a demanding job that seems to be a dead end, frustration can mount. When it seems impossible to get or do something

81

that is of much importance to you, it is easy to succumb to frustration. The average man or woman with a desire and drive to succeed or amount to something is bound to run head-on into frustration at times. Feeling frustrated is bad enough, but if you give up your self-respect because of it, you lose all. If frustration is gnawing at your self-respect, do the following.

A. Go off by yourself and analyze your problem. Make notes. Ask yourself questions, such as: How important is this anyway? Am I really going to be destroyed if this doesn't turn out the way I want? How much time and agony do I owe this situation? What will I gain if I lose my self-respect over it?

B. After this bit of soul-searching, list all the possible solutions you can think of. Also, list alternatives in case you can't resolve the problem as you wish. Get outside help if you need it. As soon as possible go to work in a constructive way on whatever is frustrating you. Action releases tension and clears the air.

C. One more question to ask yourself: Do I want self-respect or a nagging, frustrating inferiority complex? Which will do the most for me?

The right answer is obvious. When you have this answer you can deal with frustration.

TERRI HOLDEN TURNS
FRUSTRATION ASIDE

Terri Holden wanted to be a gynecologist, but she could not get into the medical school of her choice. She was frustrated, but she held onto the good opinion she had of herself and went into training as a nurse. In a few years she was nursing supervisor for a large hospital. She has the respect of the professional people around her and the respect and appreciation of her community. More to the point, she did not let frustration rob her of her self-respect. She has plenty of that and she deserves it all.

* Past mistakes. Anybody who lets a past mistake take away his or her self-respect is dealing with a ghost. The way to keep your self-respect in this case is to profit from what you've learned and get on with the job of living. Grieving over past mistakes is like crying because you can't walk on water.

* Rejection. When someone you love and respect hurts you, that hurts. But it is extremely unlikely that anyone who might have done this to you had any intention of giving you an inferiority complex. That is like self-respect—something that you give yourself.

2. LIST YOUR REASONS
FOR SELF-CONFIDENCE

One of the big reasons that a nagging inferiority complex can take over a life is that we are all too prone to magnify and exaggerate our problems and deficiencies. Here is a workable technique to avoid this gross error. Make two lists, one list of the problems that may contribute to an inferiority complex and the other a list of reasons to be self-confident. Make the list of your reasons for self-confidence first. By listing all your self-confidence reasons first, you will take a lot of the frustration and pain out of the second list before you get to it.

Don't hesitate to use your pen or pencil when

working out a problem or when doing a personality exercise. There are reasons for this. For one, writing something crystallizes your thinking. A written list or composition is always more condensed and precise than speech or random thoughts. When you write something and see it there in black and white you will remember it much better than verbal expression. Two, you can go back and refer to the written word from time to time. Nothing drives a point home more than repetition or rereading.

Model your lists after the following.

REASONS TO BE SELF-CONFIDENT
OR
WHY I SHOULD HAVE SELF-CONFIDENCE

A. I am responsible for me.
B. I am unique. There is nobody else like me.
C. I can function well.
D. I am literate and in possession of my faculties.
E. I can do more than one thing well.
F. I want success.
G. I can improve day by day.
H. Nobody is threatening me.
I. Nobody would gain anything if I had no self-confidence.
J. Whatever I am or will be is up to me.
K. I understand the importance of self-confidence.
L. I owe self-confidence to me.

Now for the second list.

3.   LIST YOUR PROBLEM AREAS

REASONS WHY I FEEL INFERIOR
OR
EXCUSES FOR AN INFERIORITY COMPLEX

A. I am not popular.
B. Other people act so superior.
C. I can never think of the right thing to say.
D. I feel left out.
E. Everybody else is a big success.
F. I live in the wrong neighborhood.
G. I am self-conscious.
H. I am not attractive.
I. I don't have a personality.
J. I don't belong.
K. I'm afraid.

Here are two lists that just about anybody with a twinge of inferiority could draw up. Now let's see how to use the two lists to dispel any notions of inferiority.

4.   HOW TO USE THE TWO LISTS

Lay the two lists in front of you with the positive number one list on the left and the negative number two list on the right. Go down the list on the right. Pick out any item. Then look at your list on your left. When you see how much you have to offset the negatives on the right-hand list you will see that you have no reasons to feel inferior.

Let's make a short comparison of the two example

lists to illustrate this point.

List number two, item A: I am not popular.

List number one, item A: I am responsible for me. This statement is the bedrock of self-confidence. Use it to become popular if that is important to you. Get involved with people. Be aggressive in meeting new people. Encourage them to talk about their interests. Then listen. You'll be popular all right.

List number two, item B: Other people act so superior.

List number one, item B: I am unique. There is nobody else like me.

If there is nobody else like you, how can other people be superior to you? Unique means one of a kind. If someone does act superior, that's all it is— an act.

List number two, item C: I can never think of the right thing to say.

List number one, item C: I can function well.

No matter what you say, not everyone will think it's "right." Say it anyway. As long as it's an honest statement, you're on safe ground.

List number two, item D: I feel left out.

List number one, item D: I am literate and in possession of my faculties.

This is justification enough to whip any nagging inferiority complex. Use your faculties much as suggested in item A of list number one where popularity is the issue. Anyone in full possession of his or her faculties need not be left out of anything unless they choose.

These four examples are enough to illustrate how you can use your two lists to be rid of any nagging inferiority problem. Write down your conclusions as you check your two lists against each other. This will help you retain your conclusions. There is a simple way to prove this. Think of twenty random unrelated words. Next write twenty random words. Tomorrow at this time see how many words you can recall from each exercise.

5. ENLARGE YOUR LIST OF REASONS FOR SELF-CONFIDENCE

No matter your age you face a new day each morning. Each day brings more experiences and more opportunities to develop a satisfying self-confidence. Which is a way of saying that you can whip an inferiority complex by enlarging your list of reasons for self-confidence through your daily experiences.

6. HOW TO ELIMINATE THE PROBLEM LIST

The place to begin to eliminate your problem list (Excuses for an Inferiority Complex) is to admit that feelings of inferiority are tormenting you. Often an inferiority complex is rationalized away by its victim, particularly teenagers and young people. They may avoid energetic, bright people by saying, "I don't like them." They may avoid challenging opportunities in the same way with an, "I don't like the idea" or "That isn't my thing." Of course such attitudes can be justified occasionally, but we are concerned with the fact that they are used as excuses. To recognize an excuse is essential in the matter of getting rid of a nagging inferiority complex. Here is a case in point.

HOW KRISSY VOGLER
ELIMINATED EXCUSES

Krissy Vogler was a beautiful high school freshman, but she was withdrawn and unhappy. She avoided the student leaders and her more popular classmates. Her reasoning (excuse) was that she didn't like the kids or the school activities. Her grades indicated a high degree of intelligence. Fortunately for Krissy, a kindly counselor took note. She made Krissy see that her parents' divorce and the emotional strain she had been through were no reasons to destroy her life. Krissy had to admit that she had a problem. With the aid of her counselor, Krissy got rid of her excuses and the excruciating inferiority complex. She continues to be an excellent student and is editor of the school paper as well as an enthusiastic cheerleader.

Any age group can fall victim to unsound reasoning and resort to excuses when they feel inferior for whatever reasons. You can get rid of your problem list when you get rid of excuses.

7.   ASSUME FULL RESPONSIBILITY
FOR YOURSELF

Do you have any desire to hang onto and nurture a ravaging inferiority complex? Of course you do not. Another question: Do you know what the difference is between a man with a destructive inferiority complex and a man bubbling with confidence and energy? One has sold himself short and lost his direction; the other takes full responsibility for himself. The self-confident man knows he may fail once in a while, but he also knows that he can overcome his mistakes. He has a purpose in life and stands ready to accept full responsibility for his life. He may not set the world on fire, but he is going to have fun trying. When you assume full responsibility for yourself you will work your way out of a nagging inferiority complex. Here is a nutshell idea that can get you moving into self-responsibility today.

* Expect to be self-confident. What you expect is what you will get.

* Communicate this expectation by action, attitude and voice. When you communicate your positive expectation you will create an atmosphere of ability and achievement. Those around you will quickly recognize the new man that you are, and they will extend to you the respect and recognition due any self-confident person who assumes full responsibility for himself. The self-responsible man defrauds neither himself nor his friends.

8.   YOU ARE MIRACULOUS

Not many of us regard ourselves as miraculous. The average man or woman is too modest for that. Assuredly it would be silly to go around wearing a big button that said, "I am miraculous!" But is it any less foolish to deny that you are a miraculous creation?

What makes you miraculous? Here is the miracle:

If you do not like what you are, you can change. You can change the way you think, the way you live, and the way you regard yourself. Now here is the sad part: You can never be miraculous, you can never change anything unless you think that you can. Sad? Yes, because there are still those who have been unable to accept this miracle of self.

HOW A DRUNK BECAME A MINISTER

There was a drunk who awoke one morning in Dallas, Texas in a strange room. He knew that he was in a house, but he didn't know how he got there. He smelled breakfast cooking. Soon a stranger came to the door and invited him to come eat. Over coffee and a warm breakfast he learned that the man, a Baptist minister, had picked him up from the street, brought him to his home, and had put him in bed. The drunk couldn't believe it. He was worthless! Why had this man befriended him and, in all likelihood, saved his life? The minister explained that through a miraculous power the drunk could change everything in his life. To make a long story short, that is what happened. The drunk did change. He too became a minister and spent the rest of his life telling people that they could change their lives. He was his own best example of this miracle.

You are miraculous. No nagging inferiority complex can void that truth—or live with it.

9. GIVE YOURSELF CREDIT

We have just mentioned in item number eight that most people are too modest to admit that they are miraculous though, indeed, we all are. Modesty is all right when it is a matter of decorum and courtesy. When carried to extremes its face changes and becomes neurotic behavior. To better understand that let's look at the definition of the word modest. Here is how one book explains it in part: "Placing a moderate estimate on one's abilities or worth; neither bold nor self-assertive; tending toward diffidence." To hammer the point home, look at the last word in this definition. Diffident means to be uncertain, to back off when you should be acting or speaking because you lack the self-confidence to be assertive or to shoulder responsibility.

Not a pretty picture, is it?

Nobody is suggesting that you embark on a campaign of abrasive conduct. You do not have to resort to this pattern in order to avoid an air of diffidence. You should, of course, be outgoing and self-assertive. It is enough to step out and insist on your rightful place through behavior that says, "Hey, I'm a competent friendly person. I'm going to give you your just due, but I expect you to recognize that I'm fully in charge of my life and mean to keep it that way." In other words, give yourself credit. This way neither you nor anybody else can load you with a nagging inferiority complex.

WHY ONE MAN SUFFERED
A HUMILIATING EXPERIENCE

I knew a young warehouse supervisor who was ambitious and loyal to his company. He worked for one of several operations owned by the same outfit. His only problem was that he was afraid of losing out in the race to the top. Once, only once, he forgot who he was and failed to take credit for what he could do. He was approached by his supervisor and told to pad every pre-paid shipment a few cents on freight charges to "help take care of the overhead." He could have said no, but he forfeited his self-confidence and did as he was told. This violated his self-respect and was enough to shoot a hole in his self-confidence. He felt put upon and inferior, but still he let it ride. You can guess who took the rap when company auditors uncovered the grubby scheme. It took him a long time to work his way out of the inferiority complex this incident clobbered him with. He admitted that the most humiliating aspect of the whole sordid affair was that he knew better, but didn't give himself credit for being able to handle it.

When you don't give yourself credit for being able to keep your self-respect, and thereby whip an inferiority complex, nobody else is going to give you much credit for anything.

10. KNOW THAT EVERYBODY FAILS AT SOMETHING SOMETIME

A common fear is that of making mistakes. The feeling is that if we make a mistake we will be less worthy, our image will be damaged, and we will be looked upon as inferior. This is not the case. No man can find meaning in his life if his sole aim is security, security from mistake and possible criticism. The secret of a self-confident man is that he is willing to assume the risk of success. If you have made mistakes you are not alone in a deep dark hole. Mistakes are necessary for mankind because the human race grows only through trial and error. Our progress through the ages has ridden upon the back of our mistakes. A mistake is no disgrace. Wallowing in fear and self-pity over a mistake is where the damage is done.

In summary: A mistake is no reason to abandon self-confidence. If it were so, the whole world would be writhing in a nagging inferiority complex.

11. HOW TO DEAL WITH SETBACKS

It hurts to get knocked down. It hurts a lot more if you don't get back up and deal with the matter. Few people have become successful and self-confident without a few painful side trips, but great numbers have reached the pinnacle of human experience despite setbacks. You can be one of them. Here are some steps that you can take when you suffer a setback.

* Forget it. Don't carry a setback around like a bag of ashes. You can't go back in time and do anything over again. You are you today. Whatever happened yesterday happened to yesterday's you. Profit from your setback. Put the experience to work for you in a positive way. Today you are wiser because of a setback. Remember that much and put the rest behind you.

* Don't harbor a grudge. If you feel that somebody else is responsible for your setback, nothing will be gained by filling yourself with hate and resentment. Hate and resentment are the twins of an infe-

riority complex. If you can't be sweet and forgive, at least be smart and neutralize your feelings toward whoever you think contributed to your setback. This will let you get your mind on recouping lost ground instead of committing mayhem.

* Avoid despondency. Grief, anger or self-condemnation will do nothing to relieve or correct a setback. These are self-destructive emotions that encourage a poor self-image.

Hugh Crowder owned a thriving auto repair shop. He had more business than he could handle so he borrowed money, bought a bigger building and more equipment. About the time that he hired three more mechanics the bottom fell out due to an economic slump and a disastrous slide in the automobile industry. Three months later Hugh went home and sorrowfully told his wife that they had lost everything. His wife smiled and said, "But we've still got you."

That expressive thought snapped Hugh out of his despondency. He got busy and salvaged what he could of his business. He soon had his old employees back on the payroll and it wasn't long until he had paid off his obligations. Today he is on solid ground. If you should feel despondent over a temporary setback, remember Mrs. Crowder's philosophy. You have still got you. And that is all you've ever owned anyway.

* Keep in mind that nobody is going to condemn you for a setback. Rather, people admire the man or woman who gets back up and keeps control of his or her life after a disaster has struck. You know how often you have heard the story of how many times Edison failed, of the many setbacks of Abraham

Lincoln, and of how many times Babe Ruth struck out on his way to becoming a home run king. Always the story ends with applause for these men. The only way that you can miss the applause after a setback is to give up and let a feeling of inadequacy and inferiority take over. This is not for you.

12. DEAL WITH AN INFERIORITY COMPLEX AS SELF-INFLICTED

I can appreciate that there may be many different opinions regarding the origin or cause of a nagging inferiority complex. There are those who lay the problem at the feet of their parents, an incompetent teacher, or any of a number of early personal abuses or deprivations. For the sake of argument we can grant some validity to an outside force (something outside yourself) that may have precipitated or contributed to an inferiority complex. Nevertheless, nobody can compel you to accept and hang onto it. That is your exclusive domain. It follows, then, that to get rid of a nagging inferiority complex you must deal with it as self-inflicted. This means that it is up to you to get rid of the monster. You can do this by maintaining a day-to-day positive outlook.

13. HOW TO DEVELOP A POSITIVE OUTLOOK

First, let's take a look at the expression "positive outlook." Positive means assured, confident, independent, unyielding to outside influence, immune to negative thinking and destructive emotions. Outlook means a personal point of view, how you see the future and your place in it.

The way to develop a positive attitude is to re-check your list of reasons for self-confidence discussed in item number two of this chapter. Keep adding to the list. Look ahead and plan where and how you will be using those positive attributes. When you look ahead you do not dwell on the past. A positive outlook does not cling to yesterday's shadows.

Take a positive look at you. Project that image into the future. When you develop a positive outlook you have a handle on the future and your place in it.

14.   DISCOUNT UNSOLICITED CRITICISM

If you take unsolicited criticism seriously it can tear you up. We make this point again. Criticism is nothing more than somebody else's opinion. If you can profit from it, that's fine. If not, discount it. Your personality is yours; your confidence is yours. Don't let some noisy critic turn it into a can of worms.

15.   STOP COMPARING YOURSELF
TO IMAGINARY IDOLS

How do people measure themselves? Always the standard has been other people. If we want to know how wise we are, we compare ourselves to someone we consider wise; if we want to know how fast we can run, we compare ourself with other runners, and so on down the line. The trouble with this is that we often overestimate those with whom we compare ourselves. We make imaginary idols of people we admire, then compulsively compare ourselves to them. Thus we lose. Don't compare yourself to imaginary idols. Comparing yourself to other people is as useless as blaming others for your troubles.

16. HANG TOUGH

You have to hang tough in spite of everything if you are going to whip a nagging inferiority complex. I know that there are such things as being born under an unlucky star to indifferent and incompetent parents, that there is injustice and cruelty in many lives. There is prejudice, illness and misfortune aplenty. Whatever you do in life must be done in spite of these ugly realities. You have to hang tough and claim your spot in the sun. You don't have to be mean about it. Self-confidence gives you serenity and peace along with a sense of personal worth. An inferiority complex ties you in little knots of fear and sends you looking for scapegoats and excuses.

Since we have admitted that there is much that is bitter and unfair in life, let's turn the rock over. There is another side to the equation. There is much that is pleasant and good and what is contemptible—including an inferiority complex—is subject to change. Right now you are building a stronger self-confidence. Hang tough.

CONFIDENCE KEYS

* An inferiority complex is a persistent, nagging illness.
* It can be whipped.

* You can't do much for someone you don't respect.
* Respect yourself.
* An inferiority complex responds best to self-therapy.
* List your reasons to be self-confident.
* List your excuses for an inferiority complex.
* Use the positive list to offset the negative.
* Writing it down crystallizes your thinking.
* Assume full responsibility for yourself.
* You are miraculous.
* Give yourself credit.
* Nobody is going to condemn you because of a setback.
* Deal with an inferiority complex as self-inflicted.
* Take a positive look at you.
* Don't compare yourself to imaginary idols.
* Hang tough.

Chapter 5
Key Self-Confidence Techniques To Influence People

Here is a key truth in your ability to influence people: *You can influence people when they believe in you.* You cannot influence people with personality fraud. You have to lay it all on the line if you are to influence people because . . .

WHAT THEY SEE IS WHAT THEY BELIEVE

People are natural skeptics. They are bombarded daily with opinions, appeals, arguments, persuasion, temptations, propositions and pressures. They want proof before they endorse or accept anything. What they see is what they believe. What they see in you is what they will believe. This is what is going to influence them. Fair enough. So what must they see in you if you are going to influence and motivate them to help you grow and to reach your objectives? Here are some keys they will be looking for.

* Self-confidence. They will not be looking at or

for their self-confidence. They will be looking to see how much of it you have. When they see that your self-confidence is solid, active and outreaching, their own self-confidence will begin to grow. As they recognize your self-confidence, their doubts and fears will be removed. When these barriers fall they will go along with you and support you. A big secret in influencing people is to share your self-confidence with them. This makes it easy for them to believe in you. Then all you have to do is point the way.

There is a story of a young lieutenant who was assigned to lecture a class of officers at one of our huge Army bases. Looking out over his audience he detected expressions of doubt and incredulity on the faces of some of the older and higher ranking men present. He began by forcefully stating that he realized that there were men who knew more about his subject than he did, but since he saw none of them present he would proceed. His confident assertion put the men at ease and gave them reason to believe in him. That they shared his self-confidence was evidenced by the attentive response of those present and his own steady rise in rank as his superiors watched his self-assured performance. Men of any rank are inclined to believe what they see.

* Excitement. People are moved by excitement. Nobody gets excited about something that he does not believe in. When you are excited about something the people you address or seek to motivate will know it. They, too, will become excited and share your enthusiasm.

A word of caution: Don't let your excitement get out of hand. Excitement does not have to be loud and noisy to be recognized. If it gets out of hand it may begin to look like an act. *Controlled* excitement keeps you in charge and arouses others to believe in you and follow you. Get excited. It not only will influence and motivate others; it will give fire to your self-confidence. That is one thing your helpers will be looking for.

* Sincerity. This is something that can move mountains. Eloquence, persuasiveness, aggressiveness and a charming personality all take second place to this quality. Of course this is not to say that you cannot, or should not, use every plus characteristic in your makeup. You can use each of these along with the sincerity you feel, and sincerity still will be easy for your audience of one or hundreds to detect. When people see that you are sincere in what you do and what you propose, they will understand that they are on safe ground in dealing with you.

* Simplicity. You will do a better job of influencing people if you keep it simple. Speech that is complicated, instructions that are too long and confusing, and pressure that builds antagonism all lead to resentment and resistance. Keep your plans simple, your language basic, and your attitude helpful as you work to influence those around you. When you operate on this level you will be reassuring. Thus, you won't be dealing with a bunch of fearful, hesitant people when they see that you are keeping it all plain and simple. Here is an example.

THE RE-EDUCATION OF A SALES MANAGER

I once had a part in the re-education of a misguided sales manager. He was a hard worker, but his problem was that he had a mistaken idea of his own role. He felt that all executives in a national organization such as the one he was in should be tough, demanding and autocratic. This is how the unhappy man fancied himself. This is the outdated image he tried to live up to as he sought to influence his salesmen and the company's customers. His instructions were long-winded, dictatorial and confusing. His manner was overbearing and patronizing. He spent long hours writing lengthy, pompous letters. He issued thick, bulky manuals and piled meaningless paper work on a harassed sales force. Unfortunately, by the time we were called in, the damage had been done. With a lot of help and persuasion the sales manager took a new direction. However, the president and the board of directors had had enough. The vice-president-sales executive was asked for his resignation. To his credit, he survived this humiliation, simplified his act, and eventually went on to another management position. He applied what he had learned and gained the support of his new people. The last I heard of him the employees were hosting a retirement party for their respected boss. When you keep it simple and honest you can expect cooperation and respect as you work to influence people in your behalf. What they see is what they believe. What and who they believe, they will support.

WHAT YOU FEEL
IS WHAT THEY WILL FEEL

If you expect to lead and influence people you must feel deeply about it. You must have a burning desire and strong conviction about any project or undertaking in which you hope to arouse people and move them. Self-confidence is no halfhearted matter. When you mean to influence others to work for you, to follow you, and to extend your power, this, too, cannot be a halfhearted affair. Leaders who influence and lead feel deeply about their ideas and their personal involvement in them.

Leading others through self-confidence techniques is more than social intelligence. It is also a matter of emotions, of feelings. If you feel determined, confident and enthusiastic, those you work with will share your feelings. When you set about to motivate and influence people, what you feel is what they will feel.

A mountain country preacher with little formal training explained his ability to attract many followers by saying, "I feel that I'm involved in the most important work in the world and I want my people to feel that way." The reverend had learned a mighty potent secret about influencing people.

AVOID TOO MUCH SHOW

When we say avoid too much show as you move to influence people, this does not mean that your performance should be as bleak as winter's garden. Just don't try to grow wings. As your self-confidence and your people strategies grow you will note that no tinsel is necessary. People will respond to your open appeal just so long as they do not feel left out. As in all things, people will want to know what is in it for them, how they will benefit by doing as you say. Let's use a hypothetical situation to illustrate the point.

Suppose you are a fund-raiser. As you know, fund-raisers can indulge in gala hoopla as they endeavor to whip up excitement and fervor in order to raise money. We have all seen them put on some real shows. However, you are heading up a project to add a wing to a growing neighborhood church. You want to present your case in such a way that pledges made will be pledges paid. So you avoid too much show. Instead, you go to work to put your campaign over by showing the congregation what they will gain by lending their support. Here are some of the benefits you may use to influence them to actively participate in the church's building program.

* Personal satisfaction in having contributed to a permanent institution dedicated to good.

* Recognition. All donors will receive public credit for their participation in a worthwhile community project.

* Contributors will have taken a stand for moral values.

* A feeling of decency for having supported a neighborhood betterment project.

* A sense of family responsibility because their children and future generations will use and enjoy the new facility.

* A personal pride in building something for the common good.

* A feeling of community because of joining friends and neighbors in a common cause.

* A spiritual satisfaction gained in building a place where others can learn and grow.

* All gifts will be tax deductible.

Appeals and benefits which are intended to influence people must be backed up by and delivered with an air of confidence. Your own self-confidence should be so evident that those you seek to influence can see the finished project and their place and part in it. This will come about as you practice, plan and eliminate show and fat from your presentation. Factual self-confidence can move more than mountains. It can move people for you.

TAKE YOUR POWER FOR GRANTED

As in all cases where your self-confidence is the key in your people strategies, you must take your power for granted. When you believe in yourself and act as if you believe in yourself, others will sense that at once. When they do, they will believe in you and they will also take your power for granted. People respect power. The point is this: Don't waste time questioning yourself. Should you do this, your ability and motives will be open to questions. Take your power for granted and take your chances. The odds are all in your favor.

HOW ELMER McELHANEY
CLOSED HIS BIG DEAL
WHEN HE TOOK HIS
POWER FOR GRANTED

Elmer McElhaney had been selling coffee for a regional manufacturer-distributor for ten years. Then he learned that the Gold Star Supermarket was for sale. Floyd Pinnell, the owner, wanted to retire to his country home. Elmer had only 10 thousand dollars but he took his power for granted. Full of confidence, he went to his banker and asked for a 50 thousand dollar loan. Mr. Pinnell would sell for 250 thousand dollars with 50 thousand dollars down. On the basis of McElhaney's long association with the business and his confident attitude, the bank agreed to the loan. McElhaney repaid the loan on schedule, paid Mr. Pinnell in full, and in five years owned two more supermarkets in adjoining towns. Mr. McElhaney took his power for granted, but didn't let it stop there. He put it to work, influenced the right people, and closed his big deal as a first step in a prosperous and gratifying career.

PEOPLE WANT TO BE INFLUENCED

Here is a key point that self-confident ambitious men and women should be keenly aware of. People want to be influenced. Making decisions and accepting responsibility is tough stuff. It's easier to turn all that over to a self-confident leader who removes fear and points the way for those he seeks to influence. When you accept the responsibility of decision-making and influencing people to act, you can see and sense their appreciation and relief. People want to be influenced. Nobody can do that better than the strong-willed man or woman loaded with self-confidence that he or she is willing to share.

HOW MICKEY ASHTON LEARNED THAT PEOPLE WANT TO BE INFLUENCED

Mickey Ashton, an aggressive young man who worked in the warehouse and shipping department of a Midwest flooring distributor, was suddenly made sales supervisor of the company's somewhat indifferent sales force. Mickey was momentarily flabbergasted by the sudden change in his fortunes, but he was full of self-confidence and energy. After a two-week period of adjustment and getting acquainted, Mickey held a sales meeting and presented a definite sales and marketing plan. Goals were explained, ideas and explanations were quick and clear, and expected performance was emphasized. Sales promptly started moving up. This didn't surprise Mickey. What did surprise him, he has often said, is the sense of enthusiasm and relief he detected in the men as he set the sales team on a definite program. Mickey's realization that people want to be influenced has added muscle and conviction to his confidence and his effectiveness. It will do no less for you.

Here is an easy way for you to see for yourself the power and the truth of the concept that people want to be—and like to be—influenced. Just turn on your TV set and watch one of the better known TV evangelists at work. Notice the attitude of the audience and the intense attentive expression on the listeners' faces. Then watch the response as he makes his final appeal. What you observe will be first-hand proof that people want to be influenced. It is also a visual demonstration of self-confidence at work influencing multitudes of people.

NO NEED TO OVERWHELM THEM

While it is true that different people respond to different tactics, most will resent unrelenting pressure and exaggerated claims. There is no need to overwhelm those you seek to influence. It is far better to present your case in a forceful, confident way that allows, indeed encourages, your people to feel that they are a part of the action. The TV evangelist that we just discussed is a classic example of how this should be done. Look at part of what he does as he leads and influences his audience to make a decision and take action.

* Holds up the expectation of eternal life in which they can participate.
* Promises joy and happiness here and now.
* Extolls the satisfaction of good works and clean living.
* Offers them love and understanding.
* Declares their intrinsic personal worth.
* Encourages them to set an example for their fellow man.
* Promises them relief from fear and worry.
* Pledges security and peace of mind to them.
* Gives them confidence for today and tomorrow.

Two key points in the evangelist's appeal are always priorities in influencing people.

1. He encourages personal commitment to his cause. He explains the benefits of individual participation in his proposal.
2. He asks the people to act now.

These two points, and the example the TV evangelist gives us, can be applied to your daily efforts to influence people. When you put these principles to work, your own self-confidence will soar as you move to influence one person or a mighty crowd.

PUT THEM AT EASE BUT NOT TO SLEEP

When you are acting to influence people you will want them to be comfortable and eager as they work with you. This does not obviate tactful aggression and persuasive force. Self-confidence breeds these two personal attributes. They are necessary tools in influencing people. You must be persuasive and forceful if your influence is to matter much to you or anybody else. You can use fire without burning your house down. Employ tact, but don't forget your purpose, which is to influence others to act in your behalf. You don't have to be as abrasive as the fellow of whom it was said that he couldn't tell you the color of his wife's eyes without making you mad. Put them at ease, but not to sleep.

DRESS THE PART

Personal appearance is a prime factor in influencing people. If you look successful it is much easier to convince them that they can be successful if they listen to and follow you. Dress the part. Don't overdress, but be careful to look like success and confidence. Do you know a shabbily dressed man or woman who successfully influences productive, competent, able people?

I personally knew a man who had only an eighth grade education who nevertheless did an outstanding sales job for a major drug company. This gentleman worked in Kansas, one of our more sparsely populated states, but he looked like a New York investment broker. His dress was impeccable and his manner impressive. He looked like success and he succeeded in influencing his customers and clients to actively participate in his success. He was self-confident and he looked it. His sales record and his loyal following testified that he understood the importance proper dress played in his ability to influence people in a territory where they are noted for rugged individualism.

TAILOR YOUR SPEECH

Speech is a self-confidence key in whatever you undertake. It is an absolute in influencing people. What you say and how you say it will determine whether you attract followers and how hard they will work for you.

Tailor your speech to fit your audience. Obviously, you would not use the same exact language in addressing a convention of truck drivers that you would in addressing a group of scientists or a room full of university professors. Good grammar and powerful delivery can be used in whatever situation though. Never speak down or up to an audience. Keep it at their level. Speak clearly, plainly and sincerely with an air of confidence and self-trust. This will get the job done for you.

Self-confidence and confident speech are so closely allied and of such importance that a whole chapter of this book is devoted to the subject. Study it closely and use it to widen your influence and add to your self-confidence.

KEEP IN CHARGE

One of the most advantageous things that self-confidence can do is to put you in charge and keep you there. The golden key to influencing people is to keep in charge of them, to influence in such a way that they will want to be your helpers and your friends.

How do you stay in charge? Here are techniques and ideas used by today's self-confident leaders in all fields of human endeavor.

ORGANIZE. Organize what you are going to do and say. Have your proposal or project outlined and ready to go. When you are organized, you inspire confidence. When you have the confidence of those you want to influence, you are in charge—in charge of the people you influence and in full charge of yourself and your affairs.

GET OFF TO A FAST START. When you get off to a fast start you remove all doubt about your ability to take charge and stay there. A fast start creates excitement and generates an air of expectation. You can influence people in short order when you lay the groundwork with a fast start.

DETAIL BENEFITS. People are easy to influence when they understand what they will gain by following you. Detail the benefits for them. When your friends understand how they will profit, you will have no trouble keeping charge. This is an inborn law of human nature.

REPEAT. Repeat your main points. Emphasize the benefits to be gained over and over again. This keeps you in charge and places your self-confidence up front. Repetition not only drives your main points home, it enhances your influence.

MAKE PROMISES THAT YOU CAN KEEP. Make promises of benefits only when you know that you can fulfill them. Once you lose credibility you lose control. As long as you deliver on your promises you can stay in charge. Once you fail to live up to the expectations of your followers you are in trouble. Promise everything that you can in order to widen your influence. As long as you deliver you will be high in the saddle.

FINISH WHAT YOU START. Finishing what you start as you work with people is much like keeping promises. As long as you do it you are in fine shape. Once you give up and abandon a project, serious questions will arise in the minds of your should-be helpers. Worse yet, if you do not finish a project, your self-confidence suffers. Finish what you start. This keeps you in charge of yourself as well as those you motivate to take action.

DON'T LOOK FOR APPLAUSE. Applause is nice, but respect is better. Besides that, it's results you are after when you take charge to influence people. Keep your eye on that.

SELF-MANAGEMENT. Self-management precedes and supersedes the management of others. Unless you can manage yourself you cannot hope to influence your co-workers to do something for you. Discipline yourself first, last and always. When you practice self-discipline you can discipline, influence and lead people, because they see in you the example of self-confidence and power they want. Self-management is staying in charge of yourself. It is a key technique in keeping charge of those you influence and lead.

EXUDE EASY SELF-CONFIDENCE

There is no such thing as a forced, strained and painful self-confidence. Self-confidence is always outgoing and relaxed.

It takes practice to develop a high degree of such satisfying self-confidence just as it takes practice to be a juggler or a ballet dancer. The juggler and the ballet dancer may perform easily and smoothly but that is because they have worked long hours to perfect their art. This same dedication is demanded of you if you are to exude easy self-confidence. When you do exude an easy self-confidence, your performance will influence others to follow and emulate you. You can prove this to yourself the next time you watch a professional speaker stir up a crowd. As he exudes an easy self-confidence you will see and feel the crowd bend to his will. With practice you can expect the same response as you apply your self-confidence in this manner.

THE MORE YOU WIN, THE MORE YOU INFLUENCE

Let's make this point as clearly and as emphatically as we can. There is nothing wrong with winning. Winners influence people. Winning adds to self-confidence.

I have known people who felt guilty about winning. They were apologetic about it. This shouldn't come as a great surprise in view of the many mistaken ideas about winners and winning. As long as there is nothing dishonest in winning it is a most commendable way of life. Ambition and self-respect demand that you be a winner. Self-confidence thrives on it. And it spreads your influence like wildfire in dry grass.

The only real hazard in winning comes about when you feel that you must win in everything at all costs. Consider this. If you won only fifty-one percent of the time you would still be moving ahead. If you productively influenced a mere fifty-one percent, your influence would still grow. Plainly, the more you win, the more you influence.

You can become a winner. Every person is the product of his actions. His beliefs are founded on his actions. If you act like a winner, you will believe that you are a winner. If you believe that you are a winner, you will be a winner. If you act like you have influence, you will believe that you have influence. When you believe that you have influence, you will have it. *Action* is the key to winning. Organized, planned and controlled action is a magic key in influencing people.

AMOS SLAVENS INFLUENCES BY WINNING

Amos Slavens had worked for five of his thirty years as a manager of a fast food store. When the owner decided to sell and leave town because of a painful divorce, the franchise went on the market. When Amos told his friends he was going to buy the store they discouraged him mightily. They advised him to try to stay on as manager for the new owner where he would have security and a guaranteed income. "Too risky," they said. "You can't win against the big, rich guys." But Amos knew that you can't win without taking risks. He pooled his savings, signed a note for the balance, and went on to become a most successful multiple-store operator. Of course, his influence in the industry is considerable. Amos will tell you that the more you win, the greater your influence will be.

KEYS TO INFLUENCE DIFFERENT TYPES

Whether you realize it or not, people move into your life. In an overcrowded and competitive world this is unavoidable. You can't always pick and choose. Further, many of them will manipulate and influence you if you let them. Down through the years you can expect them in all shapes and sizes. This is all to the good. You will need them to help you grow and to reach your personal goals. No matter the types you will want to influence on your behalf, they are individuals and will respond to you when you employ the appropriate techniques. Here are some ideas that you can use to influence different types.

* The aggressive. When you put your self-confidence to work to influence the aggressive type, you will have a strong helper. The best way to influence this type is to put them to work at once. They want a piece of the action fast, and they want to know at once what they will gain by working with you. This type is full of energy and will overrun you if you do not keep tight control. When your helpers fall in this category explain exactly what is expected of them and stay on top of the situation. They can do a lot for you.

* The fearful. The fearful don't like risk-taking and they don't like to make clear, sharp decisions. This type needs security and assurance. When you convince them that your proposition is sound, and that they have nothing to fear from you, they will be glad to give you the responsibility for their success. Facts, figures, case histories, and plain, open explanations will influence these people to work with you.

* The indifferent. This type can be a real can of worms. Before they will do much for you or for themselves you will have to jar them out of their lethargy. Benefits will have to be extolled and you will have to use showmanship, excitement and enthusiasm to influence this type. This is a challenge to your self-confidence. That fact will sweeten your victory when you influence the indifferent to move at your bidding.

* The envious. The envious type is always jealous of anybody else's success. To influence them to act on your behalf you will have to make them feel like your partners—which is what anybody you influence to follow you will always be. Play up their part in what you suggest. Feed their ego. A little gentle flattery and a bit of honest praise will erase a load of envy. With that out of the way you can influence this type to become enthusiastic helpers.

You will bump into many types as you confidently influence people in your work and in your day-to-day living. The examples just given are designed to illustrate how you can adapt your self-confidence techniques to influence any types you may encounter. Here is the master key to influencing people: It is self-influence. You, like everyone else, have been influenced by others—teachers, parents, employers, friends, plus many more who have touched your life. Still, you are what you are because of you, and whatever you may become will be because of you. Self-influence, self-management and self-confidence are of the same cloth. This is where influencing other people begins and ends.

CONFIDENCE KEYS

* People are natural skeptics.
* What they see is what they believe.
* What you feel is what they will feel.
* Take your power for granted.
* People want to be influenced.
* Encourage personal commitment to your cause.
* Ask for action.
* Keep in charge.
* Practice self-management.
* The more you win, the more you influence.
* Self-influence is a master key in influencing others.
* Self-influence, self management and self-confidence are of the same cloth.

Chapter 6
How To Build A Self-Confident Attitude

As psychologists learned long ago, the human being consists of more than, as a popular song says, "muscle and blood and bone." These are the concrete, easy-to-see, easy-to-understand elements of mankind's structure. These are the building blocks of the physical body. They are designed to carry us through a lifetime of work, play, stress, strain, sorrow and joy. These are the visible materials of the human personality, the elementary parts of our makeup—sturdy, useful, necessary. Yet there is a stronger, more powerful side to man's nature. This is the abstract. An understanding of the abstract is essential in building self-confidence. Attitude is an abstract. So here is a good place to begin.

ATTITUDE RE-DEFINED

We all know that an attitude is a matter of the mind. But it is not a matter of the brain alone; it is also a matter of emotions, of feelings, and of the spirit—hard as that is to interpret. To carry the definition further, it is a stance, or position, toward a problem, fact, challenge, belief, convention, or life itself. It is a feeling toward what life has dealt you. It is an emotional reaction to what goes on around you, what is happening to you, and what you think is happening to you. It is more potent than the physical man. It can destroy the physical or it can make of him a wondrous, productive, happy, self-confident creature. The one thing about it that concerns you and me most is this: It can be controlled. You can make it what you want it to be. You can let it destroy you, or you can harness it like the wind and put it to work for you. It can be your master or your servant. Of course, as a self-determined man or woman you will make it your servant. Here are techniques that you can use today to put this might force to work for you.

TEN WAYS TO CONTROL YOUR ATTITUDE

There are a lot of ways to control a wobbly attitude. We are going to look at ten of the most effective. But there is one thing to keep in mind above all else. You, and only you, can control your attitude.

1. Desire is the first step in controlling your attitude. Unless you *want* to control your attitude there is no way you are going to do it regardless of how much you read and learn about the subject. Now, you may ask, why should I want to control my attitude? Will it make all that much difference? And who cares anyway?

All right, we will get these questions out of the way first.

There are countless reasons why you should want

to control your attitude. Most importantly, your attitude will largely determine your success and happiness. If your attitude is positive, your conduct in business and at home will be positive. If it is destructive and depression-ridden, you will live your life on that basis. We won't belabor this point, because you can see the truth in the people around you. Also, you can find case histories in many doctors' offices to support this thesis. Besides, before you are through with this book, the evidence that a wholesome attitude is vital to your self-confidence and your well-being will be proof enough for the most determined skeptic.

Yes, controlling your attitude will make all that much difference. If your attitude changes with any and everything that hits you, you will be at the mercy of circumstances. With a strong self-confident attitude circumstances won't just happen; you will create and control them.

As for the question "who cares?" Just ask yourself this: Would you rather be around a confident, enthusiastic person or one with a hangdog attitude? When you objectively answer this question you will know that everybody who comes in contact with you will care. You can use this not-so-secret fact to great advantage every day of your life. Here is an example.

HOW DELVIN MANOR CHANGED
A DEPRESSING ATTITUDE
TO ONE OF ENTHUSIASM

Delvin Manor struggled through his days weary, depressed, resentful and heavy-hearted. His wife of forty years had died six months earlier and he had reached mandatory retirement one month after her death. Mr. Manor complained that his friends had forsaken him, and that he often wished that he could die because nobody cared. Finally, upon the insistence of his former employer, he went to see a psychiatrist. During the initial interview the doctor determined that Mr. Manor had dropped all his former activities such as golf, church, service club activities and his bowling team, and now rarely visited his beloved grandson. His major activity was complaining and indulging in self-pity, thus feeding a dismal attitude. The psychiatrist urged him to take the initiative in calling old friends, taking up his former pursuits, and by all means going to see his grandson again. He was to report back in one week with a written list of what he had done to change his outlook (attitude) as the doctor had insisted. After one week he reported that he had visited his grandson, played a game of golf, and had lunch with an old friend. Further, he had no wish to die but, instead, was looking forward to the next week. After three more weeks of consultation and self-therapy, Mr. Manor's attitude was one of self-confidence and enthusiasm. He discovered, as he says, that people do care, but that they won't run after you if all they are going to find is a blob of gloom and a sour attitude. He also confirmed that attitude is subject to change and control.

2. List your poor attitudes. You can't do anything about a problem until you get it out in the open and acknowledge it. It is human nature to rationalize when it comes to personal faults or deficiencies. It is especially hard to admit a problem so close and tena-

cious as a poor attitude. Yet this is the first step in getting rid of a weak and hurtful attitude. The quickest and best way to recognize a poor attitude is to get your pen again and make a list. On a clean sheet of paper write down any and everything that is making you resentful, apprehensive, discouraged, angry or self-pitying. Leave space under each item listed to write what you can and will do to control the problems gnawing at your attitude. To help you get started, here is a brief illustration of what your list might look like.

Attitude Problem: My husband is overbearing and makes me feel inferior. I'm beginning to hate him!

Solution: It may be that John doesn't know that he is doing this to me. Instead of shrinking from him and despising him, I will explain just how I feel and ask him to be more considerate of me for both our sakes. In any event, I will no longer permit John or anyone else to weigh me down with a depressive, resentful attitude. There, I've said it, and I feel better already!

Attitude Problem: I'm always in a financial bind and everybody else always has plenty of money.

Solution:	I will do two things. Spend more wisely and cut out so much impulse buying. Two, I will equip myself to earn more money. Further, I really don't believe that everybody has plenty of money. My gosh! Frank drives a ten-year-old car and can't even afford to play golf, but he is happy and cheerful. I am going to be like Frank, and I will learn to manage and make more money too. I'm starting right now!
Attitude Problem:	I feel that the whole world is going to the dogs.
Solution:	Now I know better than that. My friend Kurt was just made president of his company, my brother has a big raise in salary, and my wife is always happy. Come to think of it, I'm not so bad off either. I'm healthy and working, my daughter Janie graduates next week, and I'm going on vacation next month. Hurrah for me! Hurrah for the world!

This is enough to give you the idea. Use it as a model and shore up your attitude if you feel it sagging in spots. After all, it is *your* attitude.

3. Don't hide from yourself. If your attitude needs improving and you know it needs repairs, don't hide from yourself. In other words, don't latch onto an excuse and lurk behind it. Your attitude is as much a part of you as an arm or leg, and how can you hide from your arm or leg? Face up to any deficiencies in your attitude, make your list, and put your solution to work. When you do this, you are in control. When you are in control of your attitude, you are in control of you. When you are in control of you, you are in control of your self-confidence.

4. Decide how you would rather feel. Would you rather feel pessimistic than optimistic? Would you rather feel sad than happy? Would you rather feel unfriendly than friendly?

Of course, you would rather feel optimistic, happy and friendly. Anybody interested in a sound self-confidence would. This is not to say that it is as easy as ABC to feel the way you want to feel. It takes thought, determination and decision. It may occasionally take outside help. But you do have a choice and only you can make that choice. This is a privilege that we can be grateful for all our lives. Otherwise, we would have no control over our feelings or our attitude.

5. Don't be ashamed of how you feel. Don't be a self-punisher, which is what you are when you are ashamed of yourself when and if you temporarily feel out of control. You can shake this miserable attitude the minute you begin to take corrective action. Follow the self-confidence suggestions and instructions in this book and you can win control just about when

you want to. For a starter, turn back to item number one of this section and reread it. As a warm-blooded entity you will always want to do something to ensure a healthy attitude and a solid self-confidence.

6. Don't permit others to shape your attitude. Of course, you will be influenced by other people. We all are. The point is that they should not be permitted to shape your attitude. This is where you live.

There are numerous ways people can and will manipulate your attitude if you allow them to do so. They can do it through peer pressure, criticizing, boasting, fear, promises, plain old lying, and constant nagging, to name a few. Two, you should be alert to subtle outside attempts to shape your attitude. That's like messing with your personality. You are the one to build the kind of attitude that you want. You owe it to yourself to resist all efforts to tamper with your attitude so long as it is productive and keeps you and those around you reasonably content. Here is how one man did it.

HOW DOYLE PARSONS
RESISTED OUTSIDE PRESSURES
AND CONTROLLED HIS ATTITUDE

Doyle Parsons had lately become disagreeable, short-tempered and loud-mouthed. His friends had grown cool, his children feared him and his wife was growing away from him. All this came home to Doyle after a particularly hectic day and an unpleasant evening at home. He didn't like what he had become and how he felt. Though no one else knew it, Doyle's business was failing, his debtors were pressing him, and he was striking out at everything and everybody. From an agreeable man and a kind husband and father he had turned into a surly, pessimistic neurotic. Now that he had identified the reason for his abrasive behavior and sorry attitude, he made up his mind to take control. He promised himself that no matter what happened to his business, he was not going to let it so warp his attitude that he would be a monster. He would try to salvage his business, but first he would salvage himself.

The next morning Doyle got up with his old warm attitude. He embraced his family and left for work with a confident air. His personal life grew better at once. It took a year or so, but he did get his business affairs in order too. Doyle knows that he would have lost it all if he had continued to permit outside influences to shape his attitude. He controlled his attitude despite outside pressures and a few insistent people. That is the smart way to build and hang onto a self-confident attitude.

7. Refuse to be a martyr. Being a martyr can conceivably be a noble thing. However, suffering for a mistaken idea is destructive and meaningless. Although, as one who appreciates the importance of building a self-confident attitude, this will never be a worry for you, it still bears mentioning. The kind of martyr we refer to may not be so much a martyr as one who, for selfish reasons, wants to appear to be a martyr. Usually those who cast themselves in the suffering role of the martyr are starved for attention. They seek sympathy or pity through the false belief that this makes them look good and noble to other people. More often than not, the reverse is true. Such

a posture carries with it a connotation of weakness and insecurity. It is often resented. For instance, I recently was told by an eighty-four-year-old man that he still deplored the fact that his mother would always do anything to gain a bit of sympathy. The poor woman has been dead many years, yet the memory of her misdirected attitude still torments her eighty-four-year-old son.

8. List the disadvantages of a poor attitude. Make a list of all the disadvantages of a poor attitude that you can think of in five minutes. This will give you a catalogue of reasons to work hard to build and maintain a self-confident attitude. Here are some items that might appear on your list.

A. Robs me of enthusiasm.
B. Makes me a bore.
C. Weakens my effectiveness as an individual.
D. Gives me a negative personality.
E. Affects my personal appearance.
F. Makes me appear to be weak and vacillating.
G. Raises doubts about my mental stability.
H. Damages my business or professional life.
I. Plays havoc with my self-confidence.

Try this little exercise for five minutes. It can give you a lifetime of reasons to work constructively at building a strong self-confident attitude.

9. Please yourself. One of the most satisfying aspects of building a self-confident attitude is that it leads you to do things to please yourself. This is not to imply that you should use a self-confident attitude

merely for selfish gain. Self-confidence is a charitable strength. As a self-confident person you will never hesitate to help and encourage others. By the same token, you will understand that you owe it to yourself to do that which pleases you first of all, to make yourself strong enough to fulfill your own dreams and then to polish the dreams of those around you. The self-confidence to do as you please gives you the strength to go beyond yourself and to win others to your side. Build on that.

10. Use the "I can, I will" building system. Though it is true that in some cases the only way a damaged attitude can be corrected is through prolonged professional help, it is equally true that you can build a power-filled self-confident attitude yourself once you decide to do so. This is the "I can, I will" system. It sounds simple and it is. Dramatic results are often produced by simple procedures. No matter how long you may have tolerated a poor attitude or a lack of self-confidence, you can change it the moment you decide to do so. Right now you can use the "I can, I will" system, along with the other ideas and principles in this book, to build as strong a self-confident attitude as you want. And there really isn't any reason to wait, because . . .

YOUR ATTITUDE BELONGS TO YOU

Since your attitude belongs to you, you are free to do what you wish with it. You can nourish and develop it with positive thinking and direct action. Of course, not all of life is lived on a straight line. Sometimes the tail does seem to wag the dog. Nevertheless, your attitude belongs to you. You are not its slave. Which is a way of saying that even if the process proves to be slow and devious, you can still build a self-confident attitude.

Here is a good place to note that we do not mean to imply at any time that medication is never necessary. The self-help ideas and techniques in this book do work, but they are not meant to take the place of medication. Even so, medication cannot guarantee you that you will always have a self-confident attitude. Where medication is necessary, the prescription will still need help to effect lasting benefits. That help must come from the patient. Your attitude belongs to you. In the final analysis, whatever happens to it is up to you. Here is a little story to illustrate the point.

A middle-aged mother had become so overbearing and disagreeable that her husband and two children issued an ultimatum. The family had spent a small fortune on doctor bills and tranquilizers, but nothing much had happened. The woman insisted on clinging to her arrogant attitude and domineering behavior. Now the family had a conference and sat her in the middle of it. "We have done all that we can," they said in so many words. "Either you change or we go." The thought shocked the mother. She realized that she could no longer afford her old attitude which was, in reality, one of insecurity and low self-esteem. Within a week she reverted to her old self and confidently assumed her rightful role in the family. What medicine alone had failed to do the woman's self-will brought about in short order.

HOW TO MAKE YOUR ATTITUDE
WORK FOR YOU

No one can countenance a double standard while building a self-confident attitude. A double standard in this matter is where one is used for you, yet another is applied to other people. For instance, it is hiding behind a double standard when someone pouts that another individual was born with a bright attitude and a bundle of self-confidence while he was not. The truth is that we must all work to make our attitude all that it should be. This, though, is not a cause for dismay. It is a challenge and an opportunity. With that in mind let's concentrate on how you can make your attitude work for you.

* Don't spend your life on guard.

A self-confident attitude demands room to maneuver and grow. Building a self-confident attitude involves risk taking. This does not mean that you must become a death-defying daredevil in order to build a strong positive attitude. Your life won't be at stake, but you will risk some disappointment and perhaps some failures along the way. So what? Haven't men been doing that for centuries? This is the way mankind progresses. On a personal level it is the way that you will put your attitude to work for you. You cannot constantly be pointing a gun at the future. Don't miss the fun. Accept the risks that an aggressive, self-confident attitude involves. Let it work for you.

* Don't be afraid of being vulnerable.

Often those who tolerate a weak, retiring attitude are afraid to expose themselves. They are afraid that they might be embarrassed, subject to ridicule, or worse, if they exhibited a lively outgoing attitude. So they play it safe. But there is no safe place. The only safety lies in doing the best that you can with a keen confident attitude and then letting the chips fall where they may.

Don't be afraid of being vulnerable. We all are. Those who know the value of a self-confident attitude put it to work despite everyday hazards. When you put your attitude to work for you it will grow stronger, just as any part of your personality develops through usage.

HOW MARY WOOLSEY LEARNED
NOT TO BE AFRAID
OF BEING VULNERABLE

Mary Woolsey was a straight A student in high school. Mary's sense of worth was largely centered on her scholastic rating. She wanted to go to college, but she was fearful that her grades might not be straight A's. Her grandfather convinced her that her attitude was off course, that the whole of her future didn't rest on a straight A average. As a freshman she did make a few C's, but after that it was all A's again. After graduation Mary said that she learned more as a freshman than in any other year. She learned not to be afraid of being vulnerable. And that can do a lot for anybody's attitude.

* Be your own attitude analyst.

You have already learned some techniques of uncovering a personal weakness and, better yet, techniques of discovering and using the unlimited personal resources at your disposal. This is a good way to put your attitude to work for you. Be your

131

own analyst. Sit down and list everything you like about your attitude just as it is today. Take a look at anything that you may not like also. Determine how you will rid yourself of what you don't like and, more importantly, how you will put what you do like to work for you. For instance, if you are doing routine office work and find it boring, put your self-confident attitude to work and get a people job such as selling, personnel work or public relations. If you are a schoolteacher, but would rather drive an eighteen-wheel diesel, put your attitude to work and crawl into the cab of a truck. And so on down an endless chain of possibilities. It is more important to do something that a self-confident attitude fits you to do than to be president.

* Believe that these are the best of days.

You can put your attitude to work for you most effectively if you believe that these are the best of days to take action. We had all better believe that these are the best of days, because they are all we will ever be given. They will be wasted if we plod or drift through them with a negative attitude. On the other hand, if our attitude is that these are the best of days, then our attitude will make our days productive and satisfying. Memories can be sweet, the future can be rosy, but today is where we live. Put your attitude to work to make the most of that inescapable law.

* Keep your options open.

As you put your attitude to work for you, don't make one idea, one goal, or one theme the only thing. None of us can do all things, but all of us can do several things exceedingly well. Keep your options open. Then if the bottom falls out of your plans, your attitude will take you on to other goals and other successes. There was a young lady who dreamed of becoming a concert musician, but the ill health of her father suddenly cut the family's income drastically. She had to return home from the university where she was a student and go to work. However, her positive attitude told her that she still had options that were open to her. In addition to music she had studied journalism while at the university. She soon had a job with the local newspaper where she became a valuable member of the staff. Also, she accepted a position as organist in a large church and started giving private lessons in her spare time. Her life is full and she has the respect and affection of all who know her. She still keeps her attitude working for her, and she keeps her options open. This is a comfortable way to go.

MARSHAL THE FACTS

Agonize over a vexing problem if you must, but don't be pushed into doing something before you have the facts. Marshal the facts, talk them over with an expert or trusted associate if need be, then take action. Don't delay. Delay can let the fire get out of control and lead to panic. Besides, prolonged indecision can only frazzle your self-confidence. Make your decision, implement it, then get on to another constructive project.

Being under fire is not the end of the world. It means that you are very much alive and still in the game. Accept this reality, for once you see yourself as a helpless victim of circumstances or designing opponents, your attitude goes flapping away into the darkness.

* This too will pass.

Problems, grief, criticism, setbacks and frustration can all seem like eternal disaster. But whatever may be keeping you under fire, whatever the difficulty, this too will pass. More, when you face it with an attitude that spells self-confidence, you will hasten the day.

HOW TO MAINTAIN A
SELF-CONFIDENT ATTITUDE
AGAINST COMPETITION

You were born into a competitive world. You started competing before you could walk. To compete is to strive for your objectives and goals no matter the odds. Competition is a form of rivalry which is ages old. You will have to live with it all of your life. This is no cause for alarm because as long as you maintain a self-confident attitude in the face of competition you can actually enjoy it. Here are perceptions that you can use to keep a strong attitude against the competition you must surely face.

* Don't strive overmuch merely to prove your self-confidence to yourself or others. When your attitude is positive you know that your self-confidence can meet any competition head-on. A self-confident attitude supports you like a steel girder. You don't have to be dogmatic, pushy or antagonistic to validate it. Such unnecessary behavior inflames competition and invites misunderstanding. Accept the fact that you

are competent and put that attitude to work against competition. This is enough to keep you in the winner's circle.

* Everybody has a hole in their bucket. This was my grandfather's way of saying that no competitor is invincible. If you keep this in mind, you should have no trouble keeping a self-confident attitude against the stiffest competition.

* Don't think of every competitor as a personal enemy. There are good friends who go out and vie with each other every day. A classic example of this can be seen daily in the courts of our land. Two lawyers may fight each other tooth and nail all day and then have a friendly visit over dinner that night. This is not to say that you should take your competition to dinner every night. It is to say that you can maintain a self-confident attitude against the competition when you accept the fact that it is a natural part of all our lives.

A REFERENCE CHECKLIST FOR YOU

Here is a reference checklist for you. Its purpose is not to grade you, but to give you a simple standard that you can use to monitor your self-confident attitude from time to time. Add your own questions to the list if you think of any that will help you keep tabs on your attitude. Use it today, then come back periodically to check your progress. Record your answers as you go along to see where you stand today.

1. Do you agree that your emotional state can affect your attitude?

2. Do you believe that you can exercise a large degree of control over your emotions and your feelings?

3. Do you think that your mind can do much to influence your attitude?

4. Do you feel that you are a helpless victim of circumstances?

5. Do you want to control your attitude?

6. Can you admit to yourself when your attitude needs adjusting?

7. Do you often think that everyone else has it better than you do?

8. Do you permit others to unduly influence your attitude?

9. Do you think that your attitude has much to do with the state of your self-confidence?

10. Do you seek or enjoy sympathy?

11. Do you feel guilty when you do things to please yourself?

12. Are you afraid of personal exposure?

13. Do you panic when under fire?

14. Do you fear competition?

15. Do you believe that you have to be born with a self-confident attitude?

16. Do you believe that you can build and maintain a confident attitude?

If your answers were as follows, your self-confident attitude is on the right track and you should have no trouble in keeping it in good repair.

YES	NO
#1	#4
2	7

3	8
5	10
6	11
9	12
16	13
	14
	15

If you don't like your answers remember that your attitude is your exclusive property. It is yours to build as you will.

CONFIDENCE KEYS.

* You are more than muscle and blood and bone.
* An attitude is stronger than the physical man.
* You can control your attitude.
* Recognizing a poor attitude is the first step in getting rid of it.
* Your attitude is as much a part of you as an arm or leg.
* When you are in control of your attitude you are in control of you.
* Use the "I can, I will" building system.
* Not all of life is lived on a straight line.
* You can make your attitude work for you.
* Being under fire is not the end of the world.
* You were born into a competitive world.
* You can build and maintain a self-confident attitude in the face of competition.

Chapter 7
How To Use Your Self-Confidence
To Multiply Your People Power

"People power" is a term easily misunderstood. It is subject to misinterpretation by those who can think of it only as the ability to dominate, bully or abuse people. In our civilized world, and in a civilized life, this unfair connotation does not hold true. People power does not mean merely the ability to debase people, including yourself. Its meaning is much more than that, and its application wider by far.

WHAT THE TERM
"PEOPLE POWER" MEANS

Our interest in what the term "people power" means, of course, is what it means to you. Primarily it means your ability to influence, motivate, guide and lead others. It is the ability to win the respect and cooperation of other people, to win them to your way of thinking and to your way of getting things done. It does not mean that you must be the total authoritarian figure who never makes a mistake and who can brook no opposition or differences of opinion. Rather, it means the ability to eliminate opposition by convincing the "other people" that your way is better, that your thinking is sound, and that they will benefit from doing things your way. It is your ability to deal with people in a mutually profitable context. It is the way you use and share your self-confidence to set goals and get things done with the help of those around you. It is a personal power exclusively your own.

HOW YOU CAN DEVELOP PEOPLE POWER

People power is largely a matter of self-confidence. It is not determined by birth, education, wealth or the accident of good fortune. These may make the development of people power a bit quicker and easier, but this power is not restricted to, or limited by, such fortuitous circumstances. You can develop this winning trait whoever you are and wherever you are. It is to your advantage and to the advantage of other people that you do so. We discussed how you could get self-confidence in the first chapter of this book. Now let's look at some of the many self-confidence techniques that you can employ to develop people power.

GIVE YOURSELF A CHANCE

Those who have never enjoyed and shared the multiple benefits of people power have never really given it a chance. They have never opened up and put it to work. Nine times out of ten this is because they have assigned themselves a seat on the back row of life. They refuse to think that they can influence others, so they never make the effort. This is not only their loss, it is the loss of all the people around them whose lives they could make brighter.

You owe it to yourself to give yourself a chance to develop a productive people power. Your beginning does not have to be monumental, nor does it have to be minuscule. Begin with a project where you can see immediate results. You can do this by:

1. Making a speech for volunteers for a club or church activity.
2. Taking part in a fund-raising activity.
3. Asking a friend to do something for you.
4. Telling your husband or wife that you want help on a particular project.
5. Selling something to somebody.
6. Refusing a silly request (thereby influencing somebody to stop trying to take advantage of you).
7. Inducing someone to go to church or join you in a social activity.

These are small everyday possibilities, but every time you influence somebody to do something you have used people power. From such beginnings you give yourself a chance to prove that you can develop and use people power. The principle is the same whether you influence one or many, a stranger or a friend, an ally or an opponent. The point is that you have motivated somebody to do something. It is a beginning, a stepping stone, a chance to prove to yourself the power of self-confidence in moving and influencing other people. You can take it as far as you like.

It is well to note that the benefits which your people power holds forth to others is not always monetary. Financial gain is a great motivator, but it is not the only one. For example, refer back to the beginning projects just suggested.

In number one, your club or church gains needed volunteers. You gain a feeling of contributing and sharing your self-confidence and self-esteem.

In number two, the gain is financial. Your self-confident action has helped raise money.

In number three, by asking a friend to do something for you, you have made a helper of him, and probably a better friend.

By motivating your husband or wife to help in number four, you have given them a feeling of importance. You have gained a closer relationship with them.

In number five, you have filled a need for the other person. You have gained a sense of accomplishment.

When you refuse a silly request, as in number six, you have given the other person a reason to re-examine his request. It is to his benefit to see that his request is unreasonable. You have the benefit of knowing that you can be assertive.

In number seven, you have influenced someone to take action to broaden his life. In so doing, you have the satisfaction of having contributed to another person's enjoyment of life.

There are as many ways that your self-confidence

can benefit others as there are methods that you can use to multiply your people power. This gives you a basket full of reasons to give your people power a chance every day.

THROW AWAY YOUR MASK

People often talk about and wish for power, the power to impress, influence, guide and direct others. They recognize that they have the innate capacity and that people do respond to the personal power of others. But they hide behind a mask. They are afraid to open up and expose themselves. "It's risky," they say. Yes, it is risky, but so is getting out of bed on a sunny day. Life is risky. There is no escaping the fact. Fragile as life may be, however, it can be productive, forceful and full of meaning. You will never know that, though, and you will never know how exciting it can be until you take off your mask and put your self-confidence on the line.

Sounds like a miracle, you say. Yes, it is a miracle, a miracle that takes determination and a lot of work. You can develop and explode the miracle of people power when you drop the mask of self-protection.

REFUSE TO ACCEPT EVERY NO AS FINAL

When you are using people power it is vital that you learn to distinguish between "no" and "maybe." Every no is not final. Often the person or persons you choose to motivate are not saying no, but are saying, "Tell me more." Unless you thoroughly explain your proposition and detail every benefit, the people you are trying to influence will say no. Often what they mean is, "I'm not convinced so you will have to explain more fully what it is that you want me to do and what I will gain by doing it."

Don't abandon self-confidence and give up at the first no. A good way to multiply your people power is to rephrase your request, order or instructions, in a clear, easy-to-understand manner. Then keep working. When your helpers understand your proposition and how they will benefit by following you they won't say no. They will want their share of the goodies.

REFUSE TO LET A NEGATIVE
RESPONSE THROW YOU

True, it is not likely that you will strongly influence everybody every time you want to do so. No matter how much control and people power you possess, the simple law of averages will preclude one hundred percent success. This is not the most important thing. The important thing is to refuse to let a negative response throw you. When a project becomes hopelessly bogged down, that is the time to move on to another field. The world is full of responsive, reasonable people who will understand and appreciate your people power. Don't waste time grieving over a turndown. Instead . . .

REFUSE TO SET YOURSELF UP
FOR FAILURE

The essence of people power is having the self-confidence to persist. It takes personal power to persist, but then persistence builds power as it goes along. If you let the first no, or a belligerent opponent, stop or discourage you, you will have set yourself up for failure. Don't do it. The history books are filled with stories of men who succeeded only after failing many times. Abraham Lincoln is a classic example. He suffered at least nine political defeats but, as we all know, went on to become one of our most revered and honored presidents.

You may never be president of the United States, but you can attain whatever goals you set if you persist. An adroit use of people power is your best guarantee.

REPETITION BUILDS PEOPLE POWER

Repetition builds people power. Persistence is repetition. People believe when something is repeated over and over again. Repetition is a power technique. You can observe the truth of this by watching the TV ads that bombard you daily. You see the same ads telling you the same story at the same time day after day. Soon the message is fixed in your mind. The ad agencies are experts in people power. They motivate people to buy millions of products every day. Their power key is persistence and repetition. Do as the experts do. Persist and repeat. When you do you can feel your self-confidence and your people power grow.

PUT THEM TO WORK
AT THE FIRST SIGNAL

Now persistence does not mean wearing out yourself or your helpers. When you make your move to influence one or many, put them to work at the first signal. People are sending you a signal of agreement and cooperation when they ask a question, nod in approval, express an interest in how they will benefit, want to know the cost or the time it will take, or express an interest in any manner.

Be alert for these signals and put your people to work at the first sign. There is no need to persist after you have done your job. You may lose them if you keep on after they have shown that they are on your side. Repeat and persist as much as necessary, but don't tell them more than they want to know. Your people power will be much more effective when you put them to work at the first signal.

KEEP SOME SECRETS OF YOUR OWN

Keep a load of power in reserve as you prepare your presentation to motivate people to follow you. You should merit extra reasons, additional points and more benefits than you plan to present right at the start. Don't use all your power ammunition unless you must. Remember, put them to work at the first signal. The reserve persuasion that you build into your presentation is your secret arsenal in case you need more firepower. Make your presentation powerful and persuasive from the first moment, but keep some secrets of your own in case you need them.

HOW MOLLY RINKER MULTIPLIED HER PEOPLE POWER

Although Molly Rinker had been painfully shy all

her life she had managed four years of college with a business major. Then she went to work in the office of a large medical complex. Here her old habitual attitudes persisted. She was still shy to the point of being obsequious. She deferred to everyone else in the office and was unhappy with herself in the process. She was intelligent enough to realize that she was subordinating her needs to those of the people around her. She was also smart enough to know that only she could change things. She resolved that she would escape the trap she had built for herself. Here is how she did it.

Molly decided to begin with Sherry Turnbow, a co-worker who never hesitated to demand favors of anyone. She planned to insist that Sherry trade lunch hours with her the next day so that she could meet a friend for lunch and a bit of shopping. That night Molly Rinker practiced how and what she would say to Sherry the next morning. Promptly at 9:30 a.m. Molly walked over to Sherry and said, "Sherry, I want to trade lunch hours with you today."

"Well," stalled Sherry, "I don't know about that."

Molly held up a finger. "Now, remember the times I've traded with you for no reason at all. Today I'm going at eleven o'clock."

"OK," answered Sherry. "If that's how you feel."

"That's how I feel," replied Molly, surprising herself. "Thanks much." And out Molly went at eleven o'clock to meet her friend and shop for a new car.

Molly kept her new-found confidence bubbling by going alone the next day to close the deal on her new car. Molly haggled, stood her ground, threatened to forget the whole deal, stuck by her price, and finally bought the car for fifteen hundred dollars less than the salesman had first insisted was the best that he could do. She drove home feeling like a new woman.

On Thursday of the same week she decided to ask for a raise. That night she listed all the reasons why she deserved a raise, why she should be given more responsibility, and then she rehearsed the speech she planned to use when she approached Mr. Gregoroski, her supervisor. All went as planned. Mr. Gregoroski was impressed and Molly came away with more money and a new job. She also came away with a big load of self-confidence that she now knows she had been wasting for years. She has put her shyness on the back burner now that she is busy enjoying the people power she has rightfully claimed.

WHO NEEDS PEOPLE?

Who needs people? You do. I do. Everybody needs people. You can drive this people fact home with a bit of hypothesis.

Suppose that you went to work tomorrow and saw no one on the streets. Upon arriving at your office, plant, store or factory, you could find no one there no matter how desperately you searched. Would you stay and work as usual? Or suppose that you went to the supermarket and found that you were the only one in that huge store. What would your reaction be with no people in the store or anywhere in sight? Or suppose you went to church on a Sunday morning where you expected to see many friends, but only ghosts and an eerie silence greeted you. Would you stay? Or suppose you had enthusiastically arranged a meeting

147

in order to motivate and inspire a group to help you launch a wide sales promotion effort, but no one showed and you faced an empty hall alone. Would you go ahead and make your presentation anyway?

The analogy may be simplistic, but you can easily see from these imaginary situations that you need people. Other people are an extension of you, your self-confidence and your personal power to lead and motivate. They are as necessary as breathing when it comes to building personal power and getting things done.

PEOPLE ARE THE KEY

People are the key in using self-confidence to multiply your power. The only way that you can reach beyond the physical self, beyond the limitations of one's self, or beyond the strict limitations of the twenty-four hours in your day, is through people. People are the key. Here are some ideas that you can use today to unlock that key.

Idea number one: If you feel any qualms about your ability to jump right in and start motivating, working with and using people, remember this. The world is full of people who never find out how good they are, or how quickly other people will respond to a bold display of self-confidence. The reason they never find out is that they never try. This need not be your mistake. You have nothing to lose and unlimited power to gain.

Idea number two: When unlocking this secret key to more power, always make the most of the proven fact that the basic motivating force is self-interest.

The quickest way that you can multiply your people power is to show the people you choose to work with just what and how they will benefit from your leadership.

For example, if they will gain money from doing as you instruct, tell them what they must do to realize this benefit, how to do it and when to do it. Then you must dangle a dollar sign before their eyes by naming the amount of money that they can expect if they follow your leadership with enthusiasm and energy.

When prestige will be the gain you must follow the same fundamental plan. You must demonstrate exactly what your helpers must do to get this prestige, why they need it and how they will benefit from the added prestige you offer.

You can use the same basic plan in presenting any program to multiply your people power. As you utilize the self-interest of other people to influence and motivate them, keep a sharp eye on your own self-interest. The big purpose in using your self-confidence to motivate others is to meet your goals while you help other people achieve theirs. This way everybody is a winner.

HOW TOM LIGON INCREASED SALES WITH PEOPLE AS THE KEY

Tom Ligon was an above average sales executive for a textile firm specializing in women's wear. However, Tom wanted more. As a salesman he understood the value of self-confidence. He had also observed that the most successful operators in the textile field were the ones who multiplied their efforts by inspiring and motivating the people around them. Tom developed a plan to increase his company's sales by exercising his personal people power.

1. He set a company goal of a five million dollar sales increase.
2. He assigned each salesperson an individual quota.
3. To take full advantage of the self-interest appeal, he promised an extra two percent bonus to the salespeople who met and exceeded their individual quotas.
4. He gave a preview to the sales force of the helpful advertising campaign to be launched at the beginning of the sales promotion.
5. He showed samples of the new styles that the sales force would be showing.
6. He promised the salespeople backup help from everybody in the firm.
7. Tom explained there would be private interviews each week and an analysis of each salesperson's performance.
8. As a final celebration, there would be a banquet with wives and husbands of the sales team as guests as soon as the five million dollar quota went over the top.

Then, after this kickoff meeting, Tom met with each member of the sales force. At this eyeball to eyeball meeting Tom carefully explained what was expected of that individual. The salesperson's territory was reviewed and each account was targeted for a dollar amount. After that, the salesman or saleswoman was shown how much extra money the two percent bonus could produce, what an outstanding performance could mean to the individual in terms of greater self-confidence, more respect and prestige, and continued personal growth and recognition.

It is worth noting that the five million dollar quota was met six weeks ahead of schedule with each member of the sales force enthusiastically sharing in the effort. Tom had used his self-confidence to multiply his people power, thereby not only increasing sales magnificently, but also giving his people added confidence and the benefits which had been promised. Incidentally, the firm saw fit to reward Tom Ligon generously too. When self-confidence is used to influence and motivate other people you too have every right to expect the rewards that increased people power invariably brings.

PEOPLE WANT SELF-CONFIDENT LEADERS

The vast majority of people are not destined to be leaders. Nor do they want to be. What people as a whole want are self-confident leaders who will make decisions for them, give them something to get excited about, and generally improve their lot in life. They want leaders who inspire confidence and motivate them with the force of their personal power. What this means, of course, is that people want you to use your self-confidence to multiply your people power. Don't disappoint them. To do so would be their loss and yours.

WHAT SELF-CONFIDENT PEOPLE POWER MEANS TO YOU

Self-confident people power is the best tool you can have. When you influence others to do your bidding, to trust you and to work with you, then you have a great advantage in business, in your social activities and in achieving whatever goals you set for yourself. Self-confident people power means that you have a whole lot of legs and arms out there working for you. If you want to explore this magic formula further, read the biographies of great achievers. You will see that they never walked alone.

WHAT SELF-CONFIDENT PEOPLE POWER MEANT TO OLLIE LYLES

Ollie Lyles was a bookkeeper who enjoyed making speeches to service clubs, church groups and charity organizations, always for free. One day while poring over a ledger, he decided to put his love of people and his speaking ability to work for money. As an amateur he had already proven that he could enthuse and motivate people. Ollie resigned his routine job, prepared a sizzling inspirational speech, and hired an ad agency to put together a visual aid program to use with his verbal presentation. He went out on his own and booked a few small conventions. Next he sought a booking agency and was soon commanding two thousand dollars to three thousand dollars a night. His fees are considerably higher now. Ollie Lyles says that the money (which was his original goal) is only a fringe benefit. His real satisfaction is the extra self-confidence and sense of power that he now enjoys.

WHAT YOUR PEOPLE POWER
MEANS TO OTHERS

Your multiplied people power will always be more important to you than anyone else. Yet, your people power means much to others also. It means that they have found a leader, someone to lean on, one that can influence, guide, direct, encourage and motivate them to be better and to do better. More than that, it means that you have inherited the leader's responsibility to those people. The better you discharge that responsibility, the more your people power will mean to those around you and to you.

YOUR PEOPLE POWER EXPANDS
IN THE LEADER'S ROLE

One definition of a leader is a person who has commanding authority and/or influence. This is what you can expect when you use self-confidence to multiply your people power. You can also expect your power to expand as you put it to work in the leader's role. It is a law of nature that the more you use something the more it grows and expands. People power is no exception.

YOU WILL ENJOY PEOPLE POWER

You will enjoy people power as you use it more and more. You will learn how much power is required for a particular purpose. You won't use a sledge hammer to kill a fly nor will you take out after a buffalo with a BB gun. The more you learn about people power the more you will enjoy it. It is a life-long process that brings ever-increasing satisfaction.

YOUR ASSOCIATES AND FRIENDS WILL APPLAUD YOUR PEOPLE POWER

When your associates and friends see that you have real people power they will applaud you. Leaders command approbation and respect in direct relationship to their personal power. There is no stronger power than confident people power. When you use yours consistently you will hear the applause.

WHY MILDRED GILLIAM'S FRIENDS APPLAUDED HER

Mildred Gilliam's friends applauded her the minute she broke out of her shell of inferiority. When her friends ask how she managed to change from a loser filled with self-doubts to a people power person she explains, "I had a choice. I could go on reproaching myself or I could snap out of it and become an assertive self-confident woman. I chose self-confidence and people over misery and loneliness."

The confidence building techniques this young lady used to become a people-oriented business executive were these.

* She joined a self-assertive training class.
* She moonlighted as a hostess at a fancy restaurant two nights a week.
* She took a secretarial course two nights a week.

* She joined a businesswoman's luncheon club.

You will note that each of these activities involved an association with people, many of whom were strangers. Through observation and practice, Mildred Gilliam learned to deal with and manage people. In doing so, she moved from a shipping room clerk to an executive secretary with a pool of five people under her. She has never regretted the choice she made. This is mind stuff.

YOU HAVE A SELF-OBLIGATION

Your greatest obligation is always to yourself. You owe it to yourself to confidently multiply your people power. You can begin that process here and now by using the techniques and ideas in this book, plus techniques and ideas that you will develop on your own. As you do this you and those around you will be the better for it.

HOW FRED STEPHENS FULFILLED AN OBLIGATION TO HIMSELF AND WON A RAISE

Fred Stephens was a supervisor in a small engine manufacturing plant. But he had a problem. One employee, Rod Nall, resisted instructions and overtly bad-mouthed Fred. The supervisor recognized that he had an obligation to himself and to the people he supervised. He suspended Rod Nall two weeks with no pay and told him he could return to work only if he was ready to follow instructions and support Fred and the company fully. Nall came back contritely at the end of the two weeks and under Fred's watchful eye became a top producer. In fact, production improved all around when Fred put assertive people power to work. Not surprisingly, Fred's own income also improved to the tune of one hundred dollars per week as he multiplied his people power to attain his goal of more production.

AN EXERCISE
TO CHECK WHERE YOU STAND

Here is a list of fifteen questions designed to help you evaluate your attitude and progress in your campaign to multiply your people power. Each question is assigned a point value. Get a sheet of paper and head one column plus (+) and the other minus (−). After answering all the questions, add the plusses and subtract the minuses to get your score. One hundred is perfect, seventy is average, and fifty or less needs immediate work. However, a low score doesn't mean you are whipped. All it means is that you have uncovered areas that need self-confident attention from you.

1. Do you see other people as possible friends and helpers?
   +10
2. Do you relish the opportunity to stimulate, train, teach and help people?
   +15

3. Do you feel an overriding compulsion to explain and justify to other people everything that you do or say?
   −10

4. Can you hang onto your self-confidence when and if an idea is rejected?
   +10

5. Do you feel that you have to outdo and outperform everybody else before you can have people power?
   −10

6. Do you believe that people want you to succeed?
   +5

7. Do you think that people like to be influenced?
   +10

8. Do you feel trapped in a room full of people?
   −20

9. Do you want to be a leader?
   +20

10. Do you think education is all it takes to multiply people power?
    −10

11. Do you think people power means pleasing everybody?
    −10

12. Do you think nobody wants to be a follower in this day and time?
    −10

13. Do you think that an enlightened self-interest contributes to people power?
    +20

14. Do you think that you have to be born with people power in order to have it?
    −5

15. Do you believe that the majority of people don't know that they can have real people power?
    +10

Your self-confident people power like any working tool needs a periodic checkup. Come back to this exercise periodically and monitor your people power. This will help you keep it in tiptop form.

CONFIDENCE KEYS

* People power is the ability to influence, motivate, guide and lead others.
* You can develop people power.
* Repetition and persistence build people power.
* You need people.
* People are the key to personal power.
* People want self-confident leaders.
* Self-confident people power is your best tool.
* Your people power is important to others.
* You have a self-obligation.
* Check where you stand periodically.

Chapter 8
Self-Confidence Methods To Make A Strong First Impression

Psychology is a prime technique used often by determined self-confident men and women. It is an excellent tool to use in making a strong first impression. Of course, the brand of psychology you use to make a powerful impression will depend upon the people and the situation that you may be facing. The more you learn about self-confidence, and the more you employ it, the easier it will be for you to make an on-the-spot decision about the kind of psychology that is appropriate for the occasion. With practice you can quickly learn to gauge just how much psychological pressure is needed.

There are many psychological methods that you may choose from in order to make your strong first impression. For example, you may soothe, coax, demand, shock, bombard, plead, insist, control, manage, reassure, frighten, pull, push, drive, intimidate, lull, excite, imbue, enthrall, motivate, captivate, arouse, enthuse and on and on. There are as many psychological ploys as there are opportunities to make a commanding impression. Whatever self-confidence technique you elect to use, here is something to bear in mind.

THE FIRST MINUTE COUNTS THE MOST

The first impression is just that. It is the first opportunity that others have to size you up, to evaluate you, and to decide just who you are and how they will deal with you. It is also the best opportunity that you will ever have to test and to demonstrate your self-confidence. It is the opportune time for you to take control and build the kind of relationship you want. The first minute of the human encounter counts the most, because that is when lifelong impressions are forged, when roles are decided and, as psychologists might say, the pecking order is established.

HOW TO HANDLE
THE ALL-IMPORTANT FIRST MINUTE

Since the first minute is so significant let's look at some specific ways to use self-confidence to make the most of it. The basics are the same whether you are facing one or many for the first time. Here are ideas on how to handle the all-important first minute. You can put these to work today to help you make a strong, confident first impression no matter where you are or what you may be undertaking.

TAKE THE INITIATIVE

You will never have a better chance to take the initiative and make a convincing impression than the first minute of any contact. This is the moment that can open the gate for you and make everything that follows easier and simpler. This is true whether you are at a candle-lit table or taking part in a rip-roaring convention. To make it all come off, though, you will have to take the initiative at once. Here are five examples. You can use your imagination and self-confidence to enlarge upon these five basic ideas. Then you can fit them to any first encounter and produce the results you want.

EXAMPLE 1:
WHEN MEETING ONLY
ONE OR TWO PEOPLE
FOR THE FIRST TIME

When being introduced to or meeting one or two for the first time, take the initiative by stepping forward quickly. Extend your hand and acknowledge the introduction with a firm (not crushing) handshake. Give your name in a clear, easy-to-understand voice. Repeat the names of your new friends. If in doubt, ask them to spell their names. Then call them by name as you take charge of the conversation or discussion. Ask questions. Learn what their interests are, find out what is most likely to motivate them, and encourage them to tell you all you need to know about them. A big pair of ears can do much to endear you to a new acquaintance. Nevertheless, make it a point to keep the meeting moving in the direction you want it to go. You can do this by asking more questions, suggesting that you want to stay with a given subject until it is perfectly clear or when you must, by insisting that your new-found friend, or friends, stick to the business at hand. As long as you control your voice and speak confidently you can do whatever may become necessary without ruffling too many feathers.

EXAMPLE 2: BE A FRIEND

The most painless way to make a strong first impression on the people you are seeing for the first time is to make a friend. It is a burdensome mistake to anticipate that everyone you will face is going to be an antagonist. The more self-confidence you use, the easier it is to believe that any first meeting is going to be warm and to your advantage.

Be a friend, yes. But don't feel that being a friend is a matter of giving and never of getting. Friendship is a two-way street, and no way should you ever abandon self-confidence in the name of friendship. No friend is going to ask you to do that. Make all the friends you can, and meet as many new people as you can, but . . .

EXAMPLE 3: MAKE
YOUR POSITION KNOWN

Max Deckard, a veteran salesman in the Midwest, is a living example of a confident man making his position known. When calling on a new customer, he makes a strong first impression by getting to the point with, "I know you are a busy man, Mr. Buyer, and I am going to respect that. Here is why I am here." Then he proceeds to demonstrate his goods

162

and ask for the order. And Mr. Deckard does write orders.

When meeting someone for the first time, whether socially or in business, you can quickly make your position known. Get right into the conversation, transaction, negotiation or whatever, with an air of confidence. This way you will not only make your position clear, you will come on with a power impression.

EXAMPLE 4: BE PREPARED

Be prepared to make a strong first impression. When you know that you are going to meet new people, whether an individual or a group for the first time, do your homework. Study their background, find out what they do and who their associates are. Decide what you expect or want from the meeting and plan to make it happen. When you are prepared, you are an authority. Strangers respect confident authority from the first minute.

EXAMPLE 5: ASK FOR ACTION

One of the most likable salesmen I ever knew was fired outright because, as his boss sadly explained, he could never ask anyone to do anything. The poor fellow simply lacked the self-confidence to do it. Consequently, the only impression he made on customers or prospective customers was one of complete indifference or incompetence.

When you want somebody to do something the

first minute is the best time to take action. It will either get done then, or you will learn in a hurry where you must use your self-confidence to apply more persuasion.

HOW KAY UNDERWOOD
MAKES THE FIRST MINUTE COUNT

Kay Underwood is a vibrant, middle-aged woman with verve, class and superior self-confidence. She conducts seminars on self-assertiveness. Since she travels from city to city, she works largely with total strangers. This, she says, makes the first moment of contact especially important. She handles it magnificently.

When Kay faces a class she stands front center and announces, "You know why I am here and I know why you are here. There is no time to waste. The first assertive thing you are going to do this morning is come stand in front of all these people, loudly tell your name, what you do, and in ten words or less tell why you consider self-assertiveness important to you." Then she calls on each person in rotation. If they balk she goes and takes them by the hand and personally leads them to the rostrum.

Kay's classes are highly successful. Kay is a successful lady. She works on that from the first minute.

HOW TO COME ON
WITH SELF-CONFIDENCE

You do not convince anyone that you have self-confidence by telling them that you have gobs of it. They want to see it. You have to demonstrate it.

You can demonstrate self-confidence and make a strong first impression by taking a dominant stance right at the beginning. A dominant stance is not to imply that you have to clobber anybody or become unduly overpowering. You can take the lead with friendly firmness, a pleasant determination, and an unswerving, confident commitment to lead. Kay Underwood understands this. She is a prime example of how you can come on with confidence and make everybody you work with a winner.

PEOPLE EXPECT YOU TO BE ASSERTIVE

People not only expect you to be assertive, they hope that you will be. Assertive people are self-confident people. They are doers. They know where they are going. By their conduct and their manner they just naturally instill trust and confidence in others. Here is a study of a strong, confident leader whom I know. I have been around him enough to appreciate both the man and his methods.

An old and honored college had drifted into dire financial straits. The board of trustees had to find a president for the college who could and would do a financial job. They found such a man in Dr. Tom Bartowly. After Dr. Bartowly had done his job and moved on to another rewarding challenge, the chairman of the committee which hired him remembered him thus: "It's interesting that he said when he came here that he probably would stay no longer than three years. 'The first year, I'll make some of the faculty mad; the second year I'll make some of the students mad; and the third year I'll make some of the trustees mad. If I don't make them mad, I won't be doing the things which have to be done.' And he was here approximately three years."

For several years now the college has been operating in the black. It is not surprising that Dr. Bartowly is currently doing a superb job for another college in another town.

People expect the self-confident you to be assertive enough to get the job done. You owe them that much and you owe yourself no less.

HOW TO AVOID A FLABBY BEGINNING

Obviously, you won't be able to make lengthy preparation for every new encounter. Some will be spontaneous, unexpected and occasionally unwelcome. Nevertheless, you can avoid a flabby beginning.

Making a strong first impression is always largely a matter of attitude. When you accept your capacity for self-confidence and have the attitude that you can and will handle new people and new situations, then you won't do much flopping around. Work on that.

HOW TO MAKE A STRONG FIRST IMPRESSION UNDER SCRUTINY

When all eyes are upon you to see what you are going to do next, when they are boring through you to see how you will conduct yourself, or how you will respond to pressure, that is a time of testing. It does not follow that it should be a time of anxiety and discomfort. Ambitious people understand that this is routine stuff for the shakers and movers in this world. You are bound to find yourself in a position where you are being intently scrutinized by strangers. It happens to everyone sooner or later if they are doing much of anything. This is no cause for despair. It is a challenging opportunity. It is time to put your self-confidence up front and thereby make a power impression under scrutiny.

Here is something to keep in mind when you feel hot eyes upon you. Nobody bothers to scrutinize you, or to evaluate you, unless they are interested in you. Usually this means *unless they are interested in what you can do for them.* This is a direct request that you show them what you can do even as they look you over. Here are keys to make a strong first impression while you are under scrutiny.

KEY 1: RECOGNIZE THAT IT IS TO YOUR ADVANTAGE TO BE EVALUATED

There is no reason for you to fear evaluation (scrutiny). Only the insecure dread evaluation. When you are in charge of yourself and have self-confidence working for you, it is to your advantage to be closely evaluated. This is your opportunity to voice your ideas and opinions and to demonstrate that you are confident of your ability. When you do this you will make a strong impression. That is always a personal benefit of high order.

KEY 2: NEW PEOPLE ARE LOOKING FOR STRONGER FRIENDS

This is a key that can unlock many doors for you.

People are always looking for strong friends. This is the only kind that can give them confidence, help them grow, and reach goals otherwise unattainable. When you use your self-confidence to make a strong impression, then the people you are dealing with for the first time know they have met a worthwhile friend. This makes it much easier for you to spread your influence among more and more helpers.

KEY 3: YOU ARE AN INSIDER ALREADY

When you are being looked over closely at a first meeting you have the inside track. Somebody is expressing a great deal of interest in you when they give you a lot of attention from the start. This is good. When you are an insider you are in an envious position to put your self-confidence to work promptly and effectively. As an insider you can quickly make a strong impression.

KEY 4: YOU HAVE A HEAD START

When you are being scrutinized, examined, evaluated and appraised, at first contact, you are not being ignored. Your presence is recognized and appreciated. Your self-confidence is being felt. This gives you a head start in making a strong, helpful impression. This is a key placed right in your hand.

KEY 5: YOU CAN LAY THE GROUNDWORK FOR FURTHER ACTION

When you make a strong first impression under critical eyes, you have laid the groundwork for more action. You can take full advantage of such an occasion then and there by influencing and enlisting new helpers. This is a good time to define goals, extoll benefits and establish time frames for action. Once this is done you should stay on the job to be sure your instructions are followed and that your plans are being implemented. Let your self-confidence take full advantage of the impression it makes.

YOUR SELF-CONFIDENCE WINS
INSTANT CONFIDENCE FROM OTHERS

Do you know of anyone who is ever favorably impressed by a personality who is apologetic, retiring, indecisive and hesitant when meeting new friends? Do you know of anyone who likes to see a new acquaintance squirm and agonize? Of course, you do not, unless that person has a sadistic bent of mind. On the other hand, self-confidence puts new friends at ease. More than that, it wins instant confidence from new people. You can prove this to your own satisfaction by analyzing and reviewing your own reaction to these two diverse circumstances. You may be sympathetic to, and sorry for, a new acquaintance with low self-esteem, but you won't be comfortable around him. On the other hand, a self-confident man or woman will stimulate and inspire you. This personal reaction tells you that a self-confident approach will win instant confidence from others.

HOW TO MAKE THE MOST
OF A STRONG FIRST IMPRESSION

You don't have to do everything for acceptance. It is natural and good to want to please people. You should do this anytime the price is not too dear. However, being sweet is not the only way to make a strong impression. The way to make the most of a strong impression is to remember your self-obligation. You have a right to success, a right to express yourself, an obligation to act in your own behalf. Fortunately, you can most often bring this about without starting any fires. You will never be able to please everyone, but you can always look out for your own interests by making the most of a strong first impression.

HOLDING ONTO THE ADVANTAGES A STRONG FIRST IMPRESSION GIVES YOU

When you have come on and made a favorable power impression, keep the advantage by keeping control. Be polite, but don't give up the dominant position you have earned to an eager beaver who has no interest in your goals or your welfare. You can do this by the same techniques that put you out front in the first place. By being assertive without being antagonistic you can always lead the group, meeting, assemblage, convention or whatever back to the subject or program you have initiated. Do this as often as you must. Each time you may be interrupted you can acknowledge the intruder by nodding, or with a "yes, but," and go right back to your subject. If this fails to eliminate the irritating interruptions, never hesitate to stop the whole proceedings and explain in your best manner that no further interruptions can be tolerated. Then confidently proceed to make the most of your strong first impression.

USE THE FOLLOW-UP TECHNIQUE

When you have met new people and opened new opportunities, follow up the advantage. Confirm and then keep any appointments made, pursue plans that you made at first contact, and aggressively keep in touch with your prospective new helpers. This is insurance that you will make the most of your winning impression.

HOW R. W. RIMMER
USED SELF-CONFIDENCE
TO CAPITALIZE ON
A STRONG FIRST IMPRESSION

Young R. W. Rimmer had made a strong impression on his firm's new vice-president of marketing by landing a tough account older salesmen couldn't tie down. As a result, he had been asked to address the sales force at their annual home office sales meeting. As he took the floor one veteran salesman started idly thumbing through a company manual. Young Rimmer stopped his presentation. Suddenly the thoughtless page-flipper realized there was a deadly silence in the room. He looked up sheepishly. R. W. Rimmer said, "If it's OK with you, Mr. Ellis, we will get on with the business at hand." Then Rimmer proceeded with his excellent presentation without further interruption. His performance was confident and commanding. He had followed up a strong impression with a strong performance. This is an ideal way to make the most of a strong first impression.

HOW TO WIN FRIENDS
WITH A STRONG FIRST IMPRESSION

You can win friends with a strong first impression since, as we have established, people are attracted to assertive, self-confident individuals. When you meet others in an easy self-assured manner they sense at once that you are competent and able. They want you as a friend because you quickly add to their own sense of worth.

You make friends, as you make a strong impression, by acting friendly. To be condescending, or to come on as the only authority, is a mistake. This will turn people off. You should, of course, present yourself in an outgoing, assertive manner. You can do this while expressing an interest in your new acquaintances, listening to them, and asking them questions. When they see that you are interested in them, they will be interested in you. When they view you in this light they will become your willing helpers.

You can win friends with a strong display of self-confidence. And this, after all, is how you make a strong impression.

FLO MASSEY'S TECHNIQUE
TO WIN FRIENDS

Flo Massey says that she used to live on the razor's edge of life. She was lonely, uncertain and afraid of new people. She felt that they might not like her, or that they would make her feel foolish.

Flo doesn't live like that any more. She was lucky.

A co-worker in the large hospital where Flo did clerical work recognized her unhappiness. She convinced Flo to see one of the hospital's psychologists. This competent man made Flo see that her attitude was nothing less than a devastation of her own personality. He scheduled a series of sessions with her and outlined activities to get her into the mainstream of life again. He started Flo on what he called "the exposure technique."

THE EXPOSURE TECHNIQUE

The exposure technique meant that Flo was to start circulating more at once, whether at work or off-duty. Thus, she was to expose herself to new people and new situations. Flo reluctantly agreed, and she met new friends the first week right where she worked. From there Flo progressed to outside contacts. Her progress has been remarkable. Flo is now happier and busier than ever before. Her attitude is bright and her circle of friends is wide. Flo recommends the exposure technique. She vows that she will use it the rest of her life. She likes what it has done for her and those around her. Personal exposure is a sure-fire way to make friends.

THE FIRST IMPRESSION
LASTS A LONG TIME

It is hard for anyone to forget a weak, vapid first impression. Fortunately, your strong first impression will also be hard to forget. The first impression lasts a long time, because this is how your new contacts will remember you for a long time. This is another sound reason for you to put your self-confidence on the front burner every time you meet new people. Consider this too.

When you come on with confidence and self-assertiveness as you meet new individuals or new groups, you will not be thought of as being antagonistic or obnoxious. As long as you are not grossly abrasive (which you will not want to be anyway), your new friends will see the following in you.

* Self-confidence working for what it deserves.
* You as a doer refusing to be ignored.
* You refusing to be a loser.
* You as someone they are glad to know.
* You as someone to listen to and to work with.

Put the ideas and techniques in this chapter to work at every new opportunity. When you make a strong first impression you are on your way. You won't be like the poor man of whom it was said, "He has a great future and always will."

CONFIDENCE KEYS

* Psychology is a basic tool in making a strong first impression.
* The first minute counts the most.
* Take the initiative.
* Be a friend.
* Make your position known.
* Be prepared.

* Ask for action.
* People expect you to be assertive.
* You can make a strong first impression under scrutiny.
* Your self-confidence wins confidence from others.
* You make friends with a strong impression.
* Use the exposure technique.
* The first impression lasts a long time.

Chapter 9
Self-Confidence Procedures
To Make You A Leader

"The highest reward for man's toil is not what he gets for it, but what he becomes by it."—John Ruskin.

Who is a leader? A leader is any person who exercises confident authority and who acts responsibly. This person, this leader, need not be one who lives in high places, garners medals and honors, or one who achieves fame and gains public acclaim. A leader is one who acts confidently and responsibly right where he lives and works. A leader is one who controls his life and manages his own affairs. He or she sets the example for others. His self-confidence is recognizable.

This is not to say that leaders should not aspire to high goals and recognition. Indeed, they should. You have a self-responsibility to be the best and most effective leader that you can. More, you owe this much to those around you. Not everyone can, nor does everyone want to, be a leader. Such people, such friends, are looking to you for leadership. They want to share your confidence in, and enthusiasm for, what goes on around you. The higher you climb as a leader, the higher you lift those about you. This alone is more than justification for a close study of self-confidence procedures to make you a leader. Let us begin with this.

CONTROL YOUR THOUGHT PROCESSES

Our thoughts control our lives and determine who we are and what we shall become. Thoughts are an unseen power secretly working day and night. They can be good, they can be bad, they can be strong or they can be weak. They can be constructive or they can be destructive. More to the point, they can be controlled by you. It is imperative that a leader understands how to direct and control this mighty source of personal power that is his alone to do with as he will.

Amazingly, there are those who let their thoughts float at random, as a thistle on the wind. This is a costly mistake. Unless we control our thoughts, they control us. The more powerful a force, the more carefully it must be directed. Your ability to think and reason—your thought processes—is the most potent force you have. It is all you will ever need as long as you maintain control over it. Here are a baker's dozen of ideas on just how you can go about controlling your thought processes.

13 STEPS TO CONTROL YOUR THINKING

1. Recognize that what you think *is* important.
2. Keep your thinking on what you want to ac-

complish each day.

3. Discipline your mind to do your bidding.

4. Let your brain free wheel once in a while to relax and to gather ideas. The key is to turn it loose only when you want it to go.

5. Don't pattern your thinking after someone else. Learn from everybody you meet, but establish your own thought processes.

6. Know that your mind has limitless potential. It never wears out.

7. Don't be afraid to think for yourself. Not every thought will be profound, but every thought will have merit.

8. Believe that what you think does make a difference.

9. Note that a thought is not dependent upon age, education, circumstance or any external influence. Your thoughts do not recognize rank or position. They do your bidding only.

10. Write down compelling thoughts as they flash across your mind. Otherwise, you may lose them in the clutter of a demanding day.

11. Cherish your thoughts. They are what give flavor and excitement to a workaday world.

12. Keep your thoughts within the realm of what is possible from where you stand today. Leadership is a step-by-step process. As your thought processes grow, you can reach higher and higher.

13. Hold this thought close. Either you control your thought processes or they will control you.

As you master the techniques of controlling your thought processes, you will produce winning thoughts. This is a technique that develops self-confident leaders in every walk of life. It is something that you can put to work today.

NEVER BE UNDONE BY A MISTAKE

When someone has a poor perception of his personal worth every mistake is like a stinging slap in the face. His mistakes rage like clanging cymbals through his mind, further eroding his self-confidence. This should never be. Everyone makes mistakes no matter how strong they may be. You will make mistakes, but that is no reason to be undone by them. As we have all been told many times, we should learn from our mistakes instead of agonizing over them. A wholesome attitude toward mistakes is one I heard a highly successful business man, Wally Flint from Kansas, express. This confident man had made a decision involving thousands of dollars when a self-appointed critic began to rant and rail that Wally's judgment was faulty and that he was making a monumental mistake. Wally listened to the tirade, then calmly said that he had made mistakes before and had managed to survive them. Further, he stated that he felt sure that he could handle a few more mistakes along the way and learn a valuable lesson or two in the process. In this particular case it so happened that Wally Flint did not make a mistake. Instead, he made a lot of money just as he is still doing today.

The best technique to deal with a mistake is to take these three steps.

Step 1: Keep your mistake in perspective.

True, a mistake may embarrass you, hurt you financially, and trouble you mentally. It can get ugly, but it is not the end of the world or of you. Keep a mistake in perspective and go on to step number two.

Step 2: Take corrective action.

Analyze what went wrong. Explore why you walked into a mistake, then decide on a method or remedy to minimize the effect of the mistake you made. Take action to recoup your losses. Learn from your mistake. Resolve not to make the same one again. Making a mistake once is understandable. Repeating it is inexcusable. It is vastly more difficult to get up when you have been knocked down more than once by the same mistake. Nor does it do much to boost your self-confidence. Still, each corrective action will straighten out your mistakes and maintain your self-confidence as a leader. Once you embark on a course of action there is only one more thing to do with a mistake. It is step number three.

Step 3: Forget it.

When you keep a mistake in perspective and take action to correct and overcome it, there is only one thing to do. Forget it. Remember the lesson, but as for the mistake, forget it.

WESLEY STEMMONS' PROCEDURES
AFTER A MISTAKE

Wesley Stemmons, a star salesman for a stock brokerage firm, has his own routine to overcome and to profit from his mistakes. On the rare occasions when Stemmons loses a client, he goes home and analyzes his mistake carefully and, at the same time, charts his course of action to correct the error or errors. First, he gets pen and paper and then diagrams what happened and what he plans to do about it. Here is an abbreviated example of the simple chart he works from.

WHAT I DID WRONG	*STEPS TO CORRECT*
1. Made too little preparation.	1. Prepare a more convincing presentation. Use more visual aids.
2. Didn't learn enough about the client and his needs.	2. Do more research on client relative to his goals and his means.
3. Tried too hard to convince him that I was right and that he was wrong.	3. Don't make the client look foolish. Keep my side positive and friendly.
4. Chose a poor time to sell him. He was too preoccupied with a temporary problem.	4. Make an appointment when he will give me his attention.
5. Failed to emphasize all the benefits of the program I presented.	5. Itemize every benefit that I can offer the client. Go over each until I'm sure that he understands everything that he will gain.

Stemmons says that as soon as he has identified his mistake, he contacts the client and goes back to wipe out his blunder. "Mostly," he says, "it's a matter of going back and doing what I should have done in the first place."

Stemmons, like every self-confident leader, is aware that the worst thing he could do would be to allow a mistake to cause him to come undone and thereby void his self-confidence. This is a mistake no one can afford.

EVERY LEADER BLEEDS A LITTLE

The leader is not an unfeeling monster. He is subject to human frailties just as we all are. He can be hurt. You can be sure that every leader bleeds a little, but he doesn't permit that to bankrupt his life or rob him of his self-confidence.

As you put your self-confidence to work to develop strong leadership qualities, you can expect a few bumps along the way. Here are pointers on how to handle the annoying problems you may encounter from time to time as you exercise a self-confident leadership role.

* Plan for success, but be prepared to cope with a few unpleasant surprises.
* Expect success. Don't brood over possible setbacks.
* Stay with your goal. A bit of heated opposition should change nothing.

182

* Proceed with self-confidence. A self-confident attitude will wipe out most problems for you.
* Accept a little bleeding as the price of leadership. It is not fatal and it can put fire in your self-confidence.

DECIDE WHAT YOU WANT AS A LEADER

A leader doesn't just happen. A leader is a person who has made something happen because that person believed in and wanted something. Your first step as a leader must be to decide what you want from yourself and from others. A vertigo of faltering indecision can obviate the best of intentions and destroy the would-be leader. This need never happen to you, but there is great need to be aware of the danger of chronic indecision.

Making up your mind is not always the easiest thing in the world to do. It becomes easier, however, as you develop your self-confidence skills. After a bit of experience you will make quick, clean decisions and then wonder why it was sometimes so painful before. You can observe the truth of this by watching business executives as they make daily decisions which vitally affect their lives and the lives of those around them. Business leaders are not the only ones whose decisions are loaded with impact. Housewives, career women, teachers, truck drivers, accountants, lawyers, farmers, students, and everybody else who contributes anything to society must make far-reaching decisions every day. What they decide shapes their lives and influences others for better or for worse. Decision-making is a basic step in self-confidence procedures to make you a leader. Decide now to make this one of your strong points.

Here are helpful observations on decision-making that you can use today and every day.

* Decisions have no power until acted upon.
* Decisions are more than sheer logic. They involve emotions, the spiritual and your attitude.
* Facts and reality are the basis for tough, intelligent decisions.
* Decisions should be decided by what you want and expect.
* A decision made in anger, pique, sorrow or fear is no decision.
* Decisions are unavoidable.
* Your decisions carry power.

Decide what you want as a leader. Do this by getting facts, weighing consequences, assessing the odds, charting your plan, and getting into action. Decision making is not meant to be misery. It is stimulating, rewarding and satisfying. It can get you what you want.

AVOID THE SHOTGUN APPROACH

Avoid the shotgun approach as you decide what you want. Zero in on specific goals. The shotgun approach, with decisions flying like confetti, will get you something. But it may not be what you want. It is not the leader's way.

Here is an easy thought to dramatize the basic importance of making a decision based on what you want.

1. If I make a dishonest decision—one based on the line of least resistance—I will not like myself.
OR
2. I want to like myself. Therefore, I will make an honest decision based on what I want.

GO AFTER BIG GOALS FIRST

The real worth of any self-confidence program to make you a leader is how much you gain from it. You gain the most when you go after your big goals first. Once you get the cake it's easy to lather on the frosting.

One thing that the leaders of men have discovered is that self-confident action motivated by a keen ambition is often more forceful than strict competence or academic brilliance. This is not meant to discourage study or technical expertise at all. Learn all you can. Leadership is not an end. It is a journey, a journey, however, that takes you nowhere without self-confident action.

When you are selecting your big goal, don't toy with every possible detail you hope to accomplish. Select what you want more than anything else; select what is necessary to your role as a winning, dominant leader. If you entertain every popcorn item you may ever want or need you will waste energy and lose valuable time. You will be in the same position as the man who has many opinions, but no ideas. Frustrated.

Go after big goals. Do it like this.

Question:	What is my most urgent leadership goal right now?
Answer:	My goal is to organize my own company.
Question:	What leadership qualities must I exercise?
Answer:	Marketing know-how and a desire to lead others.
Question:	What is my field?
Answer:	Grocery and food products.
Question:	Where do I start?
Answer:	By recruiting a sales team and contacting principal suppliers in the industry.
Question:	When do I start?
Answer:	Now.

HOW TO DEAL WITH
RIDICULE AND DISCOURAGEMENT

Suppose that some busybody ridicules you and scoffs at your plans. Whose problem is that? Yours or his? It is his, of course. You will only shoot holes in your self-confidence and question your leadership qualifications if you accept the blame.

It has been my observation through the years that self-confident leaders listen closely to other people. They are considerate individuals who enthusiastically make friends, but they never give much credence to anyone who ridicules or attempts to belittle them. Why should they? Did you ever know a man that roasted every leader who amounted to a hill of beans?

The goal of one who ridicules and attempts to discourage ambitious leaders is to make himself look good. If he can make you lose confidence and abandon your place as a winner and leader he feels superior. Don't let this type discourage you. He is the one who is sick, not you.

Of course, no man is immune to mistakes. Honest criticism can be profitable. But all too often self-appointed critics have hidden motives that even they cannot admit to or, indeed, may not recognize. Still, as we said, that is their problem. Yours is to keep on course with self-confidence and to develop your leadership skills to a high degree.

HOW HAROLD AMES HANDLED RIDICULE

Harold Ames is a young man of thirty who looks as if he had just turned twenty-one. Harold is a marketing vice-president for a large company. He is responsible for the activities of thirty-one salespeople, all of whom look older than Harold. Because of his boyish appearance, Harold is frequently subjected to ridicule, some of it lighthearted, but much of which is cruel and senseless. Harold lumps it all together and treats it alike. First, he calls the individual into his office. In that privacy, with a one-on-one situation, he states flatly that he does not apologize for his face nor does he apologize for the way he does his job. Then he suggests that an understanding friendship would be better for all concerned, but if the offender wants to be a clown he should go where his talents might be better appreciated. Harold has never lost a salesperson because of one of these frank discussions. He is honest enough to say that he would prefer to avoid them, but that he will not succumb to ridicule or discouragement for any reason. Who can fault him for that?

HOW TO GET UP
WHEN YOU GET KNOCKED DOWN

Few, if any, leaders have made it to the top without occasionally getting knocked down along the way. That is not surprising. In a highly competitive society you should anticipate a lump or two as you assume more and more of the personal satisfaction and the personal responsibilities of dynamic self-confident leadership. Here is the surprising thing: It is not the big disasters that cause the most trouble. The things that knock an ambitious able person down more often are the annoying petty irritations that can plague the strongest among us. It is the daily routine and petty pressures of everyday living that we must guard against most intently. Amazingly, the vast majority of people possess inner resources that enable them to deal with major crises in life. As one man said, "My wife seemed utterly helpless until our house burned and we lost everything. Then, as I watched her comfort the children and rebuild our home, I realized how strong and competent she could be."

Freud is reported to have said that the duty of a human being is to endure life. My own idea is that our duty to ourselves is to make the most of life. What better way to do this than by becoming a self-confident leader of men? Thus we can not only enrich our own life, but the lives of all those we touch. This is more than reason enough to get up when we get knocked down. But how do we do this? Here are key self-confidence procedures you can use to overcome any setbacks or disappointments as you sharpen your leadership skills.

* You don't have to push and shove.

If you get knocked down, you don't have to get up and push and shove. Vendettas against those who may try to block your path are a waste of time and energy. Instead of going to war, analyze what caused your temporary failure and then take steps to eliminate the problem. It's not only people who can knock you down. There are such mistakes as inadequate planning, faulty financial management, improper timing, lack of personal preparation, unfortunate accidents, or any of a myriad of circumstances in a risk-prone world. Whatever the cause of a setback, the remedy lies in learning what went wrong, then putting your self-confidence back out front to map a campaign to regain and hold your position as a growing leader.

* You don't have to stay down to win friends.

Leaders need friends. They are experts in the field of making and motivating friends. Nevertheless, don't become a "people pleaser" just to avoid the risk of a knockdown. Consider this. There are basically two types of people pleasers. One who caves in to every demand made upon him, and one who gets up and continues to lead despite a lump or two. Concentrate on where you are going. People like determined leaders. You don't have to just lie there to have friends.

* Forget about making a big impression.

It is embarrassing, of course, to get your feet kicked from under you. The temptation is there to get up and do something spectacular to compensate for the humiliating experience. Don't do it. Forget about making a big impression. Keep a setback in its proper niche. Get up and quietly and quickly go back to work. A knockdown is a detour, not the end of the road.

* Getting knocked down is not the significant thing.

No, getting knocked down is not the significant thing. The significant thing is hanging onto your own values, keeping your self-confidence, and getting up to finish your job. You can do this when you remember who you are and what you want.

HOW LEONARD ROSS GOT UP
AFTER BEING KNOCKED DOWN

Leonard Ross was the executive officer responsible

for a highly successful and growing retirement-resort development in the lake country of a Midwest state. Out of a clear sky the corporation that owned the huge complex changed hands. Ross, along with other key personnel, was summarily dismissed. Ross was temporarily devastated by the abrupt setback. However, he quickly got up and went back to work. He secured promises from two former key salesmen for his old company that they would join him in a new venture. Next he contacted an area real estate concern. With their help he obtained financing from a local bank to buy and develop a plot of shore front property adjacent to the one he had previously put on its feet. Today Leonard Ross is manager and co-owner of the biggest retirement-resort complex for miles around. He makes more money and is happier than ever before. Ross has been heard to say that sometimes a man has to get knocked down before he finds out how much he can do.

BE YOUR OWN LEADER

There is a lot being said about "human engineering" today. This has to do with the motivation, creativity and placement of people. The best idea I've heard on the subject is that you should be your own engineer—which is a way of saying that you should be your own leader. Nobody is better qualified for the job. The individual who carries out self-imposed assignments is a doer who builds self-confidence. This person soon gets used to success.

THE LEADER WHO LIKES HIMSELF
WINS THE MOST

We have already established the importance of self-esteem (liking yourself). This is a key characteristic of leaders and those who would be self-confident leaders. The sky is full of stars, but they are millions and billions of miles apart. They are alone. Our world is full of people, but each is alone. This is especially true of the leader who stays in front of the masses. Since he operates alone and under his own guidance, it is vital that he like himself.

Being alone does not mean that those who are leaders are physically isolated creatures. An effective leader must be people-oriented. He must be involved with people for they are what make him a leader. The point is that he must do his own thinking, make decisions for himself and others, he must act and influence others to act. The better the leader likes himself, the better he will like those whom he must motivate, influence, direct and use in his role as the leader. The better you like yourself, the better others will like you, and the better leader you will be. This has nothing to do with vanity. Honest, healthy self-esteem is something apart from vanity and pretense.

The leader who has a proper self-regard wins the most because he has the confidence to act. He actively influences other people to move and work at his behest. As a leader you must be active to accomplish anything. For instance, you must actively read this book to make it work for you. If you passively read it as if you were someone else somewhere else, you will do nothing more than browse through it, then let it collect dust. If you act upon the ideas and information in it, it can be an invaluable servant to you.

As a leader with due self-respect you will be active. As a self-confident leader you will give your action direction and purpose. Otherwise, action becomes nothing more than sheer drudgery.

It is natural that you should want people to like you as a leader. You want to be regarded as good. This, too, is commendable. Still, you should not be overly concerned that everybody sees you as good. Too much emphasis in this direction can cause one to focus on what appears to be good. There is a vast difference in appearing to be good and in being good. The self-confident leader who likes himself can recognize the difference. Recognizing the difference can be the difference between winning and losing.

Man is equipped for winning. The ages have proven this. Man is a survivor and a leader. You are a member of the race. Be proud of that. Your life was never meant to be one big apology.

Attitude is a result of self-management. Your self-attitude determines how well you like yourself. When you like yourself you will be a leader who wins the most.

CONFIDENCE KEYS

* A leader is one who exercises confident authority.
* You have a self-responsibility to be the best leader that you can be.
* What you think is important.
* Cherish your thoughts.

* Everyone makes mistakes.
* Never be undone by a mistake.
* Every leader bleeds a little.
* A leader doesn't just happen.
* Your decisions make a difference.
* Decisions have no power until acted upon.
* Go after the big goals first.
* Never succumb to ridicule or discouragement.
* Anticipate a few lumps.
* You don't have to push and shove.
* Getting knocked down is not the significant thing.
* Remember who you are.
* Be your own engineer.
* The leader who likes himself wins the most.

Chapter 10
Techniques To Build A Winning Personality Through Self-Confidence

Every rational person wants a winning personality. The reasons are obvious. A winning personality makes all else easier. If you have a winning personality you are the personification of self-confidence and success. People will want to identify with you. They will readily cooperate with you. Moreover, when you have a winning personality you exude happiness, assurance and a sense of well-being. With this personality—this winner's attitude—you will make friends and attract willing helpers. It is small wonder that people dream of having a winning personality. You can do more than dream. You can have a winning personality. Here are techniques and examples to get you started today.

ACT LIKE A WINNER

Act like a winner. Do not act like the stereotyped idea of how a winner should act. A real winner is not loud, overbearing, inconsiderate, unscrupulous or prone to ride roughshod over anybody who doesn't submit to his self-ordained authority. A winner doesn't have to act like that. He has confidence in himself and shuns such negative behavior. He knows every winner needs people. They are what make him a winner and a leader. A winner is one who wins people to his side by acting as if they are important to him, as, indeed, he knows they are. Fact is, nobody succeeds at much of anything unless people want him to. Build your winning act on this truth. Make it the basis of your winning personality. Here is an example of what I am talking about.

J. T. Shikaney was the assistant to the marketing director of a manufacturing concern. The company had fifty-one salespeople in the field. Since the business was complex and highly competitive, the individuals on the sales team were frequently obliged to contact headquarters for clearance on technical questions. However, Shikaney's secretary had been instructed to "get their number" so that he could call back at his convenience. Of course, this voided many sales where immediate decisions were necessary. It wasn't long until the salespeople were routing all their calls directly to Dan Walters, the marketing director. Dan Walters always took a salesman's call and gave immediate assistance. Walters made it a point to find out why Shikaney's calls were being rerouted to him. The salespeople happily supplied the information. Shortly Shikaney was looking for a new job. The people that he thought were not important enough to listen to had put him out on the streets. He was on his way to being a winner when he lost it all because he failed to act like one. The stereotyped winner is as outmoded today as is the total authoritarian.

ACTING LIKE A WINNER
PAYS BIG FOR FAY PELLHAM

Fay Pellham hated her boss. Fay was one of ninety-nine machine operators in a clothing manufacturing concern where Bertha Cutbirth was the demanding supervisor. Cutbirth apparently took delight in finding fault. She tongue-lashed her hapless victims unmercifully on the spot and before the other employees. Turnover was high. Resentment and bitterness toward the supervisor was the rule. Fay did not like the woman and she shared the views of her co-workers. Yet, she liked her job and didn't want to be a quitter. So, consciously or not, she started acting like a winner. She encouraged her co-workers to be more tolerant of their misguided supervisor and to be as positive and productive as they could. She began to have small groups in her home where they discussed their common problem. Sure enough, they soon developed a bit of tolerance for Cutbirth's miserable personality. They noted that she never smiled, lived alone, had few friends and little real enthusiasm for what she was doing. Then Fay surprised Bertha Cutbirth by inviting her to join one of the meetings at her house. The poor woman agreed to be there. There was general uneasiness for a while, but Fay guided the conversation and avoided any direct attack on Cutbirth. Instead, the talk was positive, if not cordial. The next day all agreed that Cutbirth seemed to be more relaxed. She attended three more meetings. At the fourth, she bowled the

197

other ladies over by announcing her impending marriage. She would be resigning her position, she said, and she would recommend Fay Pellham as her successor, that is, if her fellow employees approved of the idea. The room erupted in applause as Cutbirth smiled broadly.

Fay Pellham became supervisor and later part-owner of the firm. Fay has advised a lot of beginning workers that you can't be a winner without acting like one. She knows the secret of a winning personality.

TALK LIKE A WINNER

You won't have a winning personality unless you talk like a winner. Here are key characteristics of the speech that builds a winning personality.

The winner's speech is: Positive
                        Courteous
                        Firm
                        Clear
                        Correct
                        To the point
                        Commanding
                        Pleasing
                        Convincing
                        Appealing
                        Sincere
                        Plain
                        Controlled

When the winning personality speaks, there is no whimpering, no excuse making, no plea for special favor, no "gimme a break," no doom-saying. A winning personality uses his speech to produce winning thoughts and winning attitudes.

If your speech has been a bit careless, it can be changed to project a winning personality. It is essential to practice winning speech, just as it is to practice winning thinking. Both are under your exclusive control. Select your words with care. The following lists will give you the idea.

WINNING WORDS:	LOSING WORDS:
You	Me
We	I
Possible	Impossible
We can	We can't
Ours	Mine
Love	Hate
Concern	Indifference
Money	Bankrupt
Work	Dawdle
Ambitious	Lazy
Strong	Weak
Courage	Fear
Conviction	Doubt
Act	Hesitate

Winning speech, like a winning personality, can be a habit. Talk like a winner. It will attract friends, motivate people to do what you want them to do, make you money, build your confidence, and give you a winning personality.

Study speech. Practice speech. Read and reread the chapter in this book on speech power. Then don't be afraid to speak up. As Dizzy Dean, the old-time ball player and speaking personality said, "If you've done it, that ain't braggin'." When you talk like a winner it really *ain't*.

BUILD A PERSONALITY THAT YOU LIKE

The personality that you want is a confident, winning personality. This doesn't necessarily mean winning a lot of money, winning every fight, bowling over everybody who crosses you, and going down the highway of life like a runaway bulldozer. A winning personality is one that adds confidence and good things to your life as you contribute to the lives of those around you. Does this sound like a big order? It's not. It is the recipe that the vast majority of well-adjusted people follow. It is something you can enjoy now. Here is why.

Our personalities are not an accident of birth. They are learned. They can be changed overnight, made into whatever you want, mastered by you, controlled by you, and used by you to go wherever you will. Like self-confidence your personality is your exclusive property. You are its master, not its victim.

Here are items to consider as you build a winning personality.

1. Do a periodic self-analysis.

This is more than looking for faults. Identify your good points and utilize them as building blocks.

2. Turn your imagination loose.

Imagine the personality you are building. See it as you work, greet friends, hold meetings, face strangers, sit with your family, or encounter demanding challenges. Do you like what you see? If so, you have visualized the kind of personality that you like. All that remains is to *actualize* it; that is, use your in-born self-confidence to put it to work for you. The rewards will stretch your imagination.

3. Beware the venom of self-pity.

The weakest personality is that of self-pity. Nobody wants to be around, much less work with, the person who habitually whimpers for sympathy. As an outgoing personality interested in a self-confident life, this is not likely to be of concern to you. But it does happen and it is insidious. Keep a positive attitude if unavoidable sorrow or trouble comes your way. Beware the venom of self-pity. Whatever obstacles you may face you can work around or overcome, just as successful, self-confident personalities always have.

4. Be for real.

Whatever personality you build, let it be for real. A personality is no good unless it fits you. A personality that is nothing more than an act fools no one. You wouldn't like it. There was a high school girl who was crying because she couldn't get her hair fixed like all the other girls at school. She complained to her mother that unless she did as the other girls, she wouldn't have any personality at all. She would be freaked out, she said. Her mother suggested that she simply wear it in two long braids and go to school as herself. Reluctantly, the girl consented. That night she came home ecstatic. Her classmates were so impressed that six were coming to school the next day with their hair braided. Her mother taught the young lady more than the teacher that day.

Your personality is distinctly yours. Everyone should work to build a winning personality. No one should put a false face on it.

HOLD DOWN OUTSIDE INFLUENCE

To say that we should never be influenced by anyone would be irresponsible. Any intelligent and sensitive person is influenced by others. Nevertheless, you can't be a sponge and soak up everybody's opinions, instructions, beliefs, style, mannerisms, appearance or personality. Be selective. Hold down outside influence. Absorb only that which will add strength and polish to your personality. Build on constructive influence. Don't lean on it.

VIRGIL HARPER SHAKES
AN OUTSIDE INFLUENCE

Virgil Harper owned a growing confectionery wholesale company. His father-in-law, a former small-time wholesaler himself, continually cautioned Harper to "stick with the little guys." They made more loyal and better customers in the long run, he repeatedly told Harper. Virgil listened for a while though he felt uncomfortable by such depressing influence. When he saw his competition moving into

202

supermarkets, chain stores, convenience stores, and dealing with co-ops, he shook this outside influence. Harper kept his old accounts but he hired a specialty salesman, increased his inventory, borrowed needed capital and went after his share of big accounts. His business expanded as he assumed full responsibility for his own affairs and his own personality. He is a winner in his industry. Harper is still courteous to his father-in-law, but he is not easily influenced these days.

GO WITH THE WINNERS

"Go with the winners" does not suggest that you should be a hero-worshipper. What it does say is that you should associate yourself with winners. When you go with the winners you share their spirit, their ideas and their attitudes. You become one of them. The old adage that birds of a feather flock together is still valid.

When you go with the winners you will often be with people who may be smarter than you are. Don't be uncomfortable about this. Remember you are getting smarter each day as you study techniques to build a winning personality. Also, you will note that intelligent, successful people are easy to be around. They have the self-confidence and the personality to want others to be achievers. Directly or indirectly they will help you. They want you to be a winner for a very good reason: They, too, like to go with the winners.

As you go with the winners, go as an equal. Successful, aggressive people are repelled by a subservient approach. On the other hand, they are impressed by sincere friendliness and a self-confident attitude. They are not looking for flattery. They recognize you as an equal—another human being with the self-confidence to learn and to make a personal contribution to the lives of others. That is enough to place you on a par with the winners.

Gary Pitts worked part-time at a garage to help pay his way through school. One of Gary's regular customers was L. L. Myers who owned a large travel agency in a nearby office building. Gary, who had visions of travelling, chatted amiably with Myers from time to time. He asked questions, told Myers of his interest in travel and, in short, shared his dreams with the older man. The two became good friends as Gary serviced Mr. Myers' car and visited easily with him. Myers suggested that Gary come to his office shortly before graduation. Gary was invited to work in the agency, an opportunity he grasped at once. Gary is now vice-president of L. L. Myers, travels extensively and still rubs shoulders with the winners. Gary says (no pun intended), "It's the only way to go."

DON'T FEEL GUILTY ABOUT WINNING

A feeling of guilt is a heavy and demoralizing burden carried by great numbers of sensitive men and women. Much, if not most of it, is for imaginary reasons that are wholly without justification. It is a self-imposed, deadly handicap. Unbelievable as it may sound, many good people feel guilty about winning. You should never feel guilty about winning. The guilt belongs to those who do not try to become a winning personality, those who sit on their talents and watch others work and grow. This is a waste. The world needs winners. You know that and I know it. The tragedy of good intentions spoiled by a false sense of guilt is personality destruction. When you win honorably and fairly, you put yourself in position to do much for yourself and for others. Is that a cause for guilt?

Another point. Don't be ashamed of losing once in a while. When we speak of a confident, winning personality, we do not mean that to have a winning personality you must engage in and win every argument and every encounter. Nor does a winning personality have to be sweet and winsome under any and all circumstances. The winning personality we are concerned with is a workaday personality who possesses and uses self-confidence, whose determination and ability attracts and motivates others to get things done. Even this strong character may not always win. We have covered techniques to handle occasional setbacks. Don't be ashamed of not being perfect. Above all, don't feel guilty about winning. When you put your self-confidence to work to build a winning personality, about the only thing you will be guilty of is a more satisfying life.

BE YOUR OWN BEST EXAMPLE

If you hide your real personality and try to be like

someone you think has a gung-ho personality, you will never know the satisfaction of building a strong personality of your own. Granted, one of the best ways of learning personality techniques is to learn from others. Still, you must be discriminating in what you use as you observe other personalities at work. Let others contribute to your personality, but don't be unduly influenced. Be your own best example. Here is a secret that you can use as a guideline in being your own best example of a winning personality.

* Reveal your own true self.

It is not true that your personality will suffer if you reveal your own true self. Familiarity does not automatically breed contempt. Conversely, people detest sham and pretense. Reveal your own true self, warts and all. This is not to say that you should call attention to every fault that you may have. It is enough to act natural and be natural as you use your self-confidence to build your winning personality. There is a certain risk in being self-revealing, but there can be great rewards. How else will you ever know just how strong and useful your personality can be?

FACE TOUGH SITUATIONS FAST

The toughest situation you will ever have to face may have nothing to do with your job, money, competition, disappointments, or any of the problems usually associated with personal difficulties. Here are examples of some of the toughest situations you can face in a campaign to build a winning personality.

* Anger.

I do not agree that if you feel anger boiling up in you that you should cut loose with an emotional explosion. The supposed logic offered by those who advocate or practice this degrading theory is that you will feel better if you "get it off your chest." This is simply not true when viewed in the context of the full and final results of such irrational behavior. What have you accomplished if you blow your top, create a scene and tell off someone? What will it do for your personality?

First of all, an angry emotional outburst is usually an indication of insecurity. It is evidence of a faulty personality. It is destructive. It is not, as the perpetrator believes, an assertive act. If you feel tension building up to an unbearable degree, take the advice a good doctor once gave a would-be suicide: Go for a long walk. Physical exertion will relax you and let you deal with anger more rationally. Anything that gives you control of yourself will help you build a more positive personality.

* Classifying people.

You classify people when you give them labels that you like or dislike. Everybody likes the label "superior," nobody likes the label "inferior." You may see some people as "good" while you label others "bad." Labels are relative and of no worth to you. The "superior" person has faults, the "inferior" person may possess intrinsic personal values. "Good" and "bad" may be only in the eyes of the beholder.

It is damaging to a winning personality to label people. You may thus avoid a helpful, stimulating personality because you have mislabeled someone. When you control this situation fast you will build a supportive personality, and you will gain helpful friends.

* Approval dependency.

A situation in which one must have constant approval is a tough place for any personality. This is a situation that can cost its victim many worthwhile friends and helpers. When anyone feels that he must always have the approval of others in order to feel worthwhile or competent, he is not in charge of his personality. If one seeks constant approval he will avoid strong personalities who may not always agree one hundred percent with him. Consequently, he forgoes contact with outgoing achievers and leaders who could and would contribute much to a winning personality.

The way to face this personality situation is to evaluate your attitude and your chosen associates. You do not have to give up any of your present friendships and contacts. Just be sure that you include self-sufficient individuals who have the personality and the confidence to disagree occasionally, but who do not consider disapproval a rejection of the person. This will boost your winning personality and theirs.

DON'T OVERRATE EVERYBODY YOU MEET

It's tough on a personality when the person is constantly measuring his own worth by what he thinks he sees in others. This is invariably weighted in the other person's favor, because we tend to forget that people we admire also have deficiencies. Give everybody all the credit due them. Learn from them, mingle with them, influence them, enjoy them, but don't overrate them. You don't need this. The people you exalt and overrate are almost surely seeing qualities in you that they wish they had.

An excellent way to overcome the habit of overrating others is this. Instead of saying to yourself, "How do I stack up alongside these people?" say "How do these people stack up against *me*?" This positive attitude will keep your self-belief from being shaken by unfair and unrealistic comparisons. With this approach you discover that you have every reason to be a self-confident, winning personality.

WHAT HAPPENED
WHEN HARVEY McALISTER STOPPED
OVERRATING EVERYBODY ELSE

Harvey McAlister was thirty-seven, well-educated and a competent worker. Yet, he had a habit of overrating everybody else. His problem was compounded because there were a number of company officials in the department where he worked. Though Harvey was well aware that his progress depended upon how he impressed his bosses, Harvey avoided them. He wanted to get ahead, but his behavior gave the opposite impression. He had overrated the bosses as superior to himself, and consequently felt uneasy in their presence. As his thirty-eighth birthday approached, Harvey made up his mind that it was high time that he repair his self-esteem and stop overrating his associates. One by one Harvey went to lunch with each of the officials. One by one he found that they were personable, interesting, easy-to-talk-to individuals who were looking for other interesting, easy-to-talk-to people. McAlister was surprised to find that he liked these men immensely. He also found them immensely helpful. Two years after he stopped overrating them and gave them the opportunity to know him, he was promoted to their ranks. McAlister learned a hard truth the hard way. You can't overrate somebody else without underrating yourself. And by the same token, when you overrate someone else's personality, you underrate yours.

MAKE A WORKING LIST OF
YOUR WINNING TRAITS

Most of us possess far more winning traits than we recognize, just as most people have more reason for self-confidence than they know. One of the best methods to uncover your winning personality traits is to make a working list of every one that you can think of. A working list is different from a *list*. A list means simply jotting items down on a piece of paper. A working list is a list of items that you put to work. Your list, like a winning personality trait, will mean nothing until you put it to work. Your list need not be elaborate or filled with great attributes. Fill it with your everyday traits that people will like, traits that are often commonplace, but seldom used to best effect. Here is a sample list to get you started. Start your list now and add to it from day to day as your self-confidence and self-appreciation grows. Make it work for you.

MY WINNING PERSONALITY TRAITS

Ambitious	Considerate	A learner
Independent	Unafraid	Open-minded
Self-confident	Like people	Sincere
Well-groomed	Enjoy challenges	Honest
Likable	Sociable	Thoughtful
A worker	Realistic	Kind
Determined	Tough	Aggressive
Articulate	Generous	Optimistic

Forget modesty as you start your list. Nobody else need ever see it. If you inhibit yourself as you list your worthwhile traits, you will never realize how much you have going for you. A key point is to remember that you do not have to have every desirable trait in the book to have a confident winning personality. The secret is to consciously and purposefully use the winning traits you do have. The purpose of your list is to make you dramatically aware of the many strong points in your favor.

Alma Steiner was so shy and insecure that she felt she had absolutely no winning traits. A wise counselor sent her home with instructions to write down every winning trait she had. Steiner protested mildly, but the therapist told her not to come back with a blank sheet of paper. The next day she apologetically handed her therapist a sheet with three traits on it. The three traits were "loving," "desire to change" and "I care." This was enough for her counselor friend. He helped Alma understand how much those three traits were worth. Within two weeks Alma's list had grown to forty winning traits and her personality was blossoming along with her list. Before the year was out, Alma was showing a renewed interest in her work as an accountant and was engaging in outside activities she had formerly felt too much for her. Her new-found personality is winning friends and contentment for her, which is more than this young lady ever dared hope for before she developed a working list of her winning personality traits. Alma still prizes that list.

CONCENTRATE ON THE STRONG POINTS IN YOUR WORKING LIST

Human beings can change. Other creatures are programmed for life from the time they are born until they die. You can change though, for people can be what they want to be. You can change your personality in the twinkling of an eye. It is not important that you do it instantaneously, but it is important that you make your self-confidence and your personality a winning combination. Don't go about it as if a judge in a criminal court had sentenced you to it. It must be a thing of choice and personal desire with you as the chief beneficiary. When you concentrate on the strong points in your working list (see previous heading) you can change anything about you with the possible exception of your physical body, and even that is subject to modification and development.

One definition of concentrate is to focus one's powers, efforts or attention on a particular object, goal or destination. Make your own working list of personality traits. Concentrate on the areas that will more quickly give you a winning personality. It is not necessary that you build the most winning personality in the world. It is enough to build the best personality that you can. You cannot hope to do more. You rob your personality if you do less.

•

CONFIDENCE KEYS

* A winning personality makes all else easier.
* Act like a winner.
* Talk like a winner.
* Winning speech can be a habit.
* Our personalities are not an accident of birth.
* You can't be a sponge.
* Go with the winners.
* Don't feel guilty about winning.
* Be selective in choosing personality examples or models.
* Avoid the approval dependency situation.
* Don't overrate everybody you meet.
* Keep your self-belief from unfair comparisons.
* Make a working list of your winning traits.
* Human beings can change.
* Make your self-confidence and your personality a winning combination.

Chapter 11
Enthusiasm As A Component Of Self-Confidence

"You may do foolish things, but do them with enthusiasm."

—Colette

Enthusiasm is a term easily misunderstood. It is often perceived as hyperactivity, uncontrolled zeal or an unrealistic emotional state. While some of these elements may be temporarily exhibited in a burst of enthusiasm, they are not the whole story. Enthusiasm is more than that. It is a compelling mental attitude common to those with an abundance of self-confidence. It is worthy of your time and study.

The Greeks were the first to recognize and define this strong personality trait. It so impressed these ancient psychologists that they associated it with godlike qualities. The dictionary reveals that the word derives from the Greek "entheos" (en—in, theos—god), meaning god acting in you, to be inspired, to be possessed by a god. We moderns may not think of it in such a supernatural way, but we do recognize it as a winning personality characteristic and a desirable component of self-confidence. It may not be quite the poetic ecstasy the Greeks ascribed to it, but it has lost none of its vitality and fire. It is more important to the men and women in today's world than ever before because . . .

ENTHUSIASM GENERATES SELF-CONFIDENCE

Personal enthusiasm has many uses. It opens doors, it closes sales, it motivates people to act, it adds conviction and fire to speech, it creates a happy, positive attitude, and most importantly, it generates self-confidence. Note this especially. Your enthusiasm will not only create self-confidence in you, it will create confidence in the people around you. That is, they will have confidence in you, and their own self-confidence will be bolstered as they partake of your enthusiasm. Enthusiasm generates self-confidence not only in you, but everybody whose life you touch. Ask yourself this: When you are around a person with a hangdog attitude and an abject manner, how does that make you feel? Of course, it is depressing to be around such an individual. He may arouse your pity, or your scorn perhaps, but he will not add anything to your self-confidence.

Now ask yourself how you feel around an enthusiastic, energetic person who bubbles with life and shows an interest in you and what you are doing. Doesn't this man or woman make you feel better and more confident? Enthusiasm cannot be hoarded. It is always shared. Your enthusiasm will rub off on others every time. When this happens you feel your self-confidence surge. At the same time, you can see

215

the same thing happening to those around you.

Your enthusiasm must be genuine if it is to contribute to your self-confidence, or to much of anything else, for that matter. Enthusiasm that is an act is nothing more than a balloon of hot air and fools nobody. Fortunately, nobody has to fake it. You can have an inspiring enthusiasm. That is what this chapter is all about. The more you use your enthusiasm, the more it will do for you and your self-confidence.

Tom Newhouse accepted a much-needed job in the warehouse of a large department store. He did what was expected of him in a perfunctory manner since he thought of the job as a paycheck earned on a dead-end street. However, one of his co-workers, about Tom's age and on the same educational level, exhibited unbounded enthusiasm for the work. With an air of disbelief, Tom asked Rod Kidder why so much enthusiasm for such ordinary work as storing and moving heavy appliances and big boxes of goods all day long. Kidder boomed that his job was rewarding because he was filling a needed service. It was exciting, he said, to be a part of the fast-paced traffic and activity going on all around him. Besides, he added, since he was working for an outfit with many other stores and jobs, he was happy to be learning and preparing for a better position. When Newhouse asked if he really believed that, Rod Kidder shot back that yes, he did, and added that Tom would be smart to show a bit of enthusiasm also.

Tom Newhouse thought about that all day and that night. The next day he met his friend Rod with a smile and a handshake. He worked as enthusiastically as Rod Kidder from that point. To his surprise, he found that he began to like the job and the people around him. He, too, became confident that his warehouse position could lead to better things. Six months later Tom Newhouse was made assistant manager of the store's appliance department where he became a top producer. Rod Kidder is still in the warehouse, but he is now the manager and supervisor of ten men. The enthusiasm and confidence of the two men continues to grow right along with their warm friendship.

ENTHUSIASM EXCITES PEOPLE

Enthusiasm and excitement are inseparable. How can you be enthusiastic and asleep at the same time? It can't be done. Enthusiasm means action, movement, excitement, accomplishment. Not only will your enthusiasm excite you, it will excite other people. As we have seen, enthusiasm can put excitement, interest and rewards into an ordinary workaday job. When you are enthused you will not waste time grumbling and procrastinating. You will be far too busy and excited for that. Here is a true story to illustrate this point. If you are ever in Sikeston, a small town in the bootheel of Missouri, stop in and visit the enthusiastic man who is the center of our story.

NORM LAMBERT'S
HOT "THROWED" ROLLS

Norman Lambert was an enthusiastic high school

teacher and coach in Sikeston when he decided to strike out on his own. He opened Lambert's Cafe near the downtown area and soon had one of the most popular places for miles around. He featured big, hot homemade rolls and family-style food served with enthusiasm and friendliness. One day at noon the cafe was so crowded that Norm couldn't get past the throng in the doorway to pass out a large pan of steaming hot rolls to his eager customers. A man held up his hand and waved. Norm threw him a hot roll and enthusiastically yelled, "Anybody else?" The place became electric as hands shot up and excited diners joined in to catch their hot rolls.

Norm moved to a bigger place on Business Route 60 where he and his helpers dress in black bowlers and bow ties and pass among the throngs stirring up excitement and a babble of voices as they toss hot "throwed" rolls. Tea is served in Mason fruit jars; the fried chicken is heavenly, as is a full menu of other items. The atmosphere is one of gaity and excitement in an appropriate setting. "Throwed" is deliberate. Last Christmas Norm's windows wished all a Merry Christmas and invited them to "deck them halls." His outdoor sign says, "Good Food, Good Fun." On a recent tour I asked the tour guide to stop at Norm's for lunch. The forty people on the bus voted Norm's one of the highlights of the nine-day trip. The best thing about Norm's is not the menu, good as it is. The best thing is a priceless ingredient that costs nothing. It is an exciting enthusiasm.

Enthusiasm excites people, as Norm Lambert and thousands of other outgoing, successful people will testify. It truly costs you nothing and can bring you untold rewards.

THE MORE EXCITEMENT, THE MORE SELF-CONFIDENCE

Excitement and enthusiasm go hand-in-hand. It is hard to imagine one without the other. Just as enthusiasm generates self-confidence, the more excitement you feel about life and what you are doing, the more self-confidence you will have.

Excitement, like enthusiasm, is not a substitute for intelligence or good sense. Each can make an enormous contribution to your success and to your self-confidence. They can give your thinking sparkle and conviction. Just as any power factor must be given purpose, so must excitement and enthusiasm be channelled where they will do you the most good. Practice being enthusiastic every day. Don't be afraid to get a little excited. You can't lose anything, and your self-confidence and personality will be noticeably more effective and productive.

WHAT HAPPENED WHEN CAROLYN FAY GOT EXCITED

Rose O'Neill, the inventor of the Kewpie doll, is a legend in the Ozark Mountain country of Missouri as well as in New York. Miss O'Neill is the Rose of the song "Rose of Washington Square." She was a many-talented lady and a millionaire when a million dollars was worth more than it is today. Also, she was considered to be one of the six most beautiful women in the world. She died in Springfield, Missouri in 1944.

A few years ago Carolyn Fay, a prominent and gifted lady of Springfield, was asked to give a talk before a group of her peers on a subject dear to the Ozarks. She chose Rose O'Neill.

In researching and preparing for her speech, Carolyn Fay became enthralled and excited about her animated and bewitching subject. In her excitement she became confident that she could do more than get up and make a routine talk on Rose O'Neill. So she made an authentic Rose O'Neill costume, prepared her own script and gave a first-person impression of the legendary Rose O'Neill. She excited and captivated her audience. Since then she has put on her one-woman show over two hundred times in places as far away as San Francisco. Wherever she goes she shares her excitement and enthusiasm. She is still performing and enjoying the applause and the excitement of her audiences. She has been featured on the cover of a magazine and has received numerous other honors. Carolyn Fay knows that when you get a bit excited you can put on a real show with confidence to spare.

ENTHUSIASM, LIKE SELF-CONFIDENCE, IS CONTAGIOUS

Here is a potent fact about influencing people and winning their support: Enthusiasm, like self-confidence, is contagious. When you are enthusiastic, those around you will become enthusiastic. When you are dealing with, or working with, enthusiastic people, you can motivate and influence them to cooperate with you. Remember that.

Here is something else to remember. A negative attitude and gloomy talk can also be contagious. Under these circumstances, about all you can do is motivate people to go home and wait for the worst to happen. The way to prevent this disaster is to be enthusiastic yourself. Gloomy talk and negative thinking cannot survive whenever and wherever enthusiasm is churning and sparkling. Put this principle to the test the next time you walk into a bunch of pessimistic, dispirited people. You will see their faces light up like an electric billboard when they begin to feel and share your enthusiasm.

My wife is a most enthusiastic person. A number of years ago she joined a professional group of women which held weekly luncheon meetings. She revitalized the club. In her first year she won an award for her enthusiastic support of the club. One of her accomplishments was bringing in a record number of new members. Her enthusiasm was so contagious that old members went to work and began contributing much to the club and to their profession. I once ran across a former member of the club who had moved out of town. She immediately turned the conversation to my wife and their former association. "Why," she said, "she was so enthusiastic, she could walk into a boring meeting and soon have everybody bursting with excitement and enthusiasm. I just couldn't believe it."

Well, I could believe it. I know the gal and I know what enthusiasm can do.

THE MORE PEOPLE YOU ENTHUSE, THE MORE YOU GAIN

Enthusiasm is a profitable proposition. Enthusiasm is a money-making proposition for those in business. Enthusiasm is one of the best tools a professional salesman can use. In my area of business, where motivating people is important (and when isn't it important?), enthusiasm is a key ingredient. But there is more. When you put enthusiasm to work you will also gain the following.

* More self-confidence
* Friends
* Respect
* Optimism
* Better health
* Happiness
* Personal power
* Cooperation
* Recognition
* Popularity
* Extra energy
* Self-esteem
* A positive outlook

The more you enthuse, the more you gain, because influencing people to be your willing helpers is the only way that you can multiply your personal power. Think of the people around you as an extension of your own personality and abilities. When you see them in this light it is easy to understand just how important it is to enthuse and motivate them to work with you. When you view others in this sense you will quickly recognize how much you can gain when you share a confident enthusiasm with them.

Kenneth Padgham was a door-to-door salesman of party goods in a growing metropolitan area. He was enthusiastic, made a respectable living and enjoyed what he was doing. However, as his family grew, he felt the need for more income. He recognized that he could stretch his personal sales efforts no further. So he decided to organize as a party sales promoter and employ other sales people. His everyday enthusiasm inspired his new helpers from the beginning. Ken's income quickly doubled. He says that he was still selling the same product and working with the same enthusiasm, but the difference was that he was enthusing and enlisting other people. Kenneth Padgham is one bright young man who is convinced that the more people you enthuse, the more you will gain.

HOW TO GET ENTHUSIASTIC

Being enthusiastic is not a spectator activity. You cannot be an indifferent outside observer. Enthusiasm, like success, does not come running after you. To get, and to be, enthusiastic you must do your part. Here are time-proven techniques on how you can always get enthusiastic.

* Act enthusiastic.

Don't wait for some mysterious, thrilling emotion to come over you before you become enthused. Act enthusiastic on the most ordinary day over the most ordinary event. When you do this you will see the day become extraordinarily bright and the most ordinary events become most interesting. You can prove this principle yourself. The next time you awake in a blue funk just act enthusiastic anyway. One honest self-test like this will show you that when you act enthusiastic you will get enthusiastic.

* You can control your actions.

No one can deny that your feelings can get out of control temporarily. You may not be able to repress a feeling of frustration over some great loss, or you may experience a momentary flush of anger over what you perceive as a personal injustice. Yes, you may not always be able to control how you feel, but your actions are another matter. Emotions are abstract. Actions are as solid as a rock. You can put a handle on them. Act enthusiastic and you will get enthusiastic.

* Practice getting enthusiastic.

When you practice getting enthusiastic you are acting enthusiastic. Go back and reread the first item. The difference between practicing getting enthusiastic and acting enthusiastic is that you are persevering in your determination to be an enthusiastic personality. When you practice getting enthusiastic it will become an easy and natural part of your everyday makeup.

* Associate with the enthusiastic.

As we have seen earlier, enthusiasm is contagious. Don't hang around with the cynical and the pessimistic. Associate with lively, optimistic people. You will not only get more enthusiastic yourself, you will contribute to their own enthusiasm and effectiveness.

This is not to say that you should always run from

the cynic and the pessimist. Even such as they may make some sort of positive contribution to your life. Besides your enthusiasm can do much to improve the lot of those who have not yet learned of its power and its joy. The point is that you owe it to yourself to associate with enthusiastic people. Their enthusiasm will rub off on you. Plus, the more enthusiastic you get, the more you will have to share with your associates.

* Take the emotional risk.

You have to take a few emotional risks in life. You have to expose yourself. When you get enthusiastic, you get involved with people. People are individuals. A few of them won't always agree with you, no matter how enthusiastic you may get. This is a risk you run. In reality, it is not all that great a risk, because no matter how you act there will always be some sullen, misguided soul who will manage to misunderstand you or your motives. Deal with him enthusiastically anyway. His sorry attitude is his problem, not yours. Besides, when you get enthusiastic in spite of such a disagreeable individual, your enthusiasm is bound to brighten his outlook sooner or later. Go ahead and take your chances. Get enthusiastic! Do you know one person who insists on total emotional security? If you do, you know a most discontented man.

HOW KAREN RUPP WON
WHEN SHE GOT ENTHUSIASTIC

Karen Rupp, a recent graduate with a major in advertising and communication, took a position as an account executive with a floundering regional publication. As an account executive she was to sell more advertising to a few old clients and find new advertisers for this local magazine. Advertising rates were high, the customers were tough, and this was Karen's first job. Karen had been discouraged by everyone she talked to about going with a small publication with limited resources. Nevertheless, she tackled her work with enthusiasm, sold more advertising space than the two men in her department, made suggestions to improve the content of the publication and boosted morale all around. The young lady's enthusiasm and obvious self-confidence caught the attention of the board of directors. Shortly thereafter, the magazine's masthead read, "Karen Rupp, Publisher." Karen Rupp used the same combination of enthusiasm and self-confidence in her new position as she had in the advertising department. Circulation increased, advertising revenues grew and the whole staff became optimistic and enthused. Nobody begrudged Karen the hefty raise that went with her new job.

DON'T WAIT FOR ENTHUSIASM TO STRIKE

Don't wait for enthusiasm to strike. You have to get it. You have to want it and you have to want what it can do for you. You have the ammunition in your hands right now to develop and use enthusiasm. All you have to do is supply the determination and energy. Begin from where you are sitting this minute. Look about you. Count the things that you can and should be enthusiastic about right now. How many do you see? If you are at home, be enthused about your family, your house, your car, your garden, your dog and the 1001 things that bless the place where you live. Not many people are so fortunate, are they? How about your church, your friends, your parents? Look at your job and your co-workers. Think of how important they are to you and how much all of you mean to your profession or business. Don't just sit there, man. Get enthusiastic!

HOW TO STAY ENTHUSIASTIC

You stay enthusiastic in much the same way that you get enthusiastic. You *act* enthusiastic and you practice being enthusiastic. This is a good time to point out again that enthusiasm is more than hyperactivity or an unreal emotional state. Enthusiasm can be expressed by a pleasant voice, a self-confident, assured manner, a positive attitude, an optimistic outlook and a sincere interest in the people around you. True, enthusiasm need not be hyperactive, but it is an active force. The enthusiastic man or woman is active. They are in the middle of things, motivating people, guiding others and influencing the course of events. They are involved because they know that in order to keep their enthusiasm and their zest strong, effective and appealing, they must put it to work each day. You, too, will stay enthusiastic when you put enthusiasm to work in your behalf every day. More, your self-confidence will get stronger and stronger right along with your enthusiasm, as you employ this agreeable and effective power technique.

Here are five more points that are key factors in maintaining your enthusiasm. They are neither technical nor complicated. They do point out strong, simple truths.

1. Never admit defeat before you are whipped.

Never say that it is impossible to stay enthusiastic. It can and is done by highly successful and well-known people. People who accept defeat before they are defeated tend to fall into the trap of giving up easily. This is not what you want. Enthusiasm and its partner, self-confidence, will keep you away from this self-defeating trap.

2. Don't erect imaginary barriers.

Most of the people who have paid thousands and millions of dollars to psychiatrists and psychologists discover that most of their problems arise from self-imposed imaginary barriers. They have lost their enthusiasm because they have built imaginary "I can't" walls around themselves. The graffiti on their "I can't" walls say, "I'm not lucky," "I'm afraid," "I'm not smart enough," "I don't have the money" and on and on.

Don't erect imaginary walls that proclaim that you can't stay enthusiastic. The history books are replete with stories of enthusiastic and great leaders who suffered handicaps in some form. President Roosevelt was left a cripple by polio, Lincoln was poor and largely self-educated, Beethoven was deaf. Roosevelt changed the way Americans live, Lincoln freed the slaves, and Beethoven gave us immortal music. These men kept an enthusiasm for great causes along with an unshakable self-confidence and left the world a better place.

3. Knock out your complaint department.

You can't be enthusiastic if you are complaining about the unfairness of life. Whoever said life is fair? It is not. It is much better for the enthusiastic and the self-confident however. Knock out your complaint department and forget it. It is worth less than nothing to you.

4. Stay off the negative side of life.

Keep a positive attitude and you will stay enthusiastic. Look at the gloomy might-or-could-happen aspects of life and you will be depressed and barely functional. Stay off the negative side of life. That is living on the razor's edge.

5. Enjoy.

Enjoy being enthusiastic. There is nothing wrong with doing a bit of self-promotion. Turn your enthusiasm and your self-confidence loose. You will enjoy it and so will everyone else.

MAX RAIDER'S SECRET FOR STAYING ENTHUSIASTIC

Max Raider has owned a neighborhood store in the inner city for more than forty years. As in many large cities, the neighborhood has deteriorated and fallen on difficult times. Yet Max still comes to work with the same enthusiasm that he has shown for all those years. Amazingly, he does an excellent business. Old customers drive in from bedroom towns and from the suburbs to which they migrated as the old neighborhood changed character and suffered neglect. Also, Max sees new faces as younger people move back into the inner city and re-establish homes. When asked how he has stayed so enthusiastic through it all, Max replies, "I always try to be enthusiastic *whether I feel like it or not.*"

As Max can tell you, staying enthusiastic is good business.

CONTROLLED ENTHUSIASM ADDS TO YOUR SELF-CONFIDENCE

When you *control* something you are fully in charge of it. You can send it in any direction that you wish. This means, of course, that you can use it where it will do you the most good. It isn't something that you are grabbing at and merely hoping that you will be able to use profitably.

Controlled enthusiasm means enthusiasm that has purpose and direction. It is a deep emotional conviction about somebody or something. It is a strong feeling of commitment to a project, cause or a personal objective. It is not an excited ball of fluff bouncing in the air with a "Gee, I'm glad to be alive" expression. Controlled enthusiasm is enthusiasm with a purpose. It is creative and inspiring. It puts you in charge. Most importantly, it will add to your self-confidence.

Self-confidence can wear any of a number of faces. It can be of the variety that says, "I'm gonna win at all costs. To heck with everybody else." It can be a bulldozing, abrasive attitude that fights and pushes toward a personal goal with no regard for anybody else. This rough-edged self-confidence may sometimes work, but it leaves a lot of unnecessary and senseless hurt along the way. It creates opposition and drains and weakens itself. On the other hand, when controlled enthusiasm is a component of self-confidence, it is inspiring to those around you. Your influence will be positive. You will instill trust and confidence. People will cooperate with and support you. Self-confidence is your key to success. Polish it with controlled enthusiasm.

WHEN YOU ACT ENTHUSIASTIC, YOU BECOME SELF-CONFIDENT

We have already discussed the importance of acting enthusiastic. Here is an extra point. When you act enthusiastic, you will not only become enthusiastic, you will also become self-confident. Enthusiasm does away with any feeling of helplessness or depression. It demands action and is an inseparable component of self-confidence. When you become enthusiastically self-confident, you won't sit around worrying because you have nothing worthwhile to do. You will be as busy as a robin in a freshly spaded garden. You will be exuberant.

Charlie Chaplin said it best. "I had to feel the exuberance that comes from utter confidence in yourself. Without it, you go down to defeat."

ENTHUSIASM GIVES ZIP AND FIRE TO YOUR SELF-CONFIDENCE

Enthusiasm gives zip and fire to your self-confidence because people can see and feel your confidence when you are exuding it all over the place. Can you imagine a person glowing with genuine enthusiasm and yet having no self-confidence? A skilled actor might put on a facade of enthusiasm for a while, but without self-confidence his enthusiasm will have a hollow ring.

Enthusiasm is true preventive medicine. It will keep your self-confidence full of fire and zip at all times. As we have seen, enthusiasm helps build self-confidence. With the ideas and techniques we have covered in this chapter, you can build and control all the enthusiasm you want. Which is another way of saying that you can add all the zip and fire to your self-confidence that you want. When you do this you are then in a position to get anything you want—and other people will gladly help you do just that.

A CHECKLIST
TO KEEP YOUR ENTHUSIASM BOILING

Enthusiasm, as with other strong personal characteristics, is most effective when it is put to constant and daily use. If you permit your enthusiasm to come through only in moments of exhilaration or easy successes, you will not be taking full advantage of this powerful personality trait. Enthusiasm, like living, is for every day. Here is a checklist to keep your enthusiasm boiling.

* Do you believe that you can be important to other people?

* Do you feel that you are as good as anybody else?

* Do you shake off discouragement?

* Do you act self-confident in front of strangers?

* Can you be self-motivating?

* Do you enjoy new challenges?

* Do you have realistic goals?

* Do you appreciate the importance of self-respect?

* Do you want people to like and trust you?

* Can you find something to be enthusiastic about each day?

* Do you aggressively pursue what you want?

* Do you like to be a leader?

* Do you like to be around enthusiastic and energetic people?

* Do you refuse to let depression get you down?

* Do you recognize that enthusiasm is a positive factor in self-confidence?

* Are you enthusiastic about what you are doing right now?

If you can answer yes to twelve of these questions, you have a solid foundation for a healthy enthusiasm. When your answer is yes to all sixteen of them, your enthusiasm is boiling and you know that it is. Here is a bonus thought to keep your enthusiasm shining and boiling. Your enthusiasm is all yours. It is not something given to you by somebody else, nor can it be taken from you by anyone else. The responsibility is all yours. Accept that enthusiastically because the benefits are all yours.

CONFIDENCE KEYS

* Enthusiasm is a compelling mental attitude.
* Enthusiasm generates self-confidence.
* Enthusiasm must be genuine and real.
* Enthusiasm and excitement are inseparable.
* Excitement and enthusiasm give you confidence to spare.
* Enthusing people multiplies your personal power.
* Being enthusiastic is not a spectator activity.
* When you act enthusiastic, you will become enthusiastic.
* Don't wait for enthusiasm to strike.
* To stay enthusiastic, put your enthusiasm to work each day.
* Knock out your complaint department.
* Controlled enthusiasm has purpose and direction.
* Enthusiasm gives zip and fire to your self-confidence.

Chapter 12
How To Use Self-Confidence
To Win Respect

Though the word respect has several connotations, the meaning of the term for our purposes is explicit and personal. Respect: to consider worthy of high regard, the quality or state of being held in esteem by others, commanding particular attention and consideration.

Most often respect is thought of as the regard and esteem that is accorded us by our peers. Respect is not lightly given. It is reserved for the self-confident who have demonstrated their ability to take care of themselves and to contribute to the lives of the people around them. The respect of your fellow man is not only desirable but, like self-confidence, is imperative if you are to accomplish much of anything in this world. Now here is the clincher: *Respect begins with self-respect.*

RESPECT YOURSELF FIRST

Your life would be empty and disappointing if you knew no one that you could respect. This would be like living in a can of worms. Every self-confident person recognizes the innate necessity of friends and associates who command his admiration and respect. Without going into a lot of psychiatric murk, here is a hard truth: You cannot respect or hold in esteem anybody else, no matter how good or noble they may be, until you *first respect yourself.* Which is tantamount to saying that you can have no real confidence in anybody or anything until you first have confidence in yourself.

People who lack self-respect suffer from an inferiority complex plain and simple. You have heard and read hundreds of reasons why a man or woman gropes through life with little or no self-respect. Everything from Mom and Dad to a childhood illness is used as an excuse. It may be a total surprise to anyone suffering from a loss of self-respect, but the condition has to be learned. That's right. You have to learn to feel no respect for yourself. You were not born that way. People who have no respect for themselves, no appreciation of their God-given abilities and talents, are not defective and inferior. They just think they are. That is the bad news. Here is the good news. Just as you have to learn to disrespect yourself, you can learn to respect yourself. Begin with this.

* Don't demand perfection of yourself.

Don't demand perfection of yourself before you feel self-respect. The time will never come. Nobody is perfect. Everybody stumbles and falters at some point in their life. Nobody can do all things perfectly. You know this. There is no reason to slash your wrists if you feel less than perfect. You do not demand perfection from others, even those you may see as superior. Why expect the impossible from yourself? If you feel a few pangs that come with loss of self-respect, take a good look in the mirror. You aren't all that different from strong, confident people whom you may envy. Adopt Walt Whitman's philosophy and claim a bundle of self-respect: "I am as bad as the worst, but, thank God, I am as good as the best."

* Accept your vulnerability.

Those who feel no self-respect seek to avoid other people. They sit in the darkest corner of a room hoping not to be noticed. They accept menial jobs and work far below their capacity. They are afraid of looking foolish or of failing. They are their own victims.

Accept your vulnerability and hang onto your self-respect with this thought. No man rises so high that he cannot be hurt and no man wins so much that he cannot lose. We are all fragile and vulnerable, but we are all imbued with the power to do good. Accept your vulnerability. You can have a healthy self-respect right along with it.

* Don't run after approval and assurance.

You do not need other people's approval to be a confident, self-respecting personality. Nor do you need the assurance of everybody you meet that you are a worthwhile person. Approval is nice (whatever that means), and assurance is comforting, but don't go out of your way looking for approval or assurance. You don't need it to have self-respect. What you need is to know that you are using your best judgment in doing what is best for you and for those whose lives you touch. That is more than justification

237

for self-respect.

* Do your best, forget the rest.

Each of us is the best judge of ourself. We know when we are doing our best. Anyone who does his best is entitled to self-respect, plus the respect of all who know him. Do your best, forget the rest. That is to say, do your best and don't worry that you can't do more. When you do this you will have plenty of respect from all sources.

CONFIDENTLY ACT
AS IF RESPECT IS YOUR DUE

I am a great believer in the philosophy that action establishes the fact. I have seen it happen and I have applied the theory in my own life. It works. When you observe someone acting confidently, you just naturally assume that he or she is self-confident. When anyone confidently acts as if respect is his or her due, you are most likely going to respect that person. On the other hand, when someone comes in dragging a bundle of self-doubt with him, you won't feel a lot of respect for him. You will feel uncomfortable and a bit annoyed that he is depressing you with his apologetic and uncertain demeanor. You may pity him as you would a dead sparrow, but you cannot respect him. Action can and does establish the fact. When you confidently act as if respect is your due, you will get it.

HOW MARIE RIGGS
REGAINED HER SELF-RESPECT

A divorce, even in these times, can be a traumatic

experience though both parties may wish it. It can be devastating if the principals go to war with ugly accusations and sly insinuations being hurled with reckless abandon. Marie Riggs, thirty-four and the mother of two, was subjected to a mean divorce proceeding. She says that she came out of it feeling dirty and with her self-respect shattered. She became a recluse for a year. She indulged in self-pity, resentment and apprehension. Then as her meager savings dwindled she realized that it would take more than her modest alimony to provide for her children. Gradually she forced herself to become active again. She did the grocery shopping herself instead of sending the children. She made a dental appointment, the first in nearly two years. She called her former beautician and made an appointment once more. Bit by bit she acted as if she had the self-confidence and self-respect to again take her place in the world. The next and most painful step was to line up two job interviews. Because of her former experience, she landed a position as a medical secretary. She went to work the first day filled with trepidation, but by week's end she was acting as if respect was her due, though her co-workers had all read the flaming accounts of her divorce trial. Marie Riggs is still working at the medical center. Nobody has ever brought up the ugly subject of her sticky divorce. She is grateful for that. But she is more grateful for the respect she regained when she acted as if it was her due, which, indeed, it was.

You don't have to come on like thunder rolling through the hills. When you matter-of-factly act as if respect is your due you will get it.

RESPECT IS YOUR RIGHT

Respect is your right, but it is not without self-obligation. We have seen and we still see the eroding of many traditional values. Yet there are some human ideals that do not change. Respect is an ethic built on the concept of duty to oneself and duty to others. It involves such old-fashioned, yet forever new, disciplines as those dealing with what is fair and honest, good and bad, and moral duty and obligation. Meaning, of course, that respect is your right *as long as you earn it*. You do not have to be wealthy, from a prominent family, or privileged in any sense to enjoy self-respect, self-confidence and the approbation of those around you. Doing your duty to yourself and to others as you see and understand it gives you the right to respect.

This does not call for any pussyfooting or the bending of your will to every Tom, Dick and Harry. It does mean that when you accept self-responsibility in what you do and what you project you are going to feel some responsibility for those around you. They will see and understand this and they will respect you for it. That is the stuff of a solid and enduring self-confidence.

YOU CANNOT DEMAND RESPECT

Respect, like love or self-confidence, cannot be demanded. It must be commanded, earned, deserved. Screaming or taking mean advantage of a position of authority to demand respect may get you lip service, but it won't get you respect. Parents who do no more than demand respect will get only resentment and rebellion in return. Executives and bosses who arbitrarily demand respect get disloyalty and poor cooperation. Nobody gets respect merely by demanding it, nor should they.

Another thing about respect is this. You do not have to ask anyone if they respect you. You can sense it and you can feel it. Few people are ever going to walk up to you and announce that they feel an enormous respect for you. Some will, to be sure. Be grateful for these sensitive friends, but don't think that they are the only ones who respect you. Respect is a solid emotion reflecting an honest opinion about another person. It is usually as quiet as a shadow moving across the grass. It will be there when people recognize you for the self-confident, worthy person that you are or can be.

CLIFFORD ADAMS LEARNS THAT YOU CAN'T DEMAND RESPECT

We have all been subjected to such idiotic expressions as "do your own thing," "let it all hang out," "do it if it feels good" and other equally empty-headed exhortations. The implication is that we can do, and should do, anything that pops into our minds, and that we can demand anything that we want. Baloney! Intelligent, self-confident people do not conduct their lives on this basis. Above all else, they understand that you cannot demand respect. Your personality, your confidence, plus your behavior and attitude, will command it. But demand it, no.

241

Clifford Adams learned a hard lesson when he demanded to be respected. He had been made manager of a district office of an insurance company. His first act was to hold a meeting of all the agents in the district to let them know a new man was in charge. His speech was abrasive and his attitude cocky. Adams bluntly stated that he would demand two things from everybody in the agency; namely, that they respect him and that they obey his every order without question.

Six months later Adams was called into the home office to explain the dismal drop in production that his office had suffered. Also, the president wanted to know why he had lost three of the top salesmen working under him. When Adams had no satisfactory explanation, he was terminated. Two weeks later at an aptitude counseling session Clifford Adams was told what had gone wrong and what he had to do in order to avoid a repetition of such a disaster. It was too late to save his job, but the hard lesson served him well. He no longer demands respect. He works to get it.

When a misguided soul belligerently demands that he be given something, he usually achieves the opposite effect. This attitude antagonizes self-confident, independent people. Instead of proving what they can give such a character, they are most likely to set about proving what they don't have to give him.

RESPECT IS MORE THAN FLATTERY

Flattery is excessive, meaningless praise usually heaped on someone from motives of self-interest. The self-confident person needs this like he needs a second set of teeth.

Flattery is insincere and dishonest. It fools only those who wish to be fooled. Respect, on the other hand, is as sincere and honest as a child's hug. Beware of flattery. It is meant to do you no good. Even when given with no ulterior motive it can make you look and feel foolish.

BETTY ABBOT REJECTS FLATTERY

Betty Abbot is a middle-aged woman with a pretty face and an eye-catching figure. She works as a teller in a busy bank located in the financial district of a large Southwestern city. She gets many compliments, most of which are genuine. However, there are times when a man will be too effusive. When this happens Betty keeps the line moving by saying something like, "Oh, come on now. Nobody is that gorgeous. Let's be realistic and stick to business. OK?"

Betty Abbot appreciates a compliment, but she rejects flattery. She knows that she is pretty. She also knows the difference between a compliment and designing flattery.

HOW TO TEAM
SELF-CONFIDENCE WITH RESPECT

There can be no self-respect, or respect from outside sources, without a basic self-confidence and a mite of independence. Self-confidence and respect team up in that order. Can you imagine anyone having self-respect, or respect from anyone else, without first having self-confidence? It is inconceivable. However, for one who is self-confident, or who is developing self-confidence, respect is a bonus. The two are inseparable. One heartily supports the other. Your self-confidence is most effective when teamed with respect. As your self-confidence grows so will your self-respect, as well as the respect you command from others.

In building self-confidence no one can be totally free of the thinking and opinions of the people around him. We can be totally free of *dependence* on others' thoughts, opinions and feelings, but as warmblooded, sensitive creatures we cannot be forever insensitive to or unaware of those around us. You cannot submit to every tug and pull against you. If you did so, self-doubt would replace self-confidence and respect would hide its face. On the other hand, when you have a sound and productive self-confidence, you can help others become confident achievers without giving up anything. The key is to show individuals and groups that you live and work with proper consideration for all. You can do this without permitting them to distort your judgment or sway you from your personal goals.

Here are traps to avoid as you work to team up your self-confidence with the respect that is rightfully yours.

* Avoid doing good for the sake of appearance.

Doing good for the sake of appearing to do good is self-defeating. It will fool nobody for long and it will damage your self-image. There is plenty that any self-confident human being can do for himself and for his fellow man without any pretense. You can share your self-confidence and encourage others to be enthusiastic. You can lead, motivate, guide, teach, or give money if you wish. You will never have to advertise it when you are honestly trying to be helpful. People will notice and respect you for it. They will notice when anyone is doing something for the appearance of doing good. But they won't be eager to bestow their respect.

* Never be too self-protective.

Any way that you word it, nobody else is going to feel the responsibility for you that you must feel for yourself. This is an instinct as old as time. Nevertheless, you should not be so wrapped up in self-preservation that you are reluctant to step out and take necessary risks. There is no way that an active, ambitious man or woman, filled with self-confidence and self-respect, can avoid taking risks. Nor is there one who would be content to sit on the sidelines for the sake of security. You take risks when you cross the street, when you love someone, or when you invest your money, change jobs, move to a new area or get out of bed. Never fall into the trap of being too self-protective. Should you do this, your self-respect would wither. And this you should protect against.

* Discount those who have no respect to offer.

There are unhappy people who, for reasons only a psychologist could guess at, find it impossible to respect the best intentioned of individuals. When they observe people who are more successful, more outgoing, or more outstanding in any way than they are, the only thing they feel is resentment and bitterness. Fortunately, these unhappy souls are in the minority. Should you bump into one of this type, discount his criticism or unethical behavior. He probably subconsciously or otherwise envies you and dislikes himself.

* Don't struggle overmuch for respect.

To struggle means to put forth a violent, sometimes painful, effort. It invites strife, contention and often misunderstanding. Don't struggle overmuch for respect. If you must struggle for it you are doing something wrong, or you haven't put your self-confidence up front. Of course, you should work hard to command respect. You should not strive so hard for it that you do yourself psychological or emotional damage. When you struggle too much for something it soon becomes apparent to those around you that something is lacking. Here is the secret. When you lay your self-confidence on the line and use it matter-of-factly, you automatically exhibit self-respect. Your own respect is the most important respect to be had. Respect from others is the fringe benefit that just naturally comes right along with self-confidence and self-esteem. Think of it that way. Work on it on that basis.

YOU DON'T HAVE TO LEARN TRICKS

You don't have to learn tricks when you use self-confidence to win respect. Trickery is neither a social nor a professional asset. It can destroy your very self-respect. Should that happen, your base for any respect is lost. As an intelligent individual who understands the value of self-confidence you are on solid ground. Still, it is useful to be aware of common areas of trickery that can be employed by anyone who wants respect but isn't sure that he is entitled to it. This type of unhappy and misguided individual might indulge in such as the following unethical conduct.

* Stretching the truth
* Hiding the truth
* Outright lies
* Empty promises
* Idle boasting
* Misleading statements
* Creating false impressions
* Distorting his authority

Note that each.of these categories can be indulged in without the commission of a chargeable crime. Indeed, there may be no criminal intent. The emotionally damaged person who uses tricky tactics in an effort to get attention and respect isn't after money. He doesn't plan to hurt anyone else. He is his own pitiful victim.

RICK HAUSER FINDS THAT RESPECT GOES DEEPER THAN TRICKS

After graduating with a degree in business and a year in the home office of his company, Rick Hauser was promoted to buyer for one of the firm's large stores. Rick was immensely pleased. He felt that he was on his way up and he certainly meant to have the respect he thought he was entitled to as the buyer.

The first salesman to call on him was a gray-haired scholarly gentleman from one of the store's preferred suppliers. After introducing himself, Jeff Mackay, the distinguished-looking supplier representative, spent the next ten minutes listening to Rick Hauser describe the esteem he enjoyed with the folks who ran his company. He told of playing golf with the president, frequently going to lunch at the country club with other company officers, and of how they had practically begged him to accept his current position. He ticked off first names as chummily as an old schoolmate. When he paused, Mr. Mackay explained that his call was strictly a get-acquainted call since his fall merchandise wouldn't be ready for showing for two months. Then he told Rick that he had only recently left Rick's firm after twenty years, the last five as executive vice-president. He remembered seeing Rick at his desk. Then he offered some timely advice. "If you want my respect, and if you want to keep your job, be a bit more honest with yourself. You don't have to fake it to make it with this company or anybody else." Then he was off with an understanding pat on Rick's shoulder.

Hauser was too dumbfounded to reply. He had found out in a hurry that respect goes deeper than tricks.

HOW TO DEVELOP PERSONALITY TRAITS THAT WIN RESPECT

A personality trait is a distinguishing quality or characteristic. Traits that win respect involve the total man. They are seen in the way we live, speak, work or play. Traits are elements of our everyday behavior. They affect our attitudes, goals and personal productivity. They can turn people off or they can win respect for us.

Personality traits need special attention because they are often used subconsciously. They become habitual. This is not necessarily bad, because we can discard undesirable traits and develop those that can win respect and otherwise contribute to our lives.

Here are persuasive personality traits along with ideas that you can use to take full advantage of them.

* The "Make things happen" trait.

The "Make things happen" personality is the confident mover and shaper of events. He or she gets things done. This type is not content to await circumstance; he fashions his own circumstance. There is no one more admired and respected than the individual who possesses the "Make things happen" trait.

The way to develop this trait is to set goals and objectives, then move to bring them about. This takes planning and thought, as well as action. I'm convinced that writing down your goals, objectives and plans is the most effective way to organize and shape events. When you have your goals, objectives and plans staring back at you in black and white, the next step is to write down your plan of action. This detail list should include names and phone numbers of people you plan to see, what you plan to do when you see them, and when and where you are to see them. Put dollar amounts by the name of each individual and fill in what each call should be worth to you. If the call is not strictly a business call make a note by each name of exactly what you plan to accomplish. List the steps you plan to take to bring this about in a one, two, three manner. At the end of your next working day check your lists to see where you stand and what else, if anything, you must do. The man or woman who methodically plans and persistently follows an organized plan is the one who makes things happen.

* The "Always stay in control" trait.

The "Always stay in control" trait is largely one of self-control. When you control yourself, you are able to control events and to motivate other people to respect and cooperate with you.

Keeping control of your emotions is an absolute in gaining and holding respect. To drive this point home, recall the time or times when you have seen someone break out with an emotional tirade. How much weight did you give to what he said or to what he was trying to do? How much respect have you felt for this out-of-control person since?

If you wish to stay in control, anger is the emotion to most closely guard. Anger ignores reason and distorts your vision. It is no friend of respect. It will destroy your self-respect, rob you of the respect of others, and leave your self-confidence open to question. You would have to be pretty cold-blooded to go through life without ever feeling anger boil within you because of some outrage or another. Don't worry about this. The time to worry is when you let it get out of control. When you stay in control of yourself and your emotions, you will have a trait that inspires confidence from within and without.

* The "It has to be right" trait.

The "It has to be right" trait is a noble trait. When you have this trait you will never be tempted to do anything that is questionable, offensive or intended to help you gain something by taking unfair advantage of a person or situation. This trait enriches your self-respect, generates admiration and respect from your peers, and keeps your self-confidence intact. Embrace it.

* The "I respect you" trait.

The "I respect you" trait says, without putting it into words, that you are ready to respect anyone you meet until he proves that he has no right to your respect. This is a sound and reasonable attitude. You may get fooled on occasion, but we all owe our fellow man respect and consideration until we know that he is not worthy of such high regard. Respect breeds respect. When you respect others, you have every right to expect their respect in return.

* The "I respect myself" trait.

This is the beginning of all respect. It is the beginning and the end of self-confidence. We have explored and discussed this theme, but it cannot be emphasized too often. Self-confidence thrives on self-respect. With this combination you can have all the respect you want from anybody you want.

ATTITUDES THAT BUILD
SELF-CONFIDENCE
AND WIN RESPECT

Your attitude encompasses the way you act, feel and think. It reveals your disposition, bares your opinions, and shows your mental and emotional state. It affects your self-confidence and your self-respect, as well as the respect and confidence from those around you. Here are notes on attitudes that you can use to keep your attitude or attitudes in good shape.

* People's conception of themselves affects not only their physical health and their mental well-being, it affects their attitudes, their control, their personal power and, most forcefully, their self-confidence. Your first concern, then, is to keep a strong, healthy opinion of yourself at all times. This is central to building self-confidence and winning respect.

* If one condemns himself to disrespect he will tend to lump everybody else in a dismal pit of disrespect. With this attitude the war is on. Others will strike back by rejecting this attitude and will go out of their way to avoid such a miserable personality. This does nobody's self-confidence any good. Go back and reread the preceding paragraph. You will never want to condemn yourself to disrespect, but you must always be alert to the danger.

* Friends and those you seek to influence will fill the image that you have of them. Children are not the only ones who judge themselves as they are judged by their parents and other people important to them. Adults will also strive to meet the image that you have of them. If your attitude indicates that you respect them and expect much of them, they will try to justify your good opinion. If your attitude rejects them, they will know it and you will lose whatever help and affection they might have given. To

have strong, helpful friends, let your attitude broadcast to those around you that you want them as strong helpful friends. They will try to match the good image that they feel you have of them. They will share your confidence and give you their respect.

Your attitude will always affect how you use your self-confidence to win respect. Should you ever feel your positive attitude sagging go back and review the chapter on "How to Build a Self-Confident Attitude." This subject exerts such a heavy influence on your self-confidence and respect that it should be carefully monitored.

How can you tell when you are using your self-confidence in a way that wins respect? You know that you have made the grade when relatives, friends, associates and assorted strangers find it profitable and comfortable to be near you. You will know it when you relish the opportunity to work with other people and to motivate them to work with you. You will know it because you can feel your self-confidence expand and your self-respect blossom.

CONFIDENCE KEYS

* Respect yourself first.
* Don't slash your wrists if you are less than perfect.
* Being vulnerable need not destroy self-respect.
* Don't run after approval and assurance.
* Act as if respect is your due.
* You have a right to respect.
* Respect entails self-obligation.
* You can't demand respect.

* Flattery is meaningless.
* Team your self-confidence with respect.
* You don't have to learn tricks.
* Personality traits need special attention.
* Your attitude affects your self-confidence and
  your respect.

Chapter 13
Self-Confidence Secrets To Handle Problem People

Problem people with reference to self-confidence are those people who see life only in terms of attack and counterattack or as an offense/defense matter. The problem people that we are going to discuss are not the lame, the halt or the blind, but the ones who are abusive, antagonistic, unpredictable, insulting and abrasive. Those in the first category have a problem. Those in the second are the problem

Problem people are insecure. They view the world as one big army mobilized against them. An individual of this type sees himself as one against many. He feels that others are out to get him. So he must prove that he is tough, worthy of respect, and able to take care of himself in spite of it all. His strategy is to strike out in all directions to let those around him know who he is and where he stands. He wins a few skirmishes, but he always loses the battle.

There are a variety of theories and opinions as to what produces such a destructive attitude and behavior. Be that as it may, our concern in this discussion is not to diagnose the hidden causes of this problem. Our purpose is to explore ways and means to deal with those individuals who are afflicted with it. Let us begin with this.

EXPECT TO MEET A FEW
DISGRUNTLED AND BITTER CHARACTERS

There is no way that you can go through life surrounded only by sweet, reasonable people. You cannot expect it. You can expect to meet a number of confused and bitter people in your day-to-day contacts. This is no cause for alarm. It is something that happens to us all. You can deal with such people with equanimity if not affection.

KEEP YOUR SENSE OF PROPORTION

The best thing to do when you bump into a problem person who is overbearing and rude is to keep your sense of proportion. You can do this by mentally evaluating such questions as these.

1. How important is this man's conduct anyway?
2. Whose problem is this?
3. What difference does it make what Mr. McNasty says?
4. Why should I be impressed by bully tactics?
5. Whose head is it that has come unscrewed?
6. Why should I meet him on his own terms?

OK. Now let's examine each question in order.

1. His conduct is not important. If it were, he wouldn't find it necessary to be obnoxious and un-

reasonable. As far as you are concerned, your own sense of proportion will tell you that what you can do far outweighs what anyone operating under such a tattered banner can do. Keep cool. You can't afford the luxury of shouting back. Besides, the exercise of your self-confidence makes this type of behavior on your part not only unnecessary, but distasteful as well.

2. The problem is not yours. It is a medical fact that something is basically wrong with an adult who resorts to tantrums and yelling. He is out of control. It is a mistake to feel put down because of anybody's incompetent and abrasive behavior, even your employer's or your spouse's. Which means that you should never feel the problem is yours when you are obliged to deal with someone else's personality quirk.

3. What difference does it make what Mr. McNasty does or says anyway? Good question with a simple, clean answer—none or little, at most.

Because of his volume or his attitude, the abrasive character does occasionally bowl over an unsuspecting and unprepared individual. Since you appreciate and have a respect for the solid power of self-confidence, your sense of proportion will tell you that you are in the driver's seat. You know the value of what you say and do. The person who resorts to scare tactics to influence, motivate or control people or events has more hot air than substance. Even he suspects as much.

4. You should not be impressed by bully tactics. You won't have to resort to schoolboy violence to get this across to anyone coming at you like a thunderstorm. Your self-confidence and a cool head will

keep you out of trouble here. But let me tell you a true story anyway. Years ago at a small high school the school bully was at a practice basketball session. He was running over the other boys right and left until he kicked Sid Williams, the smallest boy on the court. Sid turned around and hit him once just above the belt buckle to bend him, then decked him with a right to the chin. Can you guess who was impressed?

No, you won't have to employ Sid's tactics, impressive as they were. You can rely on your self-confidence and a stiff back bone to get the same effect.

5. There is nothing wrong with you or your head when and if you must deal with a difficult man or woman. The problem person is the one who has the screw loose. Keep that in mind and you will keep control.

6. There is never an occasion when you should feel it necessary to stoop to the antagonistic person's own terms and tactics. He is already in trouble. There is no reason for you to jump into this puddle of self-doubt and self-condemnation with him.

A victim is one that is hurt or destroyed by the adverse force of someone or something. Most of the time that force is an unexpected or uncontrollable force from outside the person of the victim. However, not all victims are authentic. The disgruntled, abrasive personality is not the real victim he sees himself to be. He is his own victim. Self-victims are usually strangers to reason and right. What they think and what they do is based upon their distorted view of society and what they feel it has unfairly done to them. This wrong-headed perception can be entertained by bright people. This is hard to understand until we remember that brilliant people can often be wrong. To illustrate, there was a California terrorist group that used a form of the word "symbiosis" (living together for mutual benefit) as part of their army's name. This is not kindergarten stuff. It is a word that the dull and uneducated never use. Of course, the people we are talking about are not deadly terrorists. They can sound bright and earnest. They won't come at you with guns blazing, but they can make you a victim unless you handle them with self-confidence. That is the point.

KEEP YOUR DIGNITY

One of the meanings of the word "dignity" is reserve of manner or language. This definition is appropriate for our discussion. Nothing is more confusing to a loud-mouthed troublemaker than running into a self-confident personality who maintains a calm and reasonable dignity in the face of all his noise and threats. He does not understand this, but he does feel the power behind it. Keep your dignity when dealing with a vociferous problem personality. When you do, you keep control.

An irrational demanding mentality may misinterpret your dignity as acceptance when you do not jump into the fray with bared fangs and an angry bellow. Hang in. When he sees that you are not caving in, he will begin to get the idea. All that you are accepting is the fact that you are facing someone with a personal problem. This is not approval. It is keeping your head while somebody else loses his.

The following notes will help you keep your dignity while handling a disjointed opponent.

* Keep sight of the fact that you are right.

When you are under pressure from a problem personality don't let him shoot a little self-doubt between your eyes. The desire to be through with an unpleasant episode can become so pressing that you may feel a slight urge to accept part of the blame for being caught in a tacky situation. Don't do it. When you are right, you are right. Nobody and nothing should be allowed to change that. Your self-confidence demands that you keep sight of the fact that you are the one in the right.

* There is nothing to be gained by anger.

Edmund Burke said that few men can afford to be angry. I don't know who he was talking about. I have never seen anyone, including myself, gain anything by anger. Feelings of helplessness, defeat, frustration, insecurity and self-abuse all feed on anger. If and when a problem person makes you angry, he is practically home free. This is because anger and self-control are incompatible. They pull in different directions. When you give in to anger, you give up control. There is little point in directing your anger at a mixed-up, obstreperous person. There is nothing to gain by it and it is hard on your self-confidence. You can use firm, determined resistance to turn the problem person around and win him to your way of thinking. Anger is not the key. A calm and reasoned self-belief is.

* Refrain from ridicule.

There is a whole bag full of nasty verbal barbs

that you could hurl at a problem personality. They would probably all be true and could be justified. But what would they do for you, besides give you the fleeting satisfaction of putting the culprit in his place? It is far better to use your self-confidence and your self-control to win the man to your side. Use the techniques in this book, along with the power instincts that boil inside you, to handle problem personalities on this basis. This way you will win without the chagrin and embarrassment of resorting to ridicule.

* Concessions won't work.

Concessions mean nothing when facing problem people. They will not regard a concession as a conciliatory gesture. They will interpret a concession as a sign of weakness and a sure sign that they are the injured party. This will merely encourage the misguided man or woman to heap on the coals. As a self-confident person you are going to take a reasonable stand right from the start. Stick with that. It is enough.

* Save your advice.

The erratic and self-serving individual has probably had tons of advice before you ever met him. It has done nothing for him and neither will yours. No matter how well-intentioned you are, save your advice. When someone's head comes unscrewed, it takes months and years for professional counselors to get it adjusted once more. You cannot hope to do it on the spot no matter how valid your advice might be. Keep your dignity, protect your own interests and do whatever you can for the miserable human being before you. Save your advice until he sees the light and asks you for it. Otherwise, save your breath and your advice.

THE DAY GLENN RAMEY
WON WITH DIGNITY

Glenn Ramey was a hard-working salesman for a regional meat packer. He had recently been assigned additional territory and was given a local grocery chain as part of his responsibilities. After three months in the new territory, the owner of the packing plant called him in and belligerently chewed Glenn out for not selling the chain more than the hundred thousand dollars he had sold during the past month. Glenn let him run down then said, "Just a minute." Whereupon he went to his files and came back with the account's folder. He pointed to the last year's total figures which amounted to five thousand dollars less than Glenn had sold them during one month. Then Glenn Ramey quietly closed the file and left the office. He didn't see the boss again for two weeks, but when he opened his pay envelope the following Friday there was a fifty dollar per week raise and a note that read, "I hope that this says I'm sorry."

As Glenn Ramey can tell, keeping your dignity in front of a problem personality is a paying proposition.

THE LOUDMOUTH IS INSECURE

Dealing with problem people is a social learning

process. We may wish that all people were considerate and reasonable, but that is not how it is. The world is full of confused and insecure individuals. The loudmouth is, above all, insecure. Of course, that is his problem, but it is helpful to have some understanding of this upsetting type. Here are practical observations.

First of all, we can concede that working with a loudmouth is about as soothing as an Oklahoma tornado. This is not fatal. It is a test of your self-confidence and your skill in handling disagreeable people. It is a step in the social learning process.

The loudmouth is insecure, but he is forever trying to prove to himself that he is not. He gets loud because this is the way that he thinks he can impress or subdue others. It is his way of gaining attention. He is not necessarily bad. He has a problem. He can be an embarrassment. But he is not cause for dismay or panic.

Problem people are quick to criticize others. This is a common trick used by those who feel insecure and lack confidence. Regardless of the medical reasons or the emotional condition of the loudmouth, you cannot accept guilt because of his criticism any more than you can shoulder responsibility for his sad state. His criticism is designed to put you down. This makes him feel superior and confirms what he sees as a correct analysis of you and your abilities.

There are two ways that the criticism of the loudmouth, or any criticism as far as that goes, can be handled. The losing way is to lose control and exchange loud insults with Mr. Problem Man. Or you can rely on your dignity and self-confidence as Glenn

Ramey did in the example just given. This should not be a difficult choice.

HOW JOE HARDIE
SUBDUED A TROUBLEMAKER

Joe Hardie was being hard pressed by a vocal employee in the office of an electronics firms. She was demanding that the supervisor, Joe Hardie, agree to let her take her vacation during June. Hardie had repeatedly explained that other employees had already filled all the June slots. On a Friday, when she came churning in for the fourth time in a week, Hardie asked her to stay for ten minutes after hours. First, he frankly said that he could not approve her vacation and would show her why. Further, he said her conduct was not acceptable to the company or to him, and that she was expected to understand that. Then he showed her a list of employees scheduled for June vacations. He pointed out that each one had more seniority than her. Also, she was reminded that she had voted for this agreement at an employee meeting the year before. Then he said that since the company was having a tough year he would make her a proposition. The deal was that he would forgo his vacation to save the firm money if she would do the same. Since she didn't like the idea of an August vacation, Joe Hardie said, she could make this helpful gesture without much sacrifice. Connie Debow, the loudmouth irritant, was taken aback. She quickly declined Mr. Hardie's offer and that was the end of her annoying campaign.

YOUR SELF-CONFIDENCE CAN
SOOTHE THE SAVAGE BEAST

One of the quickest ways to start a no-win conflagration is to jump right down the problem person's throat and try to beat him at his own game. The rational self-confident person is at a disadvantage from the start when this happens. To begin with, he is completely out of character. The troublemaker is on home turf. He likes it that way. On the other hand, when the self-confident, fair-minded individual maintains control of himself he has the advantage. He is working on his turf.

Self-confidence is more than self-defense. It is using your self-power not only to ward off attack, but to change and motivate people to be cooperative and reasonable. When you calmly and confidently turn aside or say no to a pushy, noisy man, he will be bewildered and confused. He may wonder what is wrong with you, but he will calm down after he notices that he is the only one coming apart. Your self-confidence soothes the savage beast and will bring him to his senses. That is, unless he is a hopeless madman. In that case, the only thing that you can do is call the authorities or run for your life.

LET THE MAN BLOW OFF STEAM

Let the problem person blow off steam. You don't have to accept or believe what he is saying. You don't have to give him the satisfaction of upsetting you. Nobody can upset you *unless you permit it*.

What the problem person says is not scripture. What he does is often impulsive and usually occasioned by an emotional disturbance. When you permit him to blow off steam he gets a lot of emotional release. This sometimes slows him down for a while and gives you a chance to calm him with a few quiet, confident words.

In any event, don't feel hurt and insulted when under pressure from an erratic type who may be venting his frustrations on you. This might make you want to take vengeance on him though you honestly feel that he is off his rocker. There is a story that illustrates the proper attitude when dealing with a pushy problem personality.

An old salesman asked a fledgling how he was getting along. "Terrible," the youngster answered. "I've been insulted in every place where I made a call." "That's odd," the old man replied. "I have been on the road for forty years. I've had my samples flung in the street, been tossed down the stairs and bawled out by janitors, but insulted—never!"

Nothing is more frustrating to noisy, irresponsible people than to try to overpower a confident, reasonable man who refuses to cooperate. The difference is that the problem person with his inferiority complex feels that he is fighting for his life. The self-assured person he is pressuring sees the situation for what it is: a minor episode that is nothing more than a part of life in an unpredictable day. In this, as in all other aspects of life, attitude is a key factor. You can readily understand the attitude of a problem person. His attitude is mixed up and confused because he himself is. Since he constantly feels threatened, he tries to reduce those he meets to his own state. This is mostly a subconscious reaction because of the uncertain attitude that he embraces, and because of the questions he has about his self-worth. He doesn't understand why but he knows that he feels totally inadequate when he faces a self-confident individual who discounts his behavior. Be that as it may, a strong, confident personality such as you endorse can thoroughly frustrate the most strident problem person by standing his ground with dignity and resolve. This not only preserves your integrity and protects your interest, but may eventually drive home the point to the confused mentality that he is using the wrong tactics. Don't count on this. Count on your own self-confidence and self-control. This always frustrates irresponsible people and puts you in charge.

The following imaginary exchange demonstrates how such a conflict might be resolved with firm, confident action.

Mr. Problem: "Joe, I insist that you listen to me right now. I still need that hundred dollars and I want you to lend it to me today. Don't argue. We are friends and I need the money."

You: "Carl, I've told you that I never lend money to friends or relatives. I'm sorry, but the answer is still no."

Mr. Problem: "You are the most inconsiderate person I know! You have absolutely no regard for other people. I'll pay you back as soon as I can. Now give me the money."

You: "No."

Mr. Problem: "Why not? You make me feel like a

fool and I resent that. Unless you loan me that hundred dollars right now, our friendship is over forever."

You: "I'm sorry to hear that, but I won't lend you any money."

Mr. Problem: "You are positively no good! I can't depend on you at all."

You: "Why don't you try the bank or your credit union?"

Mr. Problem: "Gee, do you really think I could get it there? Thanks a lot!"

HOW TO AMAZE THE BELLIGERENT
WITH YOUR SELF-CONFIDENCE

None of us should be surprised that we must deal with problem people from time to time. Our system of justice is in itself an adversary one. There is the offense and the defense, the punisher and the punished, the law and the lawless, the victim and the culprit. Problem people are not a rare species. They invade every area of life. Our purpose is not to eliminate them (an impossible task), but to handle them in such a way that they cannot and do not harm us. They may make us uncomfortable temporarily, or annoy us at the moment, but their bite is not terminal. You can handle them safely and effectively much to their amazement.

The most amazing thing that a troublemaker can encounter is someone who maintains absolute control and seems unimpressed by his belligerent tone and threatening attitude. You may not like the method at the moment, because your basic animal instinct is to tell the unreasonable person that he is completely off base and talking like a man with a paper head. At the same time, your self-respect and your self-confidence dictate that you must not crawl down to his level. True, you may not like the method at the moment, but use it no matter the boiling impulse. Use it because it works.

Meeting threats with threats is a destructive way to deal with problem people. Making threats at any time is a poor way to run your life. This will keep you in hot water, because if you fail to implement a threat, your bargaining power is gone forever after that. Say only what you mean and what you can enforce when you are under fire from Mr. Problem Man. Say it with quiet determination, and then back up what you say to protect your interests and your integrity.

When dealing with problem people, or anybody for that matter, do not issue ultimatums. This is a direct challenge and an open invitation to warfare. An ultimatum says, "I dare you." That drives up your opponent's blood pressure. If you must issue an ultimatum, be sure that you know in advance exactly how you will handle the problem person if you lose. It has happened more than once.

Never overestimate the authority of the problem person regardless of his title or position. Offensive, demanding behavior is an indication that the problem person feels no valid authority within himself despite rank, ribbons or titles. Just because someone is in a position of authority doesn't mean that he is omnipotent. This is not to suggest that you should challenge all authority. Conversely, as civilized individuals, we recognize and respect legal and genuine authority. As ambitious, worthy, self-confident individuals we cannot accept from any source questionable performance that indicates a warped personality.

All of which is to say that your self-confidence, coupled with logical behavior under heated circumstances, will amaze the belligerent problem person. It should not amaze you, for once you have put it to the test you know its power and its influence. It will put the lion back in the cage.

HOW J. C. BARBER
SURPRISED THE BELLIGERENT
WITH HIS SELF-CONFIDENCE

Dr. J. C. Barber, head of the art department for a college renowned for the artists it turns out, was taking a year-long sabbatical. It was his responsibility to select his temporary replacement. After careful consideration, he had chosen a talented young professor whose credentials were impeccable. Too, this young man was held in high regard by the students as well as the faculty.

The morning after the appointment was announced Donna Parkison, an assistant professor, burst into Dr. Barber's office with a "Hey, you." Then she proceeded to express her displeasure over not being the replacement. She ranted against the young man Dr. Barber had chosen and accused Dr. Barber of being biased against women. Her language was anything but scholarly and her attitude hostile.

Finally, she sputtered to an embarrassed stop. Dr. Barber, who had said nothing up to this point, simply said, "You are not feeling at all well today, are you, Miss Parkison?"

Miss Parkison wearily sank into a chair, saying, "I guess not, Doctor. I'm surprised at your attitude, but I appreciate it."

Miss Parkison arose to leave. Dr. Barber asked her if she would like to compare her file with the young professor's who was to take his place. Miss Parkison said no, that she understood, and that she was sorry for her outrageous behavior. She left a surprised and contrite young lady. Dr. Barber later remarked that he had been more surprised than she. The difference was that he amazed Miss Parkison by keeping his self-confidence intact, and had soothed her with his quiet self-assurance. This technique is invariably impressive and effective.

HOW TO WIN THE RESPECT
OF PROBLEM PEOPLE

J. C. Barber's example is an excellent model of how to win the respect of problem people. You will note that he surrendered nothing, yet allowed his antagonist leeway to regain her composure. He made his point without apology and with no squirming. This technique commands respect because it is an intelligent exercise of personal control and assertive self-confidence. It is a characteristic to be prized.

When dealing with problem people, don't feel that respect must be based on good/bad judgments. We are each a painful contradiction. We may be altruistic, but under stress or when we feel threatened, we might momentarily give way to language and conduct that embarrasses us. Problem people accept this as the normal way to handle people. You know better. As a self-confident person you will resist the mistaken temptation to gain satisfaction and respect by overcoming and humiliating people even though they may come at you with blood in their eye. Your goal should not be to decide whether an antagonist is good or bad. Your goal is to stay on top and win his respect.

One thing that frequently disturbs strong, rational individuals when dealing with problem people is this: They understand that the belligerent can honestly believe he is in the right and that his behavior is justified. Lucan said that honesty is often in the wrong. I have expressed the same thought many times by saying that more harm has been done to the human race by well-intentioned fools than by all the armies that ever marched. In the case of problem people this is usually true.

You cannot submit to problem people because they honestly think they are right. This would do nothing to change their thinking or their behavior. It could cost you dearly.

You don't have to assassinate your brains to win the respect of problem people. Nor should you let compassion stand in the way of reason. This does not mean that you can never try to help and understand belligerent personalities. Help them all you can, but understand that your welfare and self-respect are at stake. It is more important to your self-confidence to have the respect of problem people than it is to pacify them.

CONFIDENCE KEYS

* Problem people see life as attack/counterattack.
* Our concern is to deal with these people.
* Keep your sense of proportion.
* Not all victims are authentic.
* The problem person is his own victim.
* Your dignity can confuse the problem person.
* Anger will gain you nothing.
* Concessions won't work.
* The loudmouth is insecure.
* Self-confidence is more than self-defense.
* Never overestimate the authority of the problem person.
* Your goal is to win the respect of problem people.
* It is more important to have the respect of problem people than it is to pacify them.

Chapter 14
How To Use Self-Confidence To Get A Head Start

A head start means getting started before the competition begins to move against you. A competitor is not necessarily an individual or institution out to get you. However, when this is the case, a head start is a two-pronged advantage. First, it discourages the competition mightily, and second, it puts you out front right from the beginning. A head start means that you have gained ground while the competition has lost ground by doing nothing. This is a distinct advantage any way you look at it. Moreover, a head start invariably adds to your feeling of self-confidence and gives you extra momentum.

Self-confidence is often called upon to deal with abstract competitors, such as self-deception, indecision, worry, indifference or excuses. Here is where a head start is mandatory. When anyone is assailed by any such abstract competitors as these, he becomes his own competitor. And this is the competitor that must be dealt with before there can be any hope of getting a head start. This is not necessarily bad. Some of the most successful men and women I have known maintain a head start at all times because *they compete with themselves.* This is a technique I endorse highly. When you compete with yourself you not only eliminate self-imposed competition, you get a head start before an outside competitor or circumstance raises any kind of threat. So let's get on with how you might use your self-confidence to get and keep a head start by being your own competitor.

HOW TO GET A HEAD START
BY BEING YOUR OWN COMPETITOR

Being your own competitor is not a matter of fighting with yourself. Rather it is a system of self-encouragement whereby you urge yourself to ever-greater attainments and satisfaction. There is no magic to it, just as there is no great magic in developing a bold self-confidence. It is chiefly a matter of choices. It comes down to choosing what you want to be and where you want to be. The sooner you make your choice, the sooner you will be out front. Here are three techniques of self-competition that can give you a head start today.

1. Setting Goals and Surpassing Them.

When you set a personal goal, you are the only one working on it in the most strict sense. There may be helpers or others involved in reaching or exceeding your goal. Yet it is your self-confidence and dedication that decides the outcome. You are competing with yourself to get out front and stay there. This is a healthy situation entailing a strong and healthy attitude.

Keep your goals and expectations within reasonable limits as you establish them. Setting impossible goals is frustrating and a form of self-torture. The way to set realistic goals is to analyze your abilities and your prospects. Don't try to push yourself out front by demanding the impossible from yourself. Make a list of your financial and personality assets. Next make a list of the obstacles you must overcome to reach and exceed your goal. Lay your lists side by side. Compare. Keep your goals within the range of the probable. The idea is that as soon as you exceed one goal, then you are ready for the next higher rung on the ladder. This technique is known as . . .

2. Stretching.

To stretch means to reach out. As your own competitor it means that you are constantly extending yourself to reach further, quicker and more often. It means getting a head start by being willing to put your self-confidence and your abilities to the test. Just as we have indicated, you stretch each time you achieve and surpass one goal and then reach ahead by setting a new and tougher goal for yourself. Impossible goals will discourage you. Tough goals will keep you stretching. That will give you the head start you need and want.

3. Creating Your Own Opportunity.

Obviously, no one can sit around and wait for lightning to strike in order to get a head start. The person who gets ahead must use foresight and create his own opportunities. When you are your own competitor, you will always be looking for opportunities while others wait for them. This will put you ahead and keep you there.

MORE IDEAS ON HOW TO CREATE YOUR OWN OPPORTUNITIES

* Look in your own back yard.

Most people are inclined to look far afield when seeking new opportunities. This idea sounds exciting and romantic, but your best opportunity probably lies right in your own back yard. Remember the story of the man who searched far and wide only to discover acres of diamonds in his own back yard? You know more people right where you are. You know the economic conditions, who has the power and authority, who is likely to be helpful, and you know what you have accomplished right where you are. People are pretty much alike, but here you have roots. When your credentials are in order, the home territory is the first place to look for opportunities. Go elsewhere if you must, but look at what you may be leaving behind. You don't have to run away to get a head start.

* Be your own leader.

Leaders compete fiercely. Be your own demanding leader. You do this by programming yourself to be the best possible authority in your field. You may not want to be the world's richest man or a noted captain of industry. That's all right. There are plenty of self-confident people who go their own way and become the man or woman they choose to be. The point is that you should be an authority on what you want to be or do. As one interested in self-confidence and self-respect, your choice of a goal and a life style will be commendable. When you are an authority in whatever field, you can make your own opportunity. As an authority you have a head start right there.

* Go out on a limb occasionally.

Getting a head start involves risk-taking. And why not? The stakes are high and a head start stacks the odds in your favor. This is not to say that rushing pellmell into something is the way to get a head start. A head start is more than plunging wildly into a project, idea or goal. It is planning, thinking and acting before the opportunity evaporates.

Fred T. Lambeth had borrowed heavily to become a real estate developer. Years later when Mr. Lambeth was approaching retirement, he was asked how he had ever found the nerve to borrow all that money. Mr. Lambeth, now a millionaire several times over, replied that the chance he took in borrowing the money was not nearly as great as the risk he would have taken had he not gone ahead and borrowed it.

You don't have to go out on a limb blindfolded, but do accept the risks that all self-confident people know exist. In any event, don't be like the poor soul who had a wretched inferiority complex and didn't want to change, because that was all he was sure that he had.

* Indecision brings up the rear.

Indecision always brings up the rear. Indecision indicates a lack of self-confidence. Avoid it. It accomplishes nothing and can be sheer torture. There are many ideas on decision-making in this book. The most basic is to gather the needed information, then make a decision on the facts before you. As soon as a decision is reached, that is the time to move. A decision is like a gnawing problem in one respect. The sooner you act on it, the better. Life is more than a lottery. While it is true that some things are beyond human control, most of what happens to us is because of the decisions we do or do not make. Self-confidence and the ability to make decisions give you a sense of mastery over your life.

The origin of the word *decision* makes plain its urgency. It comes from the Latin *decisio* which means cutting short. The parent word decide is from the Latin *decidere*, to cut off. The simplest and most direct definition is *to make up one's mind*. The word itself demands action. Obviously, the first step in getting ahead is to confidently make up your mind.

Indecision is not only painful to the undecided. It has a domino effect. It can be distressing for all concerned to watch a poor wretch wallowing in indecision. Here's a simple little true story to illustrate this foot-dragging point. I had gone into a furniture showroom to see a friend at the Dallas Home Furnishing Show. My friend was standing by with a tired, helpless look on his face. A man and his wife were trying to decide which sofa line to buy. He said, "I just don't know." She sighed, "I just don't know." He said, "I just don't know either." She sighed, "I just don't know either." Whether they ever made up their minds is a moot question. I just don't know. I left.

HOW TO HIT THE FIRST LICK
IN A TIGHT COMPETITIVE SITUATION

Using your self-confidence to hit the first lick in tight competitive situations is one quick way to get a head start. Other things being equal, the one who gets in the first lick will win. The advantage is obvious. With that point settled let's look at how to hit the first lick.

* Don't be intimidated.

An old trick competitors still use is that of intimidating the competition. They know that if this tactic freezes their opposition then they are home free. This is especially true in sales work, but it is in no way limited to selling and marketing. In any field there is a tendency for most people, many with years of experience, to attribute far more power and prestige to the competitor than he deserves or possesses. We have all been subjected to such hackneyed admonishments as "It's a jungle out there," "It's dog eat dog," "The real world is tough today," etc., etc. Well, maybe. Be that as it may, your competitor does not possess any supernatural powers *unless you attribute them to him*.

Don't be intimidated. No matter how big and blustery the competition, when you hit the first lick you have a head start.

* Ignore rumors.

Rumor is not necessarily fact. It is often fuzzy talk based on hearsay, gossip or outright lies. Rumor ignores truth and exact knowledge. This is reason enough for you to ignore it.

When you are fed misinformation there are two things that you can do.

1. Accept the rumor as gospel and agonize about it until the opposition gets the advantage.

OR

2. Ignore the rumor and go ahead with your plans

to openly and honestly get ahead of the competition.

Your self-confidence and your native intelligence will quickly dictate your choice here.

* Be specific.

Avoid generalities when you are in a tight competitive situation. Be specific in purpose and in your course of action as you work to get in the first lick. Study this quick example. It will give you the idea.

Marty Chrisman was the housewares buyer for a huge department store. A new competitor had come to town and was boasting that Marty would have nothing to buy at the upcoming market because the new competitor was going to take the total production of her largest supplier. Marty decided to hit the first lick. First, she listed all her requirements for the next year. Then, with the market still six weeks away, she phoned her supplier that she was flying in the next day to place her annual order ahead of the market. This, she explained, would save them both time. Of course, the young lady was given the red carpet treatment. Her competition was given a surprise at the market.

* False modesty can kill you.

Nobody like a braggart, but false modesty can kill you in a tight competitive situation. You know what you can and should do. Put your credentials up front for a head start. You don't have to be brassy. You can matter-of-factly influence the people around you by letting them know what you stand for, what you can and will do, and what you expect from them. This way you get the benefit of a head start and they benefit from the experience and self-confidence that you demonstrate for them.

281

HOW WAYNE KIMBALL
HIT THE FIRST LICK TO
NAIL DOWN A BIG SALE

Wayne Kimball is a salesman who keeps posted on what is happening in his industry. He is also one of that aggressive and confident breed who likes to get a head start in a competitive situation. Wayne says timing has a lot to do with it. For example, Wayne, who sells packaging materials to a variety of manufacturers and shippers, had read in a trade journal that an electronics firm planned to open a branch in his city within the year. No doubt other salesmen read the same announcement and had made a mental note to contact the new people when they moved into town. Wayne thought differently. He hit the first lick by getting an appointment with the electronics company two weeks after he read of their plans. He flew five hundred miles for a fifteen-minute interview. The fifteen minutes was enough. Wayne convinced the company officers that he and his firm were well equipped to handle their packaging needs. When the competition came knocking on the doors of the Big M Manufacturers a year later it was too late. Wayne Kimball's head start paid off handsomely.

HOW TO USE SELF-CONFIDENCE
TO STAY AHEAD

Getting a head start doesn't amount to much unless you use the advantage to stay ahead. The self-confident man or woman who surges ahead knows that the game is not over. To really win you have to stay out front. Here is a thought that the aggressive and ambitious person knows well. There is not only more room at the top, there is also more room out front. Now let's examine more winning concepts that you can use to stay out front.

* Take advantage of time and timing.

An intense self-confidence makes you acutely aware of the value of your time. Once you have shed the flab of self-doubt, managing time becomes an element of your self-confidence. You quickly learn that "managing time" is a euphemistic term. You do not manage time. You manage what you *do* with time. It is not a matter of hours and days, it is a matter of choices, of priorities, of self-management.

Busy, time-conscious people do not fly blind. They plan, evaluate and act. Wayne Kimball's case history is an example of the effective use of time. He did something. His self-management propelled him out front while his competition waited on time. Wayne Kimball created time. How much time you can create depends on what you do.

Self-organization and planning are essential if one is to take advantage of time and timing. Long, elaborate, detailed and documented plans are seldom helpful. These can consume time. They may have a place in long-range corporate plans, but a simple, well-arranged, written list of what you propose to do will get the job done. The businessman's day plan and the busy housewife's list below illustrate this technique.

* Mr. Businessman's Next Day Plan

1. Phone Ernie before eight a.m. to cancel golf date.
2. Eight a.m., open mail and check incoming messages.
3. Write John Smith that twenty-five percent deposit will be required on future C.O.D. orders.
4. Make reservations for next month's Chicago meeting.
5. Lunch with Norm Combs at Mr. Gee's.
6. Work on the Southwick agreement one to four p.m.
7. Arrange for seven a.m. sales meeting tomorrow.
8. Home by six p.m. for Jackie's birthday party.

* Busy Housewife's Next Day Plan (list prepared at ten p.m.)
1. Enroll Jackie in kindergarten at nine a.m.
2. Beauty shop appointment at ten a.m.
3. Invite Peggy Hawthorne to lunch.
4. Balance checkbook.
5. Clean family room and living room.
6. Ask Jim to stop by grocer's.
7. Tell Moore's Dress Shop that I can work part-time since Jackie is in school.

When you write your plan, don't do it in cement. Keep organized, sure, but be flexible enough to deal with unexpected problems or opportunities. You can use a daily planning calendar or the back of a brown paper bag. Remember, it's not the list that manages time. It's what you do.

* Head off grinding repetition.

One way to use your self-confidence to stay ahead

is to head off grinding repetition. People with little or no self-confidence will tolerate dull repetition in their lives because the thought of change scares them. As a lively personality interested in a strong self-confidence, you know that this is a self-defeating attitude. You can't get ahead or stay ahead when you are living and working in a rut.

Don't flog yourself if your life is routine and sometimes monotonous. Self-blame is a twin brother to an inferiority complex. Remember that little word *do*? You can *do* something about grinding repetition. You won't have to quit your job, get a divorce or move out of town to turn things around. Great numbers have used simple techniques to head off grinding repetition. Here are some for your consideration.

1. Join a business or professional club where you know nobody.

2. Invite new people into your home.

3. Get a new job if your current one is a boring dead end. Don't do it impetuously and compromise yourself. Plan, then *do*.

4. Eat lunch at a different place with a new friend.

5. Take a trip to a place you've always wanted to see. (I went to Africa!)

6. Develop a fascinating hobby. (Mine is writing.)

7. Take a college-level course in a subject that challenges you.

8. Ask for new responsibilities where you work. (This is better than saying, "I want a new job because I'm bored with the one you gave me.")

9. Startle your husband with a new hair-do.

10. Buy your wife a present.

11. Look for new and better ways to do your job, keep your home, or to catch fish.

My first grade teacher taught us to sing, "The world is so full of a number of things, that I'm sure we should all be as happy as kings." I'm not sure about the king bit, but I know that the world is full of a number of things that anybody can do to escape grinding repetition. Choose yours and use it to keep a head start on life.

* Make the most of today.

You can't depend on tomorrow. It never comes. Yesterday is gone forever. You cannot recall it to take advantage of its time that was. Today is your day and it is nobody else's. You can't trade it for tomorrow or yesterday. You cannot ignore it. It is yours, and nobody else can handle it for you. The opportunity and the responsibility it brings are all yours. You can't trade them for anything. If you could, you would soon be rich. You can use them, though, to get ahead and stay ahead. Make the most of that. Today never offers a second chance.

USING SELF-CONFIDENCE
MAKES IT LOOK EASY

You have seen speakers, actors and entertainers who put on magnificent and difficult performances with no apparent effort. It wasn't easy. It just looked easy. What you did not see was the long training and the endless hours of rehearsal and practice. This is what happens when you study and practice using self-confidence. Self-confidence makes whatever you choose to do look easy. I have had people come up to me after a speech or after some program before a group and exclaim, "How do you do it? I wish I had that gift!" What they don't know is that at one time I had difficulty saying my name before a crowd of three. It took resolve, work and practice to shake that terrible inadequacy. I knew two things though. I knew that I must overcome that self-imposed handicap, and I knew that it could be done. I forced myself to study public speaking. I sought opportunities to address small groups. It was sheer agony at first, but I soon gained so much self-confidence that I actually enjoyed standing before an audience and pouring my heart out. The more I practiced, the more confident I became. It wasn't long until I was getting more speaking engagements than I could handle. I still enjoy getting up before groups, no matter how large, to motivate, educate or entertain people. It is not easy. I have never said that it was. It just looks easy because I had the shred of self-confidence to believe, and because I was willing to work, study, and practice. Whatever you would like to do and whoever you are, I recommend this technique to you. It is a real confidence builder. I know.

APOLOGY MAKES YOUR
SELF-CONFIDENCE SOUND WEAK

Whatever you plan to do, on the job or off, never do it apologetically. When you talk apologetically, you not only will sound as if your confidence is weak, you will act as if it is in short supply. Apologetic behavior makes you look handicapped. Putting your self-confidence to work makes everything look easy. That is an impressive way to handle a hard job and to get ahead.

MARTIN ERWIN MAKES AN IMPORTANT SPEECH LOOK EASY

Martin Erwin sells cosmetics to a classy clientele. Nearly all of the buyers he calls on are women. So when one of his biggest customers asked him to address her club on color language, of all things, Mr. Erwin promptly agreed. Martin says that it had to be his self-confidence that prompted him to do it for he knew nothing about color language. Still, he had a week to prepare. He checked three books out of the library and drove 150 miles to audit a special one-day non-verbal language class in another city. Within three days he had learned your choice of colors has a lot to say about you. On the evening of his speech Martin stood up and elaborated on such items as these.

* Red indicates self-confidence and force.
* Yellow is independent, optimistic and a people person.
* Blue is sensitive, respects tradition and likes home.
* Green follows rules but can be arrogant.
* Colors are not absolutes because people can be blends.

Further, he explained that colors and body language can be used successfully by salesmen and lawyers to size up prospects, competitors or jurors. He told the ladies how they might use color to assess personalities and relationships. Also, he suggested how they might influence others through the proper choice of colors that they personally used.

Martin Erwin's speech received an enthusiastic reception and his client-friend expressed appreciation and admiration for his confident and informative lecture. She complimented him especially because his delivery was smooth and looked so easy. Martin has his own ideas about that. He knows that the preparation and work beforehand bolstered his self-confidence and that made the speech look easy.

A HEAD START GUARANTEES A QUICK RESPONSE

The man out front gets the attention. The man bringing up the rear may get the pity, but what self-confident man or woman needs that? Attention will get you more than pity anytime. Nobody can accomplish much until he gets the attention of the people around him. Once you have the attention of the people you want to influence you are in a position to command a quick response.

When you have a head start you are the leader. As a leader, you can get a quick response to your request or order by . . .

* Showing those you are motivating that they too can get ahead with your help. You can be the best example. Explain what you expect of those you are

leading, detail your method of becoming a front runner, and carefully list the benefits they can expect by working with you. The *benefit* idea always gets a quick response whether you are talking about money, prestige, health or fun. Everybody wants to know what they are going to get.

* Share your self-confidence with your helpers and friends. You can do this by sounding confident and acting confident as you work with them. Once your self-confidence rubs off on them, they will be responsive to your ideas and suggestions.

* Ask for a quick response. No matter how far ahead of the pack you may be, your best guarantee of a quick response is to ask for it. Once you have explained your proposition, ask for action. As any star salesman can tell you, the man who gets the business is the one who asks for it. Nobody is more qualified to ask for a quick response that the one who has a head start. Another thing our star salesman can tell you is that nine times out of ten the one who gets the order is the one who gets there first. He is the one who has used his self-confidence to get out front.

HOW A CONFIDENT HEAD START
STACKS THE ODDS IN YOUR FAVOR

A confident head start means that you are doing something today. That puts the odds in your favor because ninety-four percent of the people live for the future. Note that the expression is *live for the future*. Nobody lives in the future. It is not here today. As the self-confident person recognizes that fact he has a head start on ninety-four percent of the rest of the people then and there.

Among the many odds that you pile up in your favor with a confident head start are the following.

* You discourage the competition.

When you go after anything worthwhile you will invariably have a bunch of competitors baying at your heels. Nothing discourages them more than to discover that you have already been there first. I've spent a lot of years in sales and marketing. I learned early that a head start can eliminate much competition. This has been driven home to me more than once when a competitor has said to me, "Gee, that was a nice piece of business you picked up from Mr. Hardnose. I've been aiming to go see those people, but . . ."

* You inspire people.

When you use your self-confidence to move up front, you inspire people. Every ambitious man and woman wants to be identified with the winners. When they see that you can and will perform beyond the ordinary, they will be inspired to emulate you. This puts you ahead in the motivation business because when you inspire people you inspire followers. Think of how much this kind of support can mean to you.

* You have shown interest in what you are doing.

People will believe in what you believe in. They will be interested in what you are interested in. When you put forth the planning and effort to get a head start, you have shown your self-confidence, your self-belief and your keen interest in what you are doing. People will see this and they will be interested. This is a strong point in your favor.

* You have demonstrated enthusiasm.

There are many authorities on self-fulfillment and motivation who tag enthusiasm as the single most important factor in getting ahead. There is no disputing the power of enthusiasm. It takes enthusiasm to get a head start and it takes enthusiasm to stay ahead. Monitor your enthusiasm regularly. When it sags, that means somebody or something is gaining on you. Review the chapter in this book on enthusiasm. Once you have demonstrated enthusiasm you will never want to let it go. That would be like relinquishing your head start.

* You have created extra time.

Extra time is another advantage stacked in your favor. When you get out front, you have created extra time. Your self-confidence has then put you in a position where you are not worrying about beating a deadline or catching up with somebody. When you have a head start, you can use your time for productive purposes instead of struggling merely to catch up. Extra time means extra confidence for you.

* You can get on to your next goal.

When your head start gives you extra time, you can finish one job and get on to your next project or goal. This keeps you ahead and keeps your enthusiasm and confidence bubbling. You can see this every day as you observe the way competent leaders around you work and use the extra time they gain to stack the odds for them.

* You have people in your pocket.

The odds are always yours when you pocket people. When you get a head start in whatever you do, you automatically become a leader. People want to follow a strong leader. As long as you exhibit your leadership qualities on the front line people will gladly respond by hopping into your pocket.

* You have proved your self-confidence.

You don't have to make speeches about how much self-confidence you have when you can claim the credit for your own head start. You have proved your self-confidence. That is enough to give you the winning odds.

JIMMY MINGO STACKS
THE ODDS IN HIS FAVOR

Jimmy Mingo was a young college graduate who badly needed a job. He had a major in accounting and was scanning the want-ads. There was one firm, Tri-State Professional Services, advertising for an accountant. Jimmy called and asked for the personnel director, a lady named Lucille Boohler. Jimmy pointed out that Miss Boohler would be swamped with applicants on the morrow, but that he could come in at once and ease her load for the next day. He requested no more than fifteen minutes. Of course, as a foresighted, confident young man, Jimmy had his resume and credentials typed and in order. The personnel manager gave him the fifteen minutes. Two hours later Mr. Mingo had his first job. He had stacked the odds in his favor by getting a head start. This is a winning strategy.

HOW TO SHARPEN YOUR SELF-CONFIDENCE FOR A HEAD START

There is no long and complicated secret to sharpening your self-confidence for a head start. Jimmy Mingo's story drives that home. The key is to prepare well and act quickly. You can make a more valid self-assessment of your abilities and your confidence than anybody else. Take this responsibility and go. The odds are with you.

CONFIDENCE KEYS

* Be your own competitor.
* You are the only one working on your goals.
* Tough goals keep you stretching.
* Create your own head start opportunities.
* Be your own head start leader.
* Go out on a limb occasionally.
* Indecision brings up the rear.
* Other things being equal, the first lick wins.
* Intense self-confidence makes you time conscious.
* You do not manage time. You manage what you do.
* Head off grinding repetition.
* Today never offers a second chance.

* Self-confidence makes it look easy.
* The leader out front commands a quick response.
* The odds are with you.

Chapter 15
How To Sharpen Your Contacts With Self-Confidence

You need contacts because you need people. If you are already a successful manager or leader you know this better than anyone. If you are a beginner, the sooner you recognize your need for people the better. It's OK to be a rugged individual but even this legendary character needs people. Without people no one is more than a sulking hermit in a dank cave.

Your contacts are the people you see, work with, live with, motivate, lead, push and otherwise use to extend your arms, legs, eyes and, yes, your brain. No man can grow bigger than himself except through his contact with other people. Executives acknowledge this as they delegate authority. This is why bright productive people are always seeking the company of brighter and more productive people. Before we get into detailed strategies to sharpen your contacts, let's consider the following capsule comments.

* Self-confidence is not power in itself. It becomes powerful and useful only when you contact and work with and through other people. By the same token, the more contacts you make and the more you influ-

ence other people, the more self-confidence you will have.

* Other people are always eager to make friends with self-confident men and women. They want to sharpen their contacts too. This means that as a self-confident personality you are in an enviable position.

* You can't sharpen your contacts simply by having a contest with yourself to see how many people you can meet. You can meet a lot of new people that way, but you won't do much to sharpen your contacts. To sharpen your contacts you must identify the people who can help you reach your goals. Concentrate your attention and your self-confidence on these people. That will sharpen your contacts and give you a solid power base.

* Using your self-confidence to sharpen your contacts is an all-important first step. The real test, though, is what you do after you have made the contact. For lack of a stronger, more descriptive term, you must "use" your contacts after the initial handshake. This is not to imply that you should take unfair advantage of them. Nevertheless, to sharpen your contacts you must lead, guide, control and dominate them. The happy part of this self-confident idea is that you can do just that for the mutual benefit of you and those you contact.

WHY YOU NEED STRONG CONTACTS

Do you know one prominent, successful or happy man who lives in an iron cage of isolation that he has built all for himself? I don't and I can't believe that anybody else does. Whoever you are and whatever your station in life, strong personal contacts are your best guarantee of success and happiness. People live in group association. It has always been thus from the earliest tribes to today's complex interwoven web of humanity. Here is another truth from time immemorial. In every group there have always been dominant leaders who surrounded themselves with others who did their bidding. Then, as now, self-confidence and ability were validated by the contacts one makes and keeps.

A WORD ABOUT WEAK CONTACTS

Weak contacts can undermine your influence and your self-confidence. Weak contacts are those who cannot or will not do anything for you. These are the contacts that are pleased to hang around you because they feel that you can do something for them. This may be nothing more than the reassurance and the prestige they gain from being in your shadow. There is no point in kicking such people about. Just be sure they don't take up so much of your time and attention that you neglect more worthy contacts. The contacts you make are as personal as a set of false teeth. They are your responsibility. Your sense of humanity may tell you to be polite to weak contacts, but your sense of self-responsibility will dictate that you focus on more rewarding contacts. These are the ties that bind you to success.

PLAN YOUR CONTACTS
WITH BOLD SELF-CONFIDENCE

Plan your contacts with bold self-confidence.

Strong contacts respect bold, positive action. This is because they recognize the self-confidence and determination in such an approach. They have confidence in you when they see you have a forceful confidence in yourself. One such contact can trigger a chain of events. Here is an example that happened in my part of the country. It drives home the point.

Bob Holcomb had been in the family's furniture business for most of his thirty-five years. He was a minority owner; his father and older brothers controlled the company. Bob decided to try something different inasmuch as he was ambitious and full of self-confidence. He used his vacation to visit three large case goods manufacturers and asked to represent them in his state and an adjoining one. He received two prompt offers. Bob chose the one nearest home to facilitate deliveries and to keep in close contact. Then he planned who to contact on his first week out. On his first trip this new sales rep called on Boyd's Big Discount House. Gruff John Boyd demanded, "Why should I see you when salesmen are running over me now?" Bob replied that Mr. Boyd owed it to himself to hear his story because he (Bob) knew his business and could help Boyd's Discount House make extra money. John Boyd considered that possibility and relented. Bob proceeded to sell him enough goods to beat his old salary for a full month. Then Mr. Boyd said, "I like your attitude and the way you operate. Go see my friend Bert Askins in Fort Dodge. Give him my card and tell him what I bought." Bob headed for Fort Dodge. He used the same bold approach as he made this contact. The results were more than satisfactory. Then Mr. Askins suggested that Bob see Ray's Salvage and Bargain Emporium in the next town. Here Bob walked in as if he owned the place and sold another dealer on the first contact. Bob's first contact snowballed into three good and loyal accounts. When you plan your contacts with bold self-confidence you can trigger exciting chain reactions. This is your opportunity and your self-obligation.

BE MORE THAN A NAME DROPPER!

Be more than a name dropper as you make new contacts. Name dropping is a tricky little gimmick at best. It doesn't impress strong contacts. Use the contacts you make for better stuff, such as getting what you want just as Bob Holcomb did. This will win new contacts far more than will mere words.

KEEP AWAY FROM PEOPLE
WHO TRY TO BELITTLE YOU

As you plan and execute your contacts with self-confident boldness here is a little red flag for you. When and if someone attempts to put you down, adopt the attitude of a brilliant speaker I once heard. He said that when anybody attempted to put him down he felt sorry for that person because he knew the depth of his self-doubt.

Mark Twain also had something to say on this subject. Here it is: "Keep away from people who try to belittle your ambition. Small people always do that, but the really great make you feel that you, too, can become great."

HOW INSURANCE SALESMAN
KIP RUCKER USED
BOLD SELF-CONFIDENCE AND
SHARPENED HIS CONTACTS

Kip Rucker had left the security of a guaranteed salary and a plush office at Wolfermann and Associates where he was a junior partner in the accounting and consulting firm. He had opened his new insurance office specializing in auto and truck insurance. He aimed high. His first call was to Church and Sons, a big fleet operator. Kip had researched the firm and knew how many trucks they had and what their insurance cost was. Despite his preliminary work, he called and on his first contact softly asked Mr. Church's secretary to see whether he was too busy to see him. Of course, she came back and said Mr. Church regretted that he was far too busy to grant an interview. Deeply chagrined, Kip Rucker called Church and Sons the next week. He put a bold self-confidence up front. When the secretary answered, Kip identified himself, instructed her to tell Mr. Church he needed thirty minutes as soon as possible in order to save him a hundred dollars in insurance costs on every truck he had. He pointed out that since Church operated two hundred units this amounted to a twenty thousand dollar savings per year on the same coverage. After a breathtaking ten minutes the secretary came back and asked if Mr. Rucker could make it by four p.m. that day. Mr.

Rucker could and did. Further, his display of bold self-confidence promptly landed him his first account and a good one it was.

Plan your contacts with bold self-confidence. The stronger and more valuable the contact the more likely he is to understand and work with you.

HOW TO STRENGTHEN OLD CONTACTS WITH SELF-CONFIDENCE

We have all been cautioned time and again about the error of taking old friends and clients or customers for granted. Taking any contact for granted bluntly means that we are dropping our guard and growing careless. This is bad. There are always ten thousand pairs of greedy eyes watching and hoping for this to happen. Old contacts and old friends are entitled to the same attention that we are forced to give new contacts. They have every right to expect this much. After all, they are the new contacts that have been around long enough to prove their loyalty and appreciation. To lose an old contact is a greater and more humiliating loss than losing a new one. It's much harder to get back an old friend than it was to get him the first time. It's harder by far to have to prove yourself all over again with an old contact than it is to go out and grab a new one. The hurt is always deeper when we know we have lost through our own carelessness or indifference. All of which is to say that it behooves each of us to continually strengthen our old contacts with self-confidence and ongoing enthusiasm.

Here are four techniques that can help you confidently hold onto and strengthen your old contacts.

1. Keep a list of your contacts (call them customers, clients, dealers, distributors, friends or whatever). Beside each name list the date of your first successful contact. This way you will always know how long your helpers have been with you.

2. Keep a record or file of what each contact has done for you or has enabled you to do for yourself. This reminder should keep you seeking new ways that your old contact can be worth more to you.

3. Keep a written record of your calls or contacts with your old friends. I've done this for years on three-by-five cards. It's easy to do and I have never lost a dime doing it. On the contrary, it has made me money as it strengthened my hold on my valued old contacts.

4. Keep asking yourself these basic questions each time you review an old contact.

A. How else can I use this old contact?

B. What can I do to make myself more important to this old friend?

C. Am I overlooking anything that can tie us closer together?

D. What am I doing to keep him aware of how much I am doing for him?

E. Am I asking him to do all that he can do for me?

F. Do I subtly remind him that I am helping him each time he helps me?

G. Am I maintaining the leader's role in our long association?

H. Do I have my old contact leaning on me for advice and guidance?

I. Does my old friend consider me an authority?

J. What makes this old contact important to me?

These questions and your self-confident analysis of an old contact can inspire you to make him a better and more productive helper. When working with an old contact, you are building on something you have already won. This is a winner's way to keep and strengthen his base.

LEE NICKELS' METHOD TO KEEP OLD CONTACTS SHARP

Lee Nickels says the only good contact is a sharp, productive one. He is also convinced that the only way to keep old contacts sharp is to keep contacting your contact. Nobody likes to feel neglected. The feeling is especially acute when and if you overlook or neglect an old friend who has been contributing to your success. Here's Lee Nickels' method of keeping his old contacts sharp and interested in him.

Lee uses what he calls his "Follow-up Formula." It is a row of file folders in the top drawer of his file cabinet. Each folder is labeled with a month of the year, January through December. As Lee visits or phones one of his steady contacts he records the visit or call on a sheet of 8½-by-11 paper with the customer's name, address and any other pertinent information at the top. He types in the date of each contact, the purpose of the contact, and what was accomplished. Next he notes when his old friend and helper should be contacted again and what should be covered on the next contact date. Then he places the file folder in its alphabetical order under the month the next contact is to be made. On the first of each month Lee goes through the files for that month, lines up his contacts to be made, and systematically follows up until he has again seen or talked with everyone scheduled under that particular month. Mr. Nickels says his "Follow-up Formula" not only keeps his old contacts sharp, but that it also keeps him on his toes.

Adopt Lee Nickels' philosophy. Make new friends and new contacts on a programmed basis, while cherishing and promoting the old.

POWERFUL CONTACTS
EXPAND YOUR SELF-CONFIDENCE

Here is a thought to chisel on your heart. When you establish powerful contacts, you are still the same person. The difference is that you now have new opportunities open to you. Your potential has grown. Further, as this is happening, your worthwhile contacts are expanding your self-confidence. Once you have put powerful contacts to work for you, you will never again settle for less than you can do. You have smelled the cabbage cooking.

Just this morning a beautiful lady sat in my office

and we reminisced about twenty-five years ago. We talked excitedly about how I used to call on them when she and her husband had formed a small distributing company. Now the company is a multimillion dollar corporation and the largest employer in a wide area. Too, she told with her old enthusiasm that they had just financed another million-dollar-plus expansion to accommodate an ever-growing business. She is a top executive in the firm. Her husband is president of the business, is on the board of directors of his bank, on the board of directors of a national food company, and has served as the president of a nationwide wholesalers' association. As we recalled all this, my old friend said with justifiable pride, "My husband and I sometimes felt a bit threatened as we grew bigger and bigger because neither of us had a college degree. We overcame that handicap though, if that's what it was, by making strong contacts and surrounding ourselves with highly qualified people. It's awesome what that has done for us. We are totally confident that we will keep getting bigger as long as we keep contacting the right people."

The lady is right of course. It was downright inspiring just to sit across from her and watch her self-confidence sparkle and glow as she talked of the importance of contacting and motivating people. You can do just what she and her husband have done if you can raise five hundred dollars and make the right contacts. That's all that Faye and Denzil Salem had going for them when they started. Their story is enough to encourage anyone to use their self-confidence to sharpen their contacts.

SELF-CONFIDENCE MAKES YOUR CONTACTS MUTUALLY PROFITABLE

When an enterprising person develops and perfects a strategy to sharpen his contacts, he expects and wants to share the goodies. One of the stronger points of a healthy self-confidence is that it understands that productive contacts must be mutually profitable. This does not mean that you are honor bound to split everything you gain from a contact right down the middle. It does mean that your contacts should have a chance to profit from their association with you. Otherwise, you can never have long productive contacts.

When a confident motivator sets about to gain something from a contact, he dangles the proverbial carrot on the stick. He emphasizes the benefits that his helpers will gain by cooperating with him. As a self-confident motivator you teach as well as lead when you show your contact how to gain something, whether it be money, fame, prestige or self-improvement. When anyone is motivated to move in your behalf it will be because you have taught him that an association with you can be mutually profitable.

Leaders in the direct selling field are adept at employing this concept. As leaders they have already demonstrated an abundant self-confidence and an ability to make money. At their motivational meetings they show what the new contacts can earn through their personal sales. Then they demonstrate how much more they can make as they build their own chain of contacts. Never mind that the leader gets an override on each sale. His contacts don't care how much he makes as long as they get their fair share.

Use your self-confidence in the same way to make your contacts mutually profitable. It is a strategy that works. As a friend of mine in the food supplement business says, it's the greatest idea since peanut butter.

HOW GINA PASKO MAKES HER CONTACTS PROFITABLE FOR EVERYBODY

Gina Pasko was the office manager for a food broker who suddenly decided to throw in the towel and retire to the Sunbelt. Gina was dismayed until her boss said that she could have the business if she could handle it. Gina called on her self-confidence. She contacted each principal the brokerage house represented and explained her plans to increase business. This was her first move to make her contacts profitable for everybody concerned. Next, she had a sales meeting with the five sales people who had been working for the former owner. She outlined an incentive plan whereby each salesman exceeding a monthly quota received a graduating bonus. The more a salesperson sold, the more that salesperson made. Then she offered a grand prize of a new automobile at year's end for the sales leader. This was her second step to make her contacts mutually profitable. The next step was to push deals that were especially profitable for the firm's customers.

Gina Pasko's strategy paid handsomely. Her firm now handles two prestigious lines that were offered her when her program attracted wide notice. Also, she has doubled the sales force. Gina still makes it profitable for all her contacts while she pockets a fat share for herself.

WHY WORTHWHILE CONTACTS WELCOME YOUR SELF-CONFIDENCE

Worthwhile contacts will always welcome your self-confidence. They know the difference between a cocky bravado and the genuine article. Self-confidence never needs a false front of noisy exaggeration or a battery of vocal fireworks meant to overwhelm a contact. Your own self-confidence will illustrate the point. You know when you are self-assured and on solid ground. Your contacts will also know that. They will welcome your self-confidence because it labels you as someone worth knowing and working with.

Earl Lytle, buyer for a coffee and restaurant supply wholesaler, once told me that he was always suspicious that a too vocal salesman was trying to hide something. It might be something deceitful or it might be that the man was unsure of himself in a new situation. Anyway, as Earl explained, he could never feel any confidence in anyone who came on in a nervous and driven manner. What Earl liked was a self-confident salesperson who came in exuding self-assurance and competence in a businesslike way. Earl welcomes self-confidence in the people who contact him because he himself feels more confident doing business with this type of individual.

Pleasing people in everything that you do or say is no guarantee that they will welcome you or cooperate with you. A bold and managed self-confidence is your best guarantee of a warm welcome as you establish more and more contacts in your business and your social life.

TEN CONFIDENT IDEAS
TO WIDEN YOUR CONTACTS

Surrounding yourself with competent working contacts is not total success insurance. The best of contacts, the most loyal helpers, the most dependable friends, the most enthusiastic workers in your behalf, are all subject to human frailties. Attrition affects your contacts no matter how highly they regard you or how much you respect them. They die. They move away. They make mistakes. Not many are forever. All of which is to impress upon the self-confident personality the necessity of a continuing campaign to widen his contacts. Though you may reach a plateau where you are satisfied with your contacts and with their productivity, this truth still obtains. *Nothing in life stands still.* Your contacts may be exceptional and loyal as an old dog, but your self-interest and the facts of life dictate that you must always widen your contacts. Here are ten confident ideas that can help you keep pushing your circle of contacts wider and wider.

1. Expose yourself.

You make contacts by the quantity and the quality of your self-exposure. You must expose yourself and your self-confidence daily. You must meet, evaluate, enlist and lead new people each day. Of course, you are not going to hit the jackpot every day. The point is that you cannot forget the importance of building new contacts for one day. It is necessary to expose yourself to new people, new situations and new possibilities. It is mandatory that you move about, see people, talk with them and line them up as friends and helpers. Get out and circulate though you may have no firm commitments for the day. When you expose yourself to opportunity it will meet you halfway. I've proved this to myself on more than one occasion. Here is a case point.

I was in charge of a four-state territory through my manufacturers' representative agency for a number of principals. One was a carpet mill with a contract line. On this particular Monday morning I felt that I had touched all bases for the time being. Nevertheless, I headed out. Two hours from home I went into a bank and bumped into an architect friend. After the usual greeting he asked me if I had time to see a specifier in that town. The specifier was looking for carpet for a hundred-unit office building. I had the time and the goods. I sold my biggest order of the week through the exposure technique. What do you think would have happened had I sat placidly in the office that day? You're right. I would not have made an important contact and I would have missed a nice chunk of business.

Chad Fremont uses the exposure technique often. He sells life insurance and a lot of it. While lesser men sit in the agency office sipping coffee and wishing that they had a live prospect, Chad goes out and exposes himself. He will go to a large shopping center where he can be seen and where he can make new contacts. The campus of a sixteen thousand-plus enrolment university is another favorite exposure site. Chad is noted for his college professor clients and his prospecting-by-sight technique. Exposure is his most effective means of adding to an already substantial clientele.

2. Travel.

Travelling can be hard, tiresome and boring. It can also be exciting, stimulating and rewarding. It is an excellent way to make new contacts. As you travel talk to people, learn who they are, what they do and where they live. Remember that first sentence. There are countless strangers who would like to strike up a conversation with you as you travel. They may be lonely or bored. Capitalize on this. Personally, I like to travel. I have made some of my best contacts on long trips. For instance, fifteen years ago I was in a distant city. The day had been long. A smiling gentleman stepped from a doorway onto the walk. I stopped him and asked him directions. He not only directed me to where I wanted to go, he insisted that we have coffee. He answered all my questions, added his own observations, and made the rest of my visit much easier and more productive. I still travel to that city and I still see C. N. Trotter every trip. He is a warm friend who continues to be helpful in many ways. I am looking forward to my next contact with him.

3. Talk.

Talk to people. Let your speech show that you are interested in them, in what they think, and in their ideas and plans. Ask leading questions. Learn what you have in common. You may find another C. N. Trotter.

It's important to talk. It is more important that you make your speech interesting and productive. Talking for the sake of talking is often done, I know. However, idle chit-chat doesn't develop strong contacts. When you talk, control the direction of the conversation. Then you will quickly know whether you've made a good contact or whether it's time to move on.

4. Ask for introductions.

You have competent friends and they have able self-confident friends. You can make many useful contacts simply by expressing a desire to meet your friends' friends. Ask for introductions. This is a simple, effective technique that you can use often to widen your contacts.

5. Make a priority contact list.

Nothing will do more for self-confidence than making sharp contacts and working with people who are energetic, successful leaders. This has been demonstrated time and again. I saw the miracle of this once early in my life. The lesson has stayed with me. I was in charge of a branch of a company that distributed wholesale books, magazines and other items sold through bookstores, drug houses and supermarkets. One employee, Kim Appleby, was a shy young lady who worked in the return department where she had contact with few of the other employees and saw no customers or outsiders. On a particularly hectic day I dragged her from the return department and put her on a billing assignment among our most dynamic and expansive people. She was terrified when she was given her station. By day's end Kim was a new person. As she said to me when she passed my desk on her way home, she had found that the very people she regarded as cold, superior types had been most kind and helpful. She had been accepted and had tasted her first bit of self-confidence. Before long she asked for and was given a regular position in billing and sales. I lost track of Kim when I was transferred soon after, but I've never worried about her. She had learned the value of working with sharp, aggressive people. She had made her contact, however reluctantly.

When you map a campaign to widen your contacts, make a priority list. These are the people you have tagged as having the most to offer you. They are the ones to contact. Identify, name, and go see them. You will like what happens.

6. Plan what you will do and say.

When you go after a busy contact, plan what you will do and say. Do not memorize your speech or presentation, but rather make a written outline. Use these notes to get your thoughts organized. Don't worry if you can't carry out every detail of your plan. It is enough to keep your goal in mind and to influence your new friend to move for and with you. Do as the well-trained professional salesman does. Plan your contact, make your proposal and close your sale. The most effective technique, as always, is to show what your new contact will gain by working and cooperating with you. This will get his attention and get you what you want.

7. Express sincere interest in your contacts.

You have to sell yourself to make and keep new contacts. You can't do this unless you are genuinely interested in their welfare as well as your own. The only way a new or an old contact will ever know that you are interested in them is for you to tell and show them. You express sincere interest by actions as well as words. You've heard the old maxim, actions speak louder than words. This is never more true than when you are trying to convince people that you have their interest at heart. They will understand that you are also working for your own good. Sharp contacts are not looking for a Mr. Goody Two Shoes.

8. Never try to "buy" a contact.

Lavish entertainment is not the way to widen your contacts. Any contact who will ever be worth anything to you or to himself will never expect you to wine and dine him in an effort to "buy" him. An honest contact will want to carry his fair share of the load. He knows that you can't afford to buy hundred-dollar dinners just to tell someone what a great guy he is and what you are going to do for him.

Of course, there will be times when you will entertain. Just don't go overboard. If you should ever make a deal with a new contact because you have made him feel obligated to you, he will resent it.

That means that he will be gone as soon as he can get away. As a self-confident, aggressive personality you can make a clean presentation of what you can do and of what he can expect. This is the way a vigorous, intelligent contact wants it.

9. Keep records.

Keep a written record of the contacts you have made. After you have seen a good contact, set up a simple, easy-to-use file on the contact. Jot down what you did and what you still plan to do regarding this contact. Scratch his name off your priority list since you now have him in your active file. Then keep both your active file and your priority list handy. These are both excellent tools for boosting self-confidence and winning helpers.

10. You are a valuable contact too.

As you work to widen your social and business contacts, keep in mind that you are a valuable contact too. Other ambitious, confident men and women are eager to make productive contacts. They are looking for you. You qualify. You are interested in getting ahead with the help of the understanding people that you meet. You also want to contribute to the success of others. This is the healthy attitude that puts everybody ahead. It is the attitude that makes your self-confidence visible. It also makes you a valuable contact. All of which means that your self-confidence has the inside track in making and widening your own valuable contacts.

CONFIDENCE KEYS

* You need people.

* Self-confidence is not power in itself.
* Self-confidence is powerful only when you contact and work through other people.
* Contact people who can help you.
* Self-confidence and ability are validated by the contacts you make.
* Plan your contacts with bold self-confidence.
* Never take an old contact for granted.
* Powerful contacts expand your self-confidence.
* Productive contacts must be mutually profitable.
* Worthwhile contacts welcome your self-confidence.
* Your self-interest demands that you always widen your contacts.
* You are a valuable contact too.

Chapter 16
Nine Ways To Use Self-Confidence To Get What You Want

What you want is often more important to you than what you need. Everybody understands the need for the basics: food, clothing and shelter. But as an ambitious, self-confident individual you want more than the bare necessities. Your life would be dull and frustrating if you could not also get much of what you want. This is good. It has nothing to do with greed or selfishness. It has to do with self-confidence and self-respect. It means that you are not content with mediocrity, that you want to be more than average or ordinary. You should never feel any guilt about wanting a great deal. This is the sign of a vibrant self-confidence and the hallmark of ambition. Further, everyone wins when a concerned self-confident person goes after what he wants, for this conscientious individual wants not only to enrich his life, but also to contribute to the welfare and self-importance of those whose life he touches.

Here is another thought to encourage you to put your self-confidence to work to get what you want. The one who downgrades himself for wanting too much simply does not think highly of himself. He feels unworthy of what he wants. This is the reverse of a healthy self-confidence. It is an indication of a gnawing inferiority complex and an unhappy mistrust of one's self. It is a trap to be avoided. It is not what you want.

Here is another point to emphasize. It will erase any concern that you have if you are afraid of wanting more than you should. The point is this. There will rarely, if ever, be a time when you will be totally and permanently satisfied with what you have or what you have accomplished. This truth obtains whether you have accumulated a large amount and have done a great deal or if you have little and have accomplished little. It is not the nature of self-confidence to permit an ambitious man or woman to be content with less than his or her best. Contentment and peace are achieved in the sure knowledge that you are using your self-confidence in the constant pursuit of what is best for you and those around you. This does not imply that you must always and forever run yourself ragged to prove that you can get what you want. Reason is a strong component of self-confidence. Go after what you want with all the self-confidence and power that you can muster, but do it within the bounds of the reasonable. It is unreasonable, if not unthinkable, to expect that a self-confident person could ever be content with less than his portion. In this light, you have every reason to go after what you want and to enjoy what you get. There is no reason to be satisfied with crumbs.

There is another cause that the self-driving achiever is not forever content when he gets what he wants. It is that our definitions change as our life progresses and our record of accomplishments grow. What you wanted at twenty may have lost much of its appeal when you are fifty. And so on throughout life. This is normal and to be anticipated, but it should in no way stop you from getting what you want today. Today is always important. Get what you want today. Tomorrow you will pursue a valid want and, in all probability, a higher and nobler goal. Your life would be dull and flat without that to look forward to.

The first step in getting what you want is, of course, to . . .

1. KNOW WHAT YOU WANT

We have already had a discussion on the distressing ripple effects of indecision in chapter fourteen. Conversely, knowing what you want (the ability to make decisions) has a ripple effect in the opposite direction. Knowing what you want is a positive confidence-building force that not only bolsters your own confidence, but reaches out and inspires others to believe in you. When people believe in you they will identify with you, listen to you and help you get what you want.

Obviously, an intelligent and understanding self-confident person is going to consider others as he decides what he wants. True self-confidence neither carries a gun nor wants one. Real and honest self-confidence will get you what you want without shooting anybody down. In fact, it will do more than get you what you want. It will help others get what they want.

Here are some keys that will help you identify and know what you want. They work.

* Why do I want this?

When you feel a burning desire to acquire or do something, ask yourself why it is important to you or, simply put, why you want it. If you have a sound financial or emotional want, then you are on safe ground. If what you want is something frivolous, like the biggest diamond in the world or something as ugly as revenge, discard the thought. You will not like getting what you want if it is an empty box. Worse, you won't like yourself, and there goes a mess of misspent self-confidence.

Examine why you want something. The easy way is to write down the positive arguments and, on the other side, any negative items concerning why you deeply want something. If the positives outweigh the negatives, then get going.

* Fulfilling your wants adds to your self-esteem.

Do not let anybody tell you what you want is not important. It is a starved mentality that holds that only needs matter. Survival may be man's basic instinct, but that is not what makes him happy. To reach his highest potential man must fill his wants as well as his bare bones existence. Needs may keep a man alive, but wants are what make him a progressive and growing animal. When man gets what he wants, he gets self-esteem. Without a generous helping of self-esteem he can neither get nor give. Hold this idea and you hold a key to getting what you want.

* Don't ask for the sun, the moon and the stars.

Don't ask for the sun, the moon and the stars. Nobody gets all that regardless of how badly they may think they want it. This is just another way of saying don't ask yourself for the impossible. The self-confident man or woman relies upon himself or herself to fulfill personal wants and dreams. Nobody else will do the impossible for you nor should you ask yourself to undertake such. You gain big wants in the same manner that you gain recognition and responsibility—one step at a time. Use your self-confidence to get what you want in a logical sequence. This way you may eventually get the sun and the moon and the stars, but not all at once.

* Be realistic in your wants.

This thought ties in with the preceding one. Here is a proven method to check the soundness of any want that you may have. Ask yourself the following.

Why do I want this?
What will this want do for me when I have
  attained it?
How will I be better off than I am now?
How will it affect others if I win this want?
How do I start to fill this want?
Where will I start to fill this want?
When will I start to fill this want?

Your answers will depend on your private circumstances and your personal resources. Answer each question confidently and analytically. Then if you still want whatever it is, you will know that you are on safe ground and ready to go.

PATTI WALLIS MOVES OFF DEAD CENTER

Patti Wallis had been a waitress for two years after graduating from high school. Patti had drifted into the job because her mother owned the busy coffee shop where she worked. Her mother loved the business, but Patti wanted to be an accountant. She went to her mother and told he what she wanted and why. Her mother expressed some surprise and a bit of chagrin, but agreed that she would put Patti through the local university if Patti would work weekends for her. This meant Patti would be busy seven days a week for at least four years. However, Patti knew what she wanted and quickly accepted her mother's offer. Patti is now an accountant and on her way to becoming head of her department. Patti is one of those lucky people who know what they want and are willing to do whatever is necessary to get it. This will move any self-confident personality off dead center just as it did Patti.

2. MAKE A WRITTEN SELF-COMMITMENT

Many people shy away from paper work. I can appreciate this. I am not exactly thrilled at the thought of paper work, but I do appreciate its effectiveness and its necessity. So I do it without any visible scars. I urge you to make a written commitment to get what you want. Do it today. Here are a number of items that your commitment should contain. Put everything helpful to you in it, then adhere to it. Your list will help you get what you want.

* Clearly state your want.

Unless you know exactly what it is that you want,

you can get lost. Your written commitment to get what you want should, first of all, clearly state your want. This will identify your goal and keep you on track.

* Outline your campaign.

When you have clearly in mind what you want, the next step is to outline how you plan to get it. Such an outline should include people who can help you, how you plan to get them to help you, and when you plan to contact them. Your helpers can include friends, employees, customers, community leaders and people that you approach for the first time.

* Be flexible, but determined.

Your written commitment should not be a strait jacket leaving no room for maneuvering. Rather, it should be a flexible tool that will permit you to adapt to circumstances and to change tactics if necessary. When you set about to get what you want, be flexible, but determined. You can use your self-confidence and keep your eye on what you want even as you change direction.

3. ESTABLISH TIME FRAMES

It is not enough to promise yourself that you are going to get what you want someday. It is just as important to decide when you are going after what you want as it is to decide how you are going to get it. Establish time frames when you plan a program to go after what you want. Dreams may last forever but you do not. Ask anyone over fifty. He will tell you that time flies. Time is your most precious possession. If you let it slip through your fingers like dry sand what you want may slide away with it. Don't panic if you have a few gray hairs. You still have time and it is ready to serve you. Give it direction. It is yours to use as you will.

The importance of establishing time frames was illustrated before my eyes. I had a friend who managed a paint and decorator store. He had talked for years of leaving the chain he worked for and opening his own store. I had made a purchase and was waiting for it to be loaded when I walked back to Tom Osborne's office. As I came in Tom was running his fingers through his salt and pepper hair and saying to a fellow employee, "Look at that! I still don't have my own store, but I'm going to." The other man said simply, "When, Tom?" Tom was jarred. "Within the month," he promised. He almost made it. His bright, new store wasn't ready for two months. It took a month longer than Tom's offhand schedule, but once he gave himself a time frame he did get what he wanted—his own business, and a successful one it is.

HOW PAUL NASH
MAKES TIME WORK FOR HIM

Paul Nash, a real estate salesman, was working day and night because he wanted to get ahead. He wound up in a hospital bed with a bleeding ulcer and an unhappy family. Paul had time for reflection in the hospital. He saw that he had been wildly spinning his wheels, thrashing about in all directions for any kind of prospects, and frequently listing property

325

that was grossly overpriced. He had exhausted himself by a frantic waste of time. During the two weeks he was in the hospital he planned an entirely new approach to his business. He counseled with his broker and his wife. Both were pleased with what they saw. Paul stuck with his plan. Now he goes to work promptly at eight a.m., works with his secretary to set up definite appointments, qualifies each prospect, refuses to work on overpriced property and spends most nights at home. His health is good, his family happier and his income is up dramatically. He is getting what he wants because, instead of haphazardly working all the time, he makes time work for him.

4. POWER TECHNIQUES TO LEAP FROM GOAL TO GOAL

Knowing what you want and recognizing that you have the self-confidence and ability to get it is not the end of the game. You have to establish goals and go from one to the other. There will be obstacles and resistance. Getting what you want is a competitive adventure full of excitement and action. This is not reason for discouragement. It is what gives spice and flavor to your sense of self-worth and accomplishment as you vault from goal to goal.

I like to tell about a successful and wealthy friend I have. He came up the hard way. He knows what it takes to meet a goal and move on up. He delights in seeing people succeed. He encourages them with this high compliment, "You made it happen." I like that. It puts the credit and the responsibility where it belongs.

With that, let's talk about some of the power techniques that you can use to leap from goal to goal as you work to get what you want. Consider these ideas. They make things happen.

* Power Recognition

Self-confidence is a power key in itself. It is the moving force that tells you that you can get what you want. It is the feeling of self-worth that tells you that you deserve what you want as long as you are willing to put forth the effort. Self-confidence and a sense of self-worth never expects to get what it wants for nothing. This attitude would destroy self-respect. Without self-respect there can be no self-confidence, no ambition and little accomplishment.

As we have mentioned earlier, self-confidence is not power within itself. It is a power technique that becomes power when it is used to influence people and circumstances. The recognition of the power and purposes of self-confidence is the number one technique in leaping from goal to goal. Here are others.

* How to Handle Resistance

People are defensive. They want you to get ahead, but they want to go along also. They will resist you until you give them a goal of their own. This is all right. You don't need helpers with so little spunk that they expect nothing from you. If they want nothing for themselves, why should they be interested in what you want?

When you run into resistance or indifference (which is a form of resistance) you can . . .

A. Avoid antagonizing the one who is resisting.

You do this by letting him save face. If you make him feel foolish or threatened he will go on the defensive and that will make it tougher for you. Instead of putting him on the defensive, point out that if you felt he didn't have a substantial contribution to make to your project you would never have approached him. Make him feel respected, explain how it will be to his advantage to join you, and then tell him what you want him to do. This will do no damage to your self-confidence and it will enhance his. Further, you will probably have him in your pocket right there.

B. Neutralize resistance.

When somebody is resisting you or your ideas he is saying, "Hey, I don't agree with you. You haven't sold me yet." Now, selling is a word that frightens some people. Never mind that. We are all salesmen if we get anything we want, though some of us may call ourselves teachers, preachers, fire chiefs, executives or dog catchers. Selling is convincing people. Read item "A" again. This is an example of a sales job that will neutralize resistance.

C. How to enlist people to help you get what you want.

OK. Now you have eliminated resistance, so what do you do next? Enlisting people is one thing. Motivating them to work hard to help you reach your goals is another. You do this by finding out what they want and showing how they can fulfill their wants when they cooperate with you. You've heard the current preachment that says when you give others what they want then, bingo! they will give you what you want. There is an element of truth in this, but there is another point to be made. Don't get so wrapped up in giving people what they want that what you want is ignored or sidetracked. Yes, help people as they help you but don't be a sacrificial lamb. Remember that the lamb never wins.

When you enlist and motivate people, listen to them as well as talk to them. When you listen to someone, you have taken the first step in motivating them to help you get what you want. As you listen attentively and earnestly you make the other person feel important and accepted as an equal. He will want to prove that your good opinion of him is sound. Listen to your prospective helper intently, then tell him what you want him to do and why you know that you've chosen the best man for the job. Let him share the goodies and you'll have a motivated helper for a long time. Listening is another power technique to enlist helpers who can help you get what you want.

5. DON'T IMPOSE LIMITS ON YOUR SELF-CONFIDENCE

Do you know what the greatest self-imposed limitation on self-confidence is? It is procrastination. Well-meaning, able people have lost far more through proscrastination than through lack of ability or opportunity. The feeling that many subconsciously entertain is that it is safer to stall and put off going after what they want than it is to risk failure. But what is failure except a hard lesson that can teach you what to do when you get up. Few men gain wealth and fame without suffering some painful setbacks first. Procrastination itself is a setback, sly, insidious and destructive.

Procrastination is tightly concerned with your time. One dictionary definition is: to put off doing something until a future time. When someone imposes severe limits on his self-confidence through procrastination, he loses more than time. He forfeits opportunity to those who are determined to use their self-confidence to get what they want now. The antidote is positive, timely preventive action.

There is a maxim called the eighty/twenty rule. This rule says that most people spend eighty percent of their time on the least important part of their jobs or goals. Obviously, it is just as important to focus your time squarely on what you want as it is to use your self-confidence to get started on time. Concentrate on using your self-confidence one hundred percent of the time on getting what you want. This will eliminate wasted motion that may be threatening your self-confidence.

The second worst enemy of self-confident achievement is that too often our goals are limited. We are better than we think. You are better than you think you are right this minute. Read the biography of any great man. You will find that he had neither wings nor a halo. He was equipped exactly as you are. You will also find that he set high goals for himself. He did not limit his self-confidence or his vision. Follow his example. Don't impose limits on your self-confidence.

J. C. STUART SHOOTS HIGH

J. C. Stuart is not an old man but he has definite

ideas about self-confident action and the time element. The only time he is concerned with is now. He explains that there is nothing you can do about time. It marches on inexorably. Each man has the same number of hours in his day. The pace of time cannot be altered by any man. It plays no favorites. All anyone can do with time is use it. Like self-confidence, he says, it is meaningless unless you use it.

Mr. Stuart practices what he preaches. He was a young engineer who started working for a highly regarded firm at age twenty-four. His goal was high. He wanted to be president of his own firm by age thirty. He saved his money, cultivated key men in his profession and made it a point to know his banker. At age thirty he took his money, confidently borrowed all that he could, sold stock to several business leaders, and formed his own engineering company. Today he is highly regarded in the industry. His specialty is working with municipalities and manufacturing firms. He is still a confident young man and still shooting high.

6. SELF-CONFIDENCE METHODS THAT INFLUENCE PEOPLE

A common misconception about the dominant self-confident personality who seeks to influence people is that he or she usually has ulterior motives. Nothing could be further from the truth. Of course, we have always had a few charlatans and parasites around who try to prey on people, but we are not talking about the criminal. Our concern is with the ambitious self-confident individual. Here is where you find productive, considerate, firm leaders who contribute much. Their influence is positive and beneficial. We are all indebted to them. You can use your self-confidence to join these winners by influencing people to listen to you and to work with you. Here are ideas that can help you do just that.

* Emphasize the positive.

You must be positive in your attitude, in your manner and in your speech to influence strong helpers. People believe what they see more readily than they believe what they hear. When they see you acting in a positive manner, they will feel reassured. When they see that you have a positive, enthusiastic attitude, they will respond with enthusiasm and confidence. In like manner, when your speech is earnest and positive, they will see and feel that and they will be responsive to you and your ideas.

One of the definitions of positive is: assured, confident. The more experience you have in dealing with people, the better you can influence them. Plus this: You will become more and more assured and self-confident yourself as you refine, polish and develop your personal methods and techniques to influence others. Here is an example that illustrates the positive principle in influencing others. Use the idea to sharpen your own skills.

HOW FLORENCE TAFT
EMPHASIZES THE POSITIVE

Florence Taft is responsible for the activities of a group of independent sales ladies who sell her prestigious, high-priced cosmetics and personal care items on a direct basis. When training a new group, here is how she starts the first meeting. Note the positive way that she opens up with the benefits that she can offer.

First she asks the question, "Who wants the good things of life?" All hands shoot up. Then Miss Taft emphasizes what more money can do for just about anybody. Then she uses charts, figures, diagrams and true success stories to show that the new recruits can have lots of money.

Next, Miss Taft asks, "Do you like to work?" A safe, positive question because no business lady worth her salt wants to say that she is a lazy slob. The response is nearly always one hundred percent positive. Florence Taft then covers the positive aspects of hard work, such as self-respect, financial independence, and the sense of personal accomplishment and satisfaction.

Finally, Miss Taft asks, "Do you like prestige?" As soon as the enthusiastic response is made, this convincing lady talks about the prestige of the products her helpers will be offering their clients. She is also careful to emphasize that the product line automatically lends prestige to those who sell it. A positive benefit, to be sure.

Emphasize the positive as you set about to influence people just as Florence Taft does. When you do, you'll get what you want.

* Beware the fifty/fifty deal.

As you seek to influence others, remember that you are the key decision-maker. Don't forget yourself as you use your influence to move others. It is your responsibility to be sure that the terms are fair for you as well as those you work with. Beware the fifty/fifty deal. It may be like the rabbit stew offered by a backwoods cafe. When the customer asked how much rabbit was in it, the waiter replied that it was about fifty/fifty rabbit. When the man persisted by asking what that meant, the waiter said, "Oh, one rabbit and one horse."

As the leader in any project, you deserve a better deal than that.

* Be selective.

Be selective in choosing who you will influence. Work with people who are bright, ambitious and intelligent. If you line up a few who are more intelligent than you yourself are, well, congratulations! You are using the right methods to influence people who can help you get what you want.

7. ACCEPT YOUR ABILITY TO GAIN WHAT YOU WANT

There's room to say it again. Most people are better than they think. We underestimate our abilities. It has been suggested that the average person uses no more than ten percent of his intellectual capacity. I can believe it. I've seen strong men cringe and rationalize when opportunity came banging on their door. One case comes to mind. I had a friend, college trained, able, and conscientious, who toiled for years at a safe little job. When pressed he would say, "I'm just trying to hang in until my kids are grown and out of school." He never made it. He died with two of his children still in college. His insurance took care of them, but his ability and prospects died with

334

him.

Failure to accept your ability to get what you want is damaging to the ego. Self-doubt is obvious not only to the victim but to those he would like to influence. This affliction is as hard to hide as a gorilla in your front room. But there is a bright side. No one is forced to resign himself to the back row of life. The thing to do is set some goals and move. About any goals: Set goals for a purpose. Do not set them for the sake of setting something. Consider the shape you will be in when you get there.

* Avoid the comfort zone.

This is not to imply that you should always be going and blowing like a west Texas wind. It means that there is something more for you than a no-man's land where nothing is expected of you and where you expect nothing from other people. To influence others you must expect something of them. And they are bound to expect more from you.

* Anticipate problems as you spread your influence.

Not everybody will run to stand by you as you work to influence others. Anticipate a few problems. Just don't waste time blaming yourself for the shortsightedness of some misguided troublemaker. Instead, solve the problem by working with people who can understand how much your self-confident action can do for them. Keep in mind that it is more important to be self-confident than it is to try to convince every Tom, Dick and Jane that you are self-confident.

EXPECT GOOD RESULTS

If you expect good results when you go after what you want, that is what you will get. When you expect good results as you seek to influence helpers, you will get good helpers. People who expect bad results often secretly want them. This way they don't have to cope with happiness and success. Instead they can sit back and drive everybody crazy by croaking, "I told you so."

This is not for the self-confident. Accept your ability to get what you want by influencing other people.

8. START WITH WHAT YOU HAVE

There will be few ideal situations in which to use your self-confidence to get what you want. Don't wait on the perfect circumstance. Start with what you have. I know it can be tough. I started from zero minus, not because I chose to but that is what I had and where I was. Yet I had goals and the confidence that I could make it. You might say that I've been a fortunate man, but I can tell you that it wasn't easy from my starting point. I do not tell you this story idly. Indeed, I do not like to remember it. I tell it to encourage you to confidently start with what you have and to expect no miracles. When you pay the price you will get what you want. This is front burner stuff. Now let's lay this alongside a persuasion that we have already touched on.

Work where you are today. This idea dovetails with the one just covered. We can tie them together in one sentence: Start with what you have and work where you are today. You may not find what you want right where you are today but you can confidently start preparing yourself for it today. Wherever you live and whatever your circumstances, you are more than a creature of adversity. You are a creature of choice with the most complex thinking apparatus in the world. Where you may be today does not detract from that confidence-building fact. You can decide and you can learn. Learning has been defined as changes in the behavior and mental process as a result of experience. The more you learn about your self-confidence, the more you will be convinced that geography or environment cannot erase its power.

9. CONSIDER THE ADVANTAGES

Another way to use self-confidence to get what you want is to look at the advantages an active self-confidence offers. Start with these.

* You project a positive personality.

Anyone who displays a day-to-day self-confidence comes on as a positive personality. Think of ten persons you know. Which ones impress you as being competent, trustworthy and outgoing? They will always be the ones who act and speak with the assurance of self-confidence. Your self-confidence will do no less for you.

* You win respect.

People respect self-confident achievers. You can see this all about you. When you use your self-confidence to win what you want, you will automatically win the respect of your peers. This is a solid fringe benefit.

* People will seek you out.

Self-confidence attracts people. It will win friends. This advantage is doubly important. As an ambitious

337

personality you need people. People will seek you out when they see your self-confidence bubbling and boiling.

* Your sense of self-worth grows.

Accomplishment and recognition invariably increase one's sense of self-worth. Applying your self-confidence to win what you want will cause your sense of self-worth to grow. And that makes all things easier.

* You learn that you can get things done.

When you use your abilities with determination and self-confidence, you get things done. Once you have learned this lesson you can get what you want.

* You will feel inferior to nobody.

The judicious use of self-confidence makes you productive and self-reliant. This drives home the fact that you do not have to stand on anybody's shoulder. Use your self-confidence. You can win what you want and you will feel inferior to nobody—which is as it should be.

* Your vision is lifted.

Self-confidence gets results. It influences people, moves goods, builds roads, establishes schools and runs the country. The more you do with your self-confidence, the more it will do for you. It will lift your vision beyond the commonplace and ordinary.

* You won't be dominated.

People who are dominated by others seldom get a whole lot. They sit in the shadows of life. You won't find aggressive self-confident people here. When you exercise self-confidence, you won't be dominated. You'll be a winner.

* You can handle pressure.

The person who has confidence in himself doesn't fold up and forget what he wants when he runs into pressure and obstacles. Instead, he regards pressure and obstacles as problems to be solved. Another of the advantages of self-confidence is that you can handle pressure. The techniques you have in this book will prove that to you.

* You will get what you want.

When you go after what you want with thought and self-confidence, you will get what you want. It may not fall into your lap but you can have it. You won't come up empty-handed.

CONFIDENCE KEYS

* What you want is often more important to you than what you need.
* The one who doesn't want much doesn't think much of himself.
* Know what you want.
* Fulfilling your want adds to your self-esteem.
* Make a written commitment to get what you want.
* Establish time frames.
* Set goals.
* Enlist people to help you get what you want.
* Don't impose limits on your self-confidence.
* Use your self-confidence to influence people.
* Accept your ability to gain what you want.
* Avoid the comfort zone.

* Consider the advantages that self-confidence offers.
* You don't have to come up empty-handed.

Chapter 17
How To Develop Confident Speech Power

"We rule men with words."
—Napoleon

Speech is the most powerful tool of the self-confident. It is not the only tool, but is the most effective means of putting your ideas across, explaining benefits, supporting your opinions and beliefs, influencing and motivating people, asking for what you want, demonstrating your confidence, and inspiring confidence in others. Speech is not only power, it is the button that sets all other aspects of self-confidence into motion. Use words carefully. They will do whatever you bid.

WHAT YOUR SPEECH SAYS
ABOUT YOUR SELF-CONFIDENCE

Your speech conveys to others your sense of self-confidence. When it is delivered in a warm, forceful manner it says that you are a friend who knows what he is about. If your speech is organized and concise, your listeners will be convinced of your authority and your self-confidence. This sets the stage for you to win support and to further expand your self-confidence and speech power.

Conversely, should your speech be faltering and hesitant, it will say that you yourself may have some reservations about your confidence and ability. Though the world is full of able people, there are many so filled with self-doubt that they speak weakly if at all. This is a sad loss, for anyone who is willing can learn to speak with authority and conviction. Study and practice is the answer. You are in that process right now. Let's get on with it with more ideas and examples.

* Speech attitude.

Your speech reveals your attitude in such a way that it has an attitude of its own which is inseparable from your person. The attitude that your listeners see in you will be exactly the attitude that your words, tone, inflection, gestures and vocal personality convey. When your speech is outgoing and positive, those who hear will respond in like manner. Should it be uncertain and vacillating, your attitude will waver and quake before your listeners. It doesn't take much imagination to understand what this can do to your self-confidence and to the confidence of those listening.

Don't let your speech drift like feathers on the wind. Point it straight as a pole at what you mean and want. Always ask for action. This is the quickest way to get it.

We recognize that some speech is for fun and relaxation. It makes no demand aside from enjoyment and perhaps a chuckle. That's fine. Everyone is entitled to free moments. However, our concern here is with productive speech that gets things done. This speech cannot flutter like a crippled bird. You will have no problem making this distinction.

* About platform speaking.

Platform speaking, or public speaking if you prefer, is a sure-fire way to build self-confidence. Yet, as we know, it can be an agonizing thought for many who are at ease and confident in a one-on-one situation. Think of it this way. Platform, or public, speaking is nothing more than speaking to a number of individuals instead of one or two. They are still people who want to hear you speak interestingly and confidently. They can be swayed and influenced by what you say. The difference is that your self-confidence has a wider audience and your influence can spread more quickly as you work and speak with groups.

There is no magic formula for public speaking. There are books and teachers. They can help just as this chapter will help, but the key is practice. As my old friend and co-speaker, Dr. O. M. Marchman of Dallas, would say, "There is no pill to make you a good speaker, but practice will do it." Dr. Marchman practiced what he preached. For years we met with the Senate Speakers Club at the Dallas Y.M.C.A. where every member was obliged to get on his feet and speak. Dr. Marchman had been a sought-after speaker for years, but he still practiced. The idea will work for you. Join a speech club, speak to church groups, be a volunteer, and use every opportunity to practice. As you do, your self-confidence will develop right along with your speaking ability.

CONFIDENT SPEECH GIVES YOU CREDIBILITY

Here is a plus benefit for you. As you develop strong confident speech power, it will give you a solid credibility. Here is why.

* You come on as strong and competent.

Nothing gives more credibility to a busy productive personality than confident, decisive speech. When you put the power of confident speech to work, you come on as honest and able. Think back over speeches you have heard. Which speaker did you believe, the one who filled his talk with flab and who rambled, or the one who came out on fire and headed in a straight line? Like every thinking man or woman you will give credibility to the man who sounds as if he knows where he is going. This is the reaction you can expect as you develop more and more confident speech power.

* You lose no time.

No matter what you say or how intense its importance to you, you will lose your audience if you do not respect their time as well as yours. When a speaker tries to prove or drive home a point by talking too long he loses credibility. Excess verbiage is poison. When you have made your point, that is the time to stop and ask for action or whatever it is that you want from your audience. The rules are the same whether the audience is one or hundreds.

We are not recommending dry precision. But do stop on time. This saves your time and the time of your friends.

* There will be no mush in what you say.

Confident speech gives you credibility because there will be no mush in what you say. A speaker can lose time not only in being longwinded, but by inserting irrelevant ideas as well as words into his speech. Mush has no power. It obscures ideas, puts people to sleep and destroys confidence in the speaker and what he has to say. When you make a well-organized talk backed by your self-confidence there will be no mush. You will know this and so will those you address.

* You create excitement and enthusiasm.

A confident rousing speech will create more excitement and enthusiasm than a puppy at a Cub Scout meeting. People love a powerful speaker. They will respond to him with excitement and enthusiasm. They will believe in him and what he has to offer. The way to make a talk that creates excitement and enthusiasm is to be excited and enthused. When you do, people can sense your conviction and power because your inspired self-confidence will be sending out the message loud and clear. Here is a secret worth special note: You cannot wait for excitement and enthusiasm to strike before making a speech. You must create the excitement and enthusiasm first. You do this by acting excited and enthusiastic as you practice and rehearse your presentation.

The importance of this little secret was vividly illustrated for me last week. There is a young man in the building where I have my office. He is responsible for the activities of sixteen salesmen who sell food products for two large processors and packers. Brock Connors holds weekly sales meetings with this group and any company officials who may be present. He has done this for at least five years. Yet as I passed the conference and sales room I saw Mr. Connors in the room with his props, samples and displays in place. He was alone but making a dynamic presentation that he planned to use the next day with everyone present. Brock saw me watching, grinned and asked, "How am I doing?"

"Just right, Brock," I answered. "Just right."

* You sound like a decision-maker.

When you develop strong confident speech you sound like a decision-maker. People are drawn to decision-makers. They want credible decision-makers to relieve them of the responsibility. This is another prime reason to develop confident speech power. With this you will command credibility,

HOW TO USE SPEECH MECHANICS TO ADD CONFIDENCE

Speech mechanics involve the rules and processes of speech. Obviously, since you are reading this book you are familiar with the language and its conventions. You can use the mechanics of speech without memorizing every grammatical rule and fretting over each word. Nobody likes to hear a speaker who is tense as a coiled snake. It takes more than precise and exact words to develop confident speech power. It takes thought, feelings, ideas and attitude. Speech does more than recite facts and convey information. It arouses emotions, makes impressions and tells much about the speaker. The mechanics of speech. cold as that may sound, are the building blocks of your speech. They are what give structure and form to what you say. The following deserves special attention, because the average person retains about ten percent of what is heard. Ninety percent goes in one ear and out the other or is soon forgotten.

* Speak clearly.

Unless you speak clearly it won't make much difference whether you speak correctly. Your listeners won't hear you anyway. Open your mouth and enunciate so that each consonant and vowel can do its work. You know how annoyed you are when someone speaks in a careless, indistinct voice. It is no fun when you have to strain to hear or understand half-muttered words. It is hard work. It is also an indication that the speaker attaches little importance to what he has to say. His listeners will feel the same way. Mumbling and weak speech do not come across as confidence and power. Clear, easy-to-understand speech does.

* Vocabulary.

Your vocabulary is the stock of words that you use. They do not have to be big, fat, pompous words. Strong, positive, short words will do the job. Stick to words that you know. This ensures that you will say what you mean instead of compromising your self-confidence.

You can build your vocabulary by using the dictionary often. Look up unfamiliar words that you hear or run across in reading. Write them down, repeat them aloud several times in a sentence. If you do not use the words that you look up, you are not likely to retain them. Keep in mind that the dictionary is not the absolute and final authority on words. Language changes and the dictionary did not come down from the mountain with Moses.

An excellent way to increase your working vocabulary is to listen to the many excellent speakers on television. Here you can hear the pronunciation and note the professional delivery of the speaker as well. Be selective. Don't waste your time on insipid programs. Turn on prominent newscasters. Listen to national leaders and qualified people. Here you will not only hear good speech, you can also watch self-confidence on display.

Of course, reading good books is one of the oldest and best ways to increase your vocabulary. The book won't pronounce the words for you as television personalities do, but your dictionary will give you the pronunciation as well as the meaning.

This short discussion on speech mechanics makes no attempt to cover the rules of grammar. There are many helpful books on English and ready teachers for those who wish to pursue this further. Our concern is to emphasize that confident speech power can be developed. The ideas that have been presented will hasten the process for you.

Here is one final thought to nail down the importance of observing the proper use of speech mechanics. It particularly applies to self-confident speech.

* If you are unable to explain an idea, it will die. If you can't explain to people what they are to do, they won't do it, and if you can't explain what you want you will not get it.

USE WORDS ECONOMICALLY

Practicing an economy of words does not mean that your speech should sound like a classified ad in the Sunday paper. It means that you should use enough words to say exactly what you mean. You don't want your speech to rattle like bare bones. Neither should it be adorned and frosted with words that add nothing to what you are saying. Years ago writers and speakers tended to long sentences and elegant words. Today sentences are shorter and words are usually simple and plain. Don't be too concerned that you use only short sentences and short words. The point is that your speech should fit the occasion, the audience and the subject. Whatever the case, though, redundancy is to be avoided. Words alone do not convince, motivate, describe or explain. The order, and your choice of words, backed by confidence and enthusiasm are what give your speech power. Look at this example:

In my book, *Lloyd Purves on Closing Sales*, I tell the story of Timothy Coleman, a young salesman who was energetically competing for a ten-day expense-paid vacation in Hawaii. Tim sold a coffeemaker that was the secret to winning the contest. He had been knocking himself out to win because his wife was excited at the prospect of a trip to Hawaii. But he was still in third place with two weeks to go when his wife said, "Sell me a coffeepot."

Tim enthusiastically jumped into the sales presentation that he had been using. He explained that the coffee-maker offered a new concept in brewing coffee, that it was, in fact, an indispensable appliance. It was decorative as well as functional. It featured the latest electronic devices and was precisely engineered. It had professional design. The beautiful appliance was as modern as space-age technology could make it. Here his wife stopped him.

"Does it make good coffee?" she asked.

Tim stopped in amazement. He got the point. The next week his presentation went like this.

"This unit makes delicious coffee. Once your customer tries it she will never want to be without it. And she will tell her friends about it. Let's make a pot. It will take only a few minutes. I have everything we need right here."

Tim won. His wife was rewarded by the trip to Hawaii—which she deserved.

You will notice that Tim used a fast-action low-vocabulary presentation to win. This technique will make you a winner, especially if you back up your words with proof as Tim did when he made a pot of coffee during his sales talk.

An economy of words embraces neither long rambling sentences nor too many short, choppy sentences. You must exercise judgment. Long, wordy sentences will bore your listener and you will lose him. If you use only short jerky sentences this will interfere with the smooth transmission of ideas and thought. Study the following two illustrations.

1. Long sentence.

One of the things that is important to a leader is self-confidence, because if he does not have self-confidence he cannot be a leader no matter how hard he tries, for education and titles are not as important as self-confidence to a leader.

2. Revision.

Self-confidence is more important than education or titles to a leader, because without self-confidence he cannot lead.

The revised sentence in this example has been tightened and stripped of useless words. Now read each sentence aloud. Which sounds better? The revision, of course, is more powerful speech though it contains less than half as many words as the original.

Confident speech power is speech that comes naturally to the speaker. It is not strained and full of pretense. Strained, affected speech fools no one, least of all the one who has resorted to this tacky device. Strained, affected speech is to be avoided. It is risky business. The one who uses affected speech is pretending to be someone or something that he is not. Most of all he is pretending that he is full of self-confidence. He is not and he is weakening whatever power he had. He is suffering from self-delusion.

I witnessed the humiliating effect that an affected, strained speech can have. A young man in Fort Worth, Texas was given a promotion which carried a bit of authority and prestige. Overnight he became a haughty Englishman. At least, he tried to sound like one. An Englishman in Fort Worth, Texas yet! The effect of his affected speech was not what he had hoped. Nobody took him seriously. He was chided when he answered the phone and snickered at in the office. He reverted to Texas English shortly. He could handle this. I'm glad to report that he continued his climb up the corporate ladder after this embarrassing episode in his life. And he has stuck with plain, direct speech through it all.

HOW JESS BRAZEAL
LEARNED TO SPEAK CONFIDENTLY

Jess Brazeal was a twenty-year-old high school graduate when he went to work for Tri-State Grocery Associates. Jess was a warehouse worker with dreams of being a customer's man for his company. But Jess was painfully shy and slow of speech. After much coaxing from an old family friend he enrolled in an adult education course at a college near his home to study speech and composition. He hoped to overcome his shyness and to learn to speak forcefully. When he submitted his first paper he used big unfamiliar words and wrote in a stilted manner that was unlike his day-to-day speech. The same thing happened when he made his first little talk before the class. His speech was stiff, his words were heavy and clumsy, and his theme lost in what he had intended to be an impressive discourse. Fortunately for Jess he had an instructor who understood his problem. He counseled Jess to develop his natural speech and to be less concerned with making an overwhelming impression. Jess listened. He followed his teacher's advice. His grades improved as he developed confidence and speech power. Today he is in customer relations for his company. Jess is still on his way up and speaking confidently. He has learned that big hollow words do not get things done nor do they contribute to self-confidence and personal power.

TONE IS IMPORTANT

Your voice is the mirror of your attitude, your thinking and your personality. It reflects your ambition, your dreams and your hopes. It broadcasts your self-confidence or whispers your lack of it. It is more than words. It is volume, quality and tone. Tone says what you really feel. If your words say one thing and your tone another, your listeners will believe your tone and expression. For instance, if you are attempting to convey respect or admiration, but your tone shows contempt, contempt is what the one who hears will feel and believe. If your words are asking for action but your tone is indifferent, the only thing you will get is indifference. Tone talks. Give it the consideration it deserves and it will give your speech power, appeal and fire.

Tone is not volume alone. Granted, there will be times when extra volume will be needed to set the tone of your speech or to give added emphasis to what you say. A monotone is deadly. Flat speech lulls an audience to sleep or pushes them into boredom.

Give your speech the tone of hills and valleys. Varying your tone will keep your audience alert and attentive whether you speak to one or many.

Tone evokes an emotional as well as a mental response. A harsh tone can evoke anger, fear and resistance. It says, "I don't like you!" It is no friend of confidence—yours or anybody else's. Too loud a voice irritates; a voice that is too low is tiring. A wavering, tremulous voice conveys timidity and a lack of confidence. A firm friendly voice denotes confidence and determination. It will evoke confidence in your listeners and motivate them to follow you. Emotions are strong stuff. The tone of your voice has hidden power. You can use that power to develop a confident speech habit.

Let's take a look at the word *habit* right here. *Habit* has a number of definitions or applications. We are concerned with how habit can apply to and affect the tone of your speech. Habit is something that comes about through repeated use. It is done automatically, often without conscious thought. This is where the danger lies. A disagreeable tone can be so habitual that the afflicted individual may not be aware of it. Here are some examples that you will recognize in individuals you have observed.

* A well-meaning parent who habitually uses a tone of disapproval. The child feels rejected and his self-esteem suffers.

* The businessman whose tone is always gruff and officious. Consequently, his associates avoid him and are reluctant to work hard in his behalf.

* The individual who glows with self-confidence

every day and whose tone conveys a sense of trust and well-being. This is a habit to develop. It does much for the speaker and for those who hear.

These few examples are enough to point out that we should all be aware of the tone (attitude) of our voice. Make a conscious effort to listen to yourself. You can evaluate the tone of your voice and only you can determine its quality and power. This is a responsibility that the self-confident recognize.

BODY LANGUAGE ADDS POWER TO SPEECH

As we have seen, there are many elements that can effect confident speech power. Some of these do not involve the voice itself. Body language adds power to speech. Body language (gestures) is the movement of the body, or part of the body, to emphasize ideas or express emotions. It can be anything from rolling the eyes or pointing a finger to pounding a podium or wildly jumping up and down. It is almost impossible for a confident, enthusiastic speaker to speak and stand like a statue. Like tone, body language should be studied and monitored. This should be no problem for you. You instinctively use body language in your everyday speech. This comes without effort as you emphasize a point. You may become acutely aware of your body language when making a public speech unless you are already an experienced speaker. A bit of practice beforehand will eliminate any worry in this department and give you the needed confidence. Here are three particular areas to guard against.

1. Repeating meaningless gestures nervously. For example, waving your hand up and down as you talk, or constantly drumming a finger against a table top.

2. Excessive emoting. If you express forced emotion throughout your speech you will make an audience uncomfortable. Do not, however, go to the other extreme and let no emotion cross your face or your lips. The stone man is not an effective speaker.

3. Hyperactivity. Hyperactivity is excessive motion. If you are hyperactive as you speak, your listeners are likely to be more impressed by your acrobatics than by what you say.

Finally, do use body language. It will relieve tension and give emphasis to what you say. Look upon body language as an aid in developing confident speech power. It can give your speech warmth, flavor, excitement and appeal.

STICK TO EASY-TO-GRASP WORDS

Stick to easy-to-grasp words for maximum speech power. You do this not because your listener is stupid or inferior, but because no one likes to struggle to understand what someone else is saying. Nevertheless, it is a mistake to talk down to those you seek to move or influence. We are not discussing something that is elemental and simple here. When we say stick to easy-to-grasp words, we are talking about good, confident speech. It is more work to present your ideas in plain unadorned language than it is to ramble around until you hit the point. The power-laden speech uses compelling, muscular words that are adequate for the audience and the circumstances. Puffy words have no place here.

Let's call upon our imagination to illustrate the difference between easy-to-grasp words and pompous speech blurted in the dim hope of convincing you. Suppose that you are in a store to buy a widget for your home. The salesperson leads you to one and begins, "We can say without any fear of successful contradiction that this is, without question, the most outstanding, stupendous, superlative bargain that you will ever find during your lifetime even if you live to be one hundred years old as we most sincerely hope you will."

Now, you are shopping, so you go to another store. A smart-looking salesperson leads you to the widgets and pulls one out so that you can examine it. Then he says, "This is a good buy."

Which salesman would win your confidence and get your business?

USE WORDS THAT GET TO THE POINT

Use words that get to the point. If, for example, you should be soliciting contributions for a building fund, you would not say that the building would be "nice," that it would be a "super place" for everybody, that it would be a "tremendous thing" and "just wonderful" for the community. These are cotton words that say nothing. Instead you would say

357

that the building was well-planned, that it would be large enough to accommodate everyone, that it would be a major accomplishment and an asset to the community. This statement uses words that describe concrete appeals and sound reasons for supporting the proposed building.

Jigsaw speech is weak and confusing. It is filled with puffy words. The poor listeners must go back and put the words together like the pieces of a jigsaw puzzle to get sense from the speech, or more likely it will be tossed in the waste basket of their minds.

Words that get to the point contribute to the development of confident speech power. All else give the mouth a hundred-yard advantage over clarity.

USE ACTION WORDS THAT
GENERATE CONFIDENCE

Words deserve careful handling. They can be manipulated, impregnated with bias, bent for accommodation, twisted by emotion, or weighted with power and truth. Words have been called hideously efficient tools. I do not particularly like this term. They are hideous only by design. As one dedicated to developing and using confident speech power, your words will be weighted with truth and power. These are the words that deserve special consideration. But no words should be taken for granted and handled like excess baggage. All words are loaded with power. You are the one who pulls the trigger.

Verbs are words of action. Adverbs and adjectives

are mostly adornments of speech. They have their place when used sparingly and purposely, but verbs get things done. They are the words you use as you influence, motivate, instruct and win people. Look at that sentence again. Influence, motivate, instruct and win are verbs. Do is a verb. When you use action words such as "do," people will do what you want.

Always know what you want and how you will say it when you want something done. Don't be like the old lady who said, "Now, how should I know what I'm talking about until I hear what I say?" Do not memorize your speech. Know your subject, what you want to accomplish, who you want to influence and then use action words. This will start the wheels turning.

Action words should be short and pithy. They demand urgency and movement. They walk and run. Look at these.

Win—see—benefit—give—get—do—run—go—stop—start—work—satisfy—leap—move—smile—fight—weep—dare.

Here is a true story that I recently read. It vividly drives home the necessity for clarity in speech if it is to get action and generate confidence.

Under the heading, "Men's Clothing and Furnishings, Retail," there was the listing, "Bank Joseph A. Clothiers, Inc." in the Atlanta Yellow Pages. Someone from the store called Southern Bell Telephone Company and instructed that the listing be changed to "drop 'Inc.' " Sure enough, in the next edition of the Yellow Pages it was changed to "Drop, Inc."

359

Napoleon knew how to inspire with action words. He issued three instructions to his secretaries who had the responsibility of transmitting orders to his troops. Here is his set of instructions.

1. Be clear.
2. Be clear.
3. Be clear.

CONFIDENCE KEYS

* Speech is your most powerful tool.
* Your speech reveals your self-confidence.
* Public speaking is a sure-fire way to build self-confidence.
* Confident, decisive speech gives you credibility.
* Speech mechanics give structure and form to what you say.
* Use words economically.
* Avoid strained, affected speech.
* Tone says what you really feel.
* Body language adds power to speech.
* Stick to easy-to-grasp words.
* No one likes to work hard to understand you.
* Use words that get to the point.
* Action words generate confidence.

Chapter 18
How To Make The Most Of Your Self-Confidence On A Day-To-Day Basis

Self-confidence is not something that you can put on a shelf and run and get when you want it. If it is to be anything at all it must be working for you every day. This is not to say that you must slay a dragon or do some monumental deed every day. It does mean that you should face each day with an assured confidence that you can handle it and come out on top. Self-confidence is something that you go to bed with and get up with each morning. If it comes and goes, it belongs to no one. Here are standards that you can use to make the most of your self-confidence on a day-to-day basis.

KEEP YOUR IDEAS ALIVE AND UP-TO-DATE

The world is full of great ideas. Your head is full of them. Think for a moment of the ideas that have flashed across your mind. At the time they seemed inspired and of tremendous import. But what happened? You probably nursed them for a while and then either forgot them or decided to do something about them "sometime." This is what happens to most of the ideas that we have. There has never been a shortage of ideas. The reason that nobody hears this abundance is that their authors lack the initiative and the confidence to pursue them. Procrastination kills more ideas than rejection. Keep your ideas alive. Give them a chance. This idea alone will go a long way toward making the most of your self-confidence.

Ideas are the most valued commodity on the market. They not only create and sustain confidence, they command money in the marketplace. Your idea does not have to be world-shaking to have far-reaching everyday impact. Years ago I read of a laborer who had a simple idea that brought him promotions, money and self-esteem. Management was complaining that much money was being lost because tools that were used each day regularly disappeared. Nobody could put their finger on the culprit or culprits. Then one laborer had an idea. It was so amazingly simple that he wondered why the bosses hadn't thought of it. Or, he reasoned, maybe they had tried it and had dropped it because the workers objected. Nevertheless, he didn't let the idea die. He went to the supervisor and laid his idea before him. His suggestion was that each man be required to sign for any tools issued him and then be required to check them in each night. His idea was promptly adopted. The losses stopped. Shortly thereafter the man was on his way up all because he had an idea and the self-confidence to do something about it.

This is one of the prime secrets in making the most of your self-confidence on a day-to-day basis.

Consider this thought. You can use it to keep your ideas alive and up-to-date. Nothing is more common than unsuccessful men with ideas. The reason is that they don't give their ideas a chance to succeed. This is another way of saying that they don't give their confidence much of a chance on a day-to-day basis. The happy thought is that this need never happen to you.

TAKE ADVANTAGE OF IMAGINATION

Self-confidence and creativity are working partners. Creativity is the capacity to make something new or to change something known into a new and better form. Imagination has always played a major role in creativity just as self-confidence has. Historically, famous inventors have imagined better ways of creating or doing things. It took supreme self-belief to persist in the face of peers who often jeered and ridiculed their imaginative ideas. You may never invent a light bulb, a telephone, or a new microchip, but you can take advantage of your imagination. It will keep your self-confidence growing on a day-to-day basis.

Imagination is not daydreaming. Webster's defines it vividly as the act or power of forming a mental image of something not present to the senses or never before wholly perceived in reality. By contrast, daydreaming is wishful thinking, usually for something personally desired, but in all probability something far removed from reality. It is largely fantasy. Imagination, when used constructively, is earnest and hard work. It is a productive process of the mind. It is not escapism as daydreaming often is. Rather, imagination is a means of unbuttoning your mind.

Take advantage of your imagination. Let it soar. Set your heart on worthwhile goals and imagine what it will be like when you reach them. Let your imagination explore new means and techniques of getting you where you want to go. Jot down your unusual ideas and try them. Never be hesitant or embarrassed by what you may imagine. Not everything will be brilliant or practical, but much of what your imagination does will lead to things beyond the ordinary. Shutting off your imagination is like locking the door of your mind against all that is new and exciting.

HOW LEONA CHOATE USED IMAGINATION

Leona Choate is a high school counselor who has an uncanny knack for turning indifferent students and wallflowers into popular, enthusiastic scholars. She is much admired in her community and among her associates. This busy lady is frequently called upon to address meetings and/or workshops. One of the questions most often asked is, "How do you do it?"

Leona Choate welcomes this question. She answers that when she is working with a discouraged child she lets her imagination take over. She doesn't see the fat, shy girl before her. She imagines what the girl could look like. Then she begins by talking about the girl's warm smile or beautiful hair or her secret dreams. She doesn't talk about her fat or her laziness. She calls upon the girl's imagination to see herself as she could be. She becomes the good parent who always imagines his or her child as full of possibilities and undeveloped talent. When the child leaves she has a different vision of herself. Of course, much more is involved—more counseling, more work, more time. But the goal that Leona Choate's imagination sets is seldom lost. What imagination has put in motion becomes reality. The child's attitude and personality changes. Because her imagination has stirred she is destined to be a well-rounded, confident adult.

Miss Choate works along the same lines with boys. When a belligerent or sullen boy stands before her, she sees him with her imagination and uses the same technique as on girls who come, or are sent, to her. As Miss Choate says, imagination is not hampered by sex, race or age. She has confidence in that.

HAVE GREAT EXPECTATIONS

You make the most of your self-confidence on a day-to-day basis when you have great expectations each day. We have already determined that what you expect of yourself is just about what you will get. Operate within the bounds of the possible for that is where self-confidence thrives. But do have great expectations for yourself each day. A great expectation need not be something that will go down in the history books. It can be making ten thousand dollars extra that day or simply giving a needy family or the Salvation Army ten dollars. It can be moving out of town or doing better right in Corn County. It can be a resolve to go back to school again or to help somebody else go to school. A great expectation is to look forward to something constructive in your life every day.

Try this. When you go to bed tonight promise yourself that you will do something that you have been wanting to do, or that you will do something that you know that you should do. Get up with the expectation that you will succeed. This is a great expectation. You can make it a great habit. When you do, you will also make a day-to-day habit of self-confidence.

DO YOUR OWN FORECASTING

As any self-confident, aggressive personality can vouch, there are always doomsayers around to predict that you may be headed for disaster. Don't be unduly influenced by this. It's your life. You know what you want and where you want to go. As a self-believer you are in charge of you. Do your own forecasting. Then rely on your best judgment and your day-to-day self-confidence to make your plans materialize. Don't indulge the fearful thoughts of lesser people.

Every self-confident person faces an endless chain of challenge and opportunity. When one goal is reached, another is set. When one challenge is met successfully, another is sought. This is because self-confidence brings ongoing purpose and meaning to life. You are aware of this principle or you would not be reading this book. You can see how sharply the principle applies to your own life by asking yourself this question. "What would I do and what would happen to my self-confidence if I had no goals or purpose in life?" The answer to this question is also the answer to the question, "Why should I be concerned about using my self-confidence on a day-to-day basis?"

I have a friend, Carl Wiggins, who is an entrepreneur. He has organized and developed a number of businesses. Carl usually sells his business once he has taken it about as far as it will go. Shortly thereafter he will begin a new enterprise. As is always true, some of his projects have paid more handsomely than others. Still, over the years, Carl has accumulated a sizable estate. When asked why he always sells out and begins anew, he is quick to explain that he thrives on challenge. Once he has built a profitable, going concern, he misses the excitement and challenge of creating a new one. So he sells that business and goes after another opportunity. Carl, or "Wig" as he is called by close friends, likes money, but he also likes the day-to-day challenge of new goals, new purposes and new excitement. Obviously, he is full of self-belief. He enjoys that too. His favor-

367

ite expression is that it's more fun to plan and build something than it is to sit on it. Plainly, he needs no one to tell him what is going to happen.

TEAR DOWN YOUR FENCES

There is no perfect human being nor will there ever be. Everyone is subject to the limitations of mortality. Everyone has limitations, handicaps, hangups, problems, and 1001 things that could destroy self-confidence if not dealt with constructively. Don't let this overwhelm you. Nothing can destroy your self-confidence *unless you let it do so*. Don't blow problems up in your mind until you become self-destructive. Self-confidence is the confidence to tear down your fences.

Here are examples of the fences that can hamper and weaken self-confidence, along with encouraging reasons to tear them down. Study these and then re-think any hangups that may be nagging you. Tear down any fences that hold you prisoner so that you can make the most of your self-confidence.

* Do you think that you have to be born lucky to be successful?

This fence is a subconscious cop-out. Luck has nothing to do with success and self-confidence. Of course fortunate things do happen. If they happen to you, then make the most of it. But believe this. Luck, success and self-confidence are by and large what you make happen. This is the attitude that makes the most of self-confidence. The stronger this conviction, the luckier you will be and the more you will get done.

* Do you feel that you are no good unless everybody likes you?

This is a fence of confusion. It is simply not true, because there is no one that everybody likes and praises. Remember that they crucified Christ because of disapproval and hatred, yet we are taught that he was the only perfect one. Don't expect everybody to like you or to approve of you in all things. It never happens to anyone no matter how much confidence they have or how noble their motives. But this is not the all-important thing. The important thing is to make the most of who you are on a day-to-day basis. The giants can do no more.

* Do you agree that it is smart to always agree with others?

This fence has holes in it. Always agreeing with others whether or not you mean it is a sure sign that you have abandoned your individuality and your confidence. Disagreement is not necessarily dislike of a person or disapproval of him. It is no more than a difference of opinion. Self-confidence is entitled to that.

* Do you believe that people who have nothing make better workers than others?

This fence is an age-old myth. The facts show that ambitious, self-confident people who have attained a degree of status and a bit of the material comforts of life are most often more aggressive and hard-working than those who have nothing. There are many causes of poverty, but it is not a guarantee that a man will work harder than his self-confident counterpart. Self-confidence finds no comfort in resigning itself to an abject poverty of money or mind.

* Do you believe that one should never admit a mistake?

The worst mistake is to refuse to acknowledge a mistake. Self-confidence has no reason to defend mistakes. Instead, the self-confident admit their mistakes and then correct them. Kick this fence over.

* Are you convinced that good luck is what builds confidence?

Don't walk into this fence. It is barbed. Self-confidence is built on solid stuff such as work, determination, desire, ambition, intelligence and personal responsibility.

* Do you hold that what other people think of you is all that counts?

This is a fence without foundation. Yes, the self-confident man or woman values the good opinion of others, but that is not where his self-confidence functions. Self-confidence understands that self-love, or self-esteem, comes first. Without that you can neither receive nor give respect. This is not selfishness. It is a psychological fact.

* Do you think that it is all right to feel sorry for yourself?

During a lifetime we all experience trouble and despair. It's true that some have been helpless victims of circumstance, painful losses or illness. In whatever form though, or from whatever cause, self-pity is a losing proposition. It turns people away after a while and, worse, it destroys self-confidence. No matter why one may feel self-pity there is something he or she can do. *Action* is the best antidote. When you act, you will accomplish. With accomplishment comes self-confidence. When self-confidence comes, self-pity crawls away.

* Do you believe that if you are criticized it means that you are no good?

This is another shaky fence. All criticism will ever be is one man's opinion. If it is valid and helpful you may profit from it. If not, forget it. Do not attach undue importance to it.

* Do you think that you either have self-confidence or you do not?

No, self-confidence is not predestined. If you have read this far, you know that self-confidence was not settled for you before you were born. You are not condemned to hide behind this fence.

The fences that hem you in and handicap your self-confidence are founded on a code of mistaken values and faulty opinions. Tear them down and claim your self-confidence.

RESPECT THE MECHANICS
OF SELF-CONFIDENCE

The mechanics of self-confidence deal with the application and techniques of self-confidence. It is the physical act of using your self-confidence on a day-to-day basis. You should respect the mechanics and rules of self-confidence, but at the same time leave room for spontaneity. When you are working to influence warm-blooded human beings, you cannot be a mechanical man. A robot gets his job done, but he does not inspire enthusiasm and cooperation. If your self-confidence is to have power, it must be organized and purposeful. This is where the mechanics come in. Yet it must be given warmth, conviction, and emotional appeal to move people to your side. This is where spontaneity comes in. To act spontaneously is to act from a personal and natural feeling. It is acting without external controls. It is a self-act controlled from within you. This permits you to be outgoing and spontaneous without flaunting the mechanics and conventions of your personal self-confidence. Respect the mechanics of self-confidence, but load them with your personality. This gives extra power to your day-to-day self-confidence.

MAKE DEMANDS ON YOU EVERY DAY

When you were a child, you made few demands on yourself. The shape of a child's life is such that decisions are made for him and certain demands are made upon him. As an adult, people will still make demands on you, but these are not nearly as productive as the demands you make on yourself. Demands from other people are for their benefit. Demands made by you on yourself are for your benefit. Your decisions are yours. Don't horsewhip yourself but decide what you want and demand that you get it. When you do, you will feel the keen surge of self-confidence that always comes with self-discipline.

372

WHAT BART CHILTON DEMANDS OF HIMSELF

Bart Chilton is seventy-nine years old and a top-notch sales producer for a wholesale distributor of tobacco and a broad line of sundry merchandise. What Bart Chilton does at his age is more a matter of personal pride and self-satisfaction than it is a matter of money. He demands of himself that he will try to sell at least one new account each week and that he will introduce a new item each week to every old customer on his route. Mr. Chilton has been making the most of his self-confidence on a day-to-day basis for a long time. An indication of the effectiveness of such self-discipline was expressed by Chilton's boss when Bart recently told his supervisor he wanted to go on a part-time basis. The sales manager patted him on the shoulder and said, "That's OK, Bart. You will still sell more than anybody else we have."

HOW TO AVOID HIGHS AND LOWS

Mental rigidity is a handicap. It restricts your ability to grow and to accept inevitable change. When an individual's mind is set in a concrete mold, he will feel good and be productive only when events are going his way. A bad day loaded with the unexpected will send him into despair. He is comfortable only on the days when his routine and rigid thinking are undisturbed. Otherwise, his attitude and his self-confidence can fluctuate wildly.

We know that the world is going to be a better

place because of you as a determined self-confident person. We also know that this is no guarantee that the world is going to smile on you every day. Life is never lived on a static plane, but that is no reason to let your self-confidence soar one day and sink the next. Here are some quick points that will help you avoid highs and lows in your self-confidence.

* Work. Don't just work, but learn to like to work. The chances are that you already like work since you are keenly interested in self-confidence and self-development. Work even though you may not be doing exactly what you would like to do at the time. Work each day with open eyes and an open mind. This way you won't have the time or inclination to discount yourself. As long as you like to work, your self-confidence won't fly high one day and take a beating the next. Anybody who likes to work will always like himself.

* Be flexible. Don't let your needle stick on one goal only. Just as you can share your heart with many people, you can be productive and happy in more than one field or one vocation. If one goal is wiped out because of a catastrophe beyond your control, don't commit mental or emotional suicide. There is more than one road to town. One of them will get you there.

* Be energetic in productive ways. Don't energetically go off in all directions. This would be better than moping, but purposeful action is what keeps your self-confidence on a high plane.

* Have regard for the physical man. Go to a good doctor and let him help you keep physically sound.

Have a thorough yearly checkup. It's hard to be high one day and low the next when your mind and body are healthy. Just knowing that you are in good shape will make it easier for you to make the most of your self-confidence on a day-to-day basis.

LIFE IS A DAY-TO-DAY BUSINESS

Most big goals are reached only after time and experience have qualified one for the responsibilities and recognition that come with such achievement. It is true that some are catapulted into prominence and success overnight. These are the people you read about, hear about and see on television. The majority of us are never exposed to national acclaim and publicity when our dreams and aspirations are fulfilled. This is probably to the good. Sudden fame is often short-lived. Even so, there is nothing wrong with sudden fame or the quick realization of your ambitions. If it comes your way, take full advantage of it. The point we make here is that most earnest, self-confident people reach their goals in life through days and days of preparation, trial and error, learning and an iron-clad self-confidence. The daily challenge can be, should be, a great part of the joy of arriving. Life is a day-to-day business spread over the years. Make the most of your self-confidence on a day-to-day basis and live your life accordingly. Don't wait until you reach the big balloon at the top of your mountain. Somebody may stick a pin in it. But today is yours. Make the most of that.

HOW TO HANDLE A BAD DAY
WITH CONFIDENCE

If you are old enough to read, I know that you have had some bad days. It is a slice of life. It is not the end of the road nor should it be the end of self-confidence. You have suffered bad days—as all mortals must—but you made it through them. The same ideals, goals and dreams you had before are still there for you. Nobody is going to tell you that disappointment and personal tragedy do not hurt. But there are living examples around you of happy, enthusiastic people who have lived through the pain of more than one bad day, yet continue to confidently face each new day. Take a good look at these people.

Not every day of our life will be as quiet as a sleeping baby's breath. Nor can anyone make it so. There will be upsetting days in spite of our best efforts. To name a few of the common upsetting events that can spoil a day, consider these.

* An automobile accident
* Embarrassing mistakes
* Death
* Illness
* Loss of friends
* Disappointment in others
* Misplaced trust
* A financial disaster
* Weather
* Physical hurt
* A senseless tongue-lashing

You can handle days plagued by such ordinary incidents as these with confidence. I question that you could long survive days of placid monotony. It is not the nature of self-confidence to sit with folded hands.

Oscar Wilde said, "Misfortunes one can endure—they come from outside. They are accidents. But to suffer for one's own mistakes—ah, there is the sting of life."

Note that Oscar Wilde did not say that the sting was fatal. Be that as it may, I have more confidence in the prayer of a minister I have known. This wise and kindly man lived a long time and embraced each day with faith and confidence. He was the Reverend Dr. Charles Riepma, former rector of Christ Episcopal Church in Springfield, Missouri. I commend his prayer to you.

"Oh, Lord our God, deliver us from the fear of what might happen, and give us the grace to enjoy what is now and to keep striving after what ought to be."

BLESSED ARE THE LITTLE CHILDREN

Observe a child for an inspiring example of how to get through a not-so-good day. Children awaken with trust and confidence. They have an unwavering capacity to put a bad day behind them. I saw a tiny example of this recently when I went to Andrea's grandmother's house. Grandmother was upset and scolding. "Andy" shrank from her and crept upon my lap. I left shortly. The next day I came back. Grandmother was bustling about baking cookies and smiling cheerfully. Andy was sitting on the cabinet near the mixing bowl and chattering away. As I came in she held a warm cookie toward me and beamed, "You oughta taste what she is doing. It's good!"

Andrea, like other children, knows what to do about a bad day.

HOLD ONTO YOUR IDENTITY

Hold onto your identity as a self-confident and able individual. Make the most of that label every day. Do not self-label yourself with a derogatory identity. More to the point, do not permit anyone else to ruin so much as one day by hanging a bogus label around your neck. This would border on the irrational. Self-confidence gives you the answer to who you are, what you are and what you can be.

Here is a truth that can enforce your determination to make the most of your self-confidence on a day-to-day basis. It is not so much what you don't believe about yourself as it is what you do believe about yourself.

When you believe in yourself and make the most of your self-confidence, you will hold no postmortems. You won't waste your days brooding over regrets. Rather, you will cherish your identity as did the unknown author who beautifully expressed his own confidence with these words:

I'm not afraid of tomorrow
Because I've seen yesterday
And I love today.

378

CONFIDENCE KEYS

* Self-confidence is not something to put on a shelf.
* Keep your ideas alive.
* There has never been a shortage of ideas.
* Let your imagination soar.
* Have great expectations.
* Do your own forecasting.
* Nothing can destroy your self-confidence unless you let it do so.
* Tear down the fences.
* Respect the mechanics of self-confidence.
* Leave room for spontaneity.
* Mental rigidity is a handicap.
* Be flexible.
* You can handle a bad day.
* Hold onto your identity.
* It is not so much what you don't believe about yourself as it is what you do believe about yourself.

TRIVIA MANIA: TV GREATS

TRIVIA MANIA: I LOVE LUCY   (1730, $2.50)

TRIVIA MANIA: THE HONEYMOONERS   (1731, $2.50)

TRIVIA MANIA: STAR TREK   (1732, $2.50)

TRIVIA MANIA: THE DICK VAN
DYKE SHOW   (1733, $2.50)

TRIVIA MANIA: MARY TYLER MOORE   (1734, $2.50)

TRIVIA MANIA: THE ODD COUPLE   (1735, $2.50)

Available wherever paperbacks are sold, or order direct from the Publisher. Send cover price plus 50¢ per copy for mailing and handling to Zebra Books, Dept. 1667, 475 Park Avenue South, New York, N.Y. 10016. DO NOT SEND CASH.

MORE BESTSELLING ROMANCE BY JANELLE TAYLOR

SAVAGE CONQUEST (1533, $3.75)

Having heeded her passionate nature and stolen away to the rugged plains of South Dakota, the Virginia belle Miranda was captured there by a handsome, virile Indian. As her defenses melted with his burning kisses she didn't know what to fear more: her fate at the hands of the masterful brave, or her own traitorous heart!

FIRST LOVE, WILD LOVE (1431, $3.75)

Roused from slumber by the most wonderful sensations, Calinda's pleasure turned to horror when she discovered she was in a stranger's embrace. Handsome cattle baron Lynx Cardone had assumed she was in his room for his enjoyment, and before Calinda could help herself his sensuous kisses held her under the spell of desire!

GOLDEN TORMENT (1323, $3.75)

The instant Kathryn saw Landis Jurrell she didn't know what to fear more: the fierce, aggressive lumberjack or the torrid emotions he ignited in her. She had travelled to the Alaskan wilderness to search for her father, but after one night of sensual pleasure Landis vowed never to let her travel alone!

LOVE ME WITH FURY (1248, $3.75)

The moment Captain Steele saw golden-haired Alexandria swimming in the hidden pool he vowed to have her—but she was outraged he had intruded on her privacy. But against her will his tingling caresses and intoxicating kisses compelled her to give herself to the ruthless pirate, helplessly murmuring, "LOVE ME WITH FURY!"

TENDER ECSTASY (1212, $3.75)

Bright Arrow is committed to kill every white he sees—until he sets his eyes on ravishing Rebecca. And fate demands that he capture her, torment her . . . and soar with her to the dizzying heights of TENDER ECSTASY!